D1539941

Architectural Rendering

D1539957

Architectural Rendering

The Techniques of Contemporary Presentation

ALBERT O. HALSE

SECOND EDITION

a NA
2780
H3
1972

E77860

887797

McGRAW-HILL BOOK COMPANY

New York   St. Louis   San Francisco   Düsseldorf   Johannesburg
Kuala Lumpur   London   Mexico   Montreal   New Delhi
Panama   Rio de Janeiro   Singapore
Sydney   Toronto

ST. PAUL PUBLIC LIBRARY

Library of Congress Cataloging in Publication Data

Halse, Albert O.
  Architectural rendering.

  Bibliography: p.
  1. Architectural rendering. I. Title.
NA2780.H3 1972   720'.28   76-39900
ISBN 0-07-025628-4

Copyright © 1972, 1960 by McGraw-Hill, Inc. All Rights Reserved.
Printed in the United States of America. No part of this publication
may be reproduced, stored in a retrieval system, or transmitted, in any
form or by any means, electronic, mechanical, photocopying, recording,
or otherwise, without the prior written permission of the publisher.

1234567890 HDAH 765432

*The editors for this book were William G. Salo, Jr., and Lydia
Maiorca, and its production was supervised by Stephen J. Boldish.
It was set in Caledonia by Progressive Typographers.*

*It was printed by Halliday Lithograph Corporation and bound by
A. Horowitz & Son Bookbinders.*

Contents

THIS BOOK is devoted to an analysis of the pictorial method of design study used by the architect. Called rendering, or delineation, this pictorial study makes it possible to visualize structures while they are still in the design stage. It is an indispensable tool for the architect.

Few books have been available for those who wish to learn about the art of rendering, and most of these have dealt with a single medium per volume. Often the technique illustrated has been that of one man. The present volume attempts to supplement these books by providing in a single place information about many media and techniques. The author hopes that such a general overview of the field of delineation will be of great value to architects, designers, professional delineators, and teachers of architecture and their students, as well as to others whose work includes the study of design. In addition, it is hoped that the general public will gain a new appreciation of this important aspect of architecture.

The author has attempted to simplify the study of rendering by separating it into its component parts. There are chapters devoted to perspective, composition, color theory, light, rendering entourage, equipment, and general approach. All of these elements apply to all media. In addition, a separate chapter is devoted to each medium, while still another chapter describes various combinations of media. Each chapter contains a suggested list of materials, advice for purchasing them, simple exercises for using the medium, and a close analysis of student renderings. In most chapters, a number of renderings made by leading professional delineators are included. The last chapter contains a gallery of such work.

The author wishes to stress that while he has tried to make this book as complete as possible, rendering is done in many more ways than those described. A look at the first chapter — which is, in fact, a concise history of architectural drawing and rendering — shows the many changes that have occurred over the centuries. There is little doubt that new materials, new media, and new inventions will cause similar changes in the future. Like all other arts, rendering is constantly being modified.

Throughout the book the reader will find illustrations of methods for drawing and painting various textures required in rendering. These are basic. Although it was not possible to illustrate the texture of every material used in construction, the reader who studies this book conscientiously from beginning to end, and tries to apply the information he has found, should acquire the skill and confidence to experiment successfully whenever a new material is met.

It is the author's hope that all who read these pages will find in them inspiration and encouragement. Application of the principles discussed should be made as quickly and as often as possible. Like many similar skills, facility in rendering increases in direct proportion to its use.

Albert O. Halse

Foreword

Acknowledgments

The illustrations identified as student work throughout this book were made at the School of Architecture of Columbia University under the direction of the author, and are reproduced herein with the kind permission of that school. This book was, to a large extent, made possible by cooperation of this nature, and the author wishes to thank Leopold Arnaud, Dean Emeritus of the School of Architecture and Ware Professor Emeritus; James Grote Van Derpool, Professor Emeritus of the Faculty of Architecture; Kenneth A. Smith, Dean of the School of Architecture; the school staff; and each student whose work is included here.

It has not always been possible to identify the buildings and architects on which student renderings were based. Frequently students took such liberties with building designs as to make such identification inappropriate, even if possible. And some renderings actually represent the students' own designs.

Sincere apologies are extended to those architects who may still recognize some of their uncredited designs in the student work; if such omissions are called to the author's attention, he will be glad to make amends in future editions.

The author also thanks the professional delineators and architects whose work is represented for their sincere interest and cooperation.

Finally, he wishes to acknowledge his debt to the sources of many of the illustrations for Chapter 1, Who Invented Rendering? These sources are indicated below; fuller information will be found in the Bibliography, pages 320–321.

Figure	Source
1.1	Capart, Jean: *Egyptian Art*
1.2	Davies, N. de Garis: "The Rock Tombs of El Amarna"
1.3	Carter H. and Cardiner, A. H.: "The Tomb of Rameses IV and The Turin Plan of a Royal Tomb"
1.4, 1.7 1.8, 1.22	Burford, James: "The Historical Development of Architectural Drawing to the End of the Eighteenth Century"
1.5	Goodspeed, George S: *A History of the Babylonians and Assyrians*
1.6	Jordan, Henricus: *Forma urbis Romae, regionum XIII*
1.9	Willis, Robert: *Facsimile of the Sketchbook of Wilars de Honecort*
1.10	Moller, Georg: *Bemerkungen über die aufgefundene original-zeichnung des domes zu Koeln*
1.11, 1.16	Uffizi: *Disegni di architettura*
1.12	Frey, Dagobert: *Bramantes St. Peter entwurf und seine apokryphen*
1.13	Mariani, Valerio: *La Facciata Di San Pietro Secondo Michelangelo*
1.14	Falda, Giovanni Battista: *Le chiesa di Roma*

1.15,1.20	Schmitz, Hermann: *Baumeisterzeichnungen des 17 und 18 jahrhunderts*
1.17	Piranesi, Giovanni Battista: *Roman Architecture, Sculpture and Ornament*
1.18	du Cerceau, Jacques Androuet: *Les plus excellents bastiments de France*
1.19	le Pautre, Anthoine: *Les oeuvres d'architecture d'Anthoine le Pautre*
1.21	Blomfield, Reginald: *Architectural Drawing and Draughtsmen*
1.23	Malton, James: *An Essay on British Cottage Architecture*
1.24	Kip, Johannes: *Britannia Illustrata*
1.25	Fouche, Maurice: *Percier et Fontaine, biographie critique*
1.26	Viollet-le-Duc, Eugene Emmanuel: "Compositions et dessins de Violett-le-Duc"
1.27,1.28	Brisebach, August: *Carl Friedrich Schinkel*
1.29	"Techniques and Tradition in British Architecture". Courtesy of Alan G. Thomas, present owner, and Roger Senhouse, former owner, of original
1.30	Gandy, Joseph: *Designs for Cottages, Cottage Farms and Other Rural Buildings, including Entrance Gates and Lodges*
1.31	Adams, Maurice B.: "Architectural Drawing"

Chapter 1

Who invented rendering?

ART HAS BEEN PRACTICED by mankind in various forms since Paleolithic times. At first man's efforts were confined to achieving beauty and symmetry in the tools he used. Later, he found enjoyment in the use of color on his body and in his clothing, as well as in ornament. Evidences of his first expressions in painting and sculpture have been found in caverns in Spain and France, where, with the help of artificial light, he painted numerous pictures in color, chiefly of animals. His paints were made by mixing red and yellow ochre with animal fat.

During the Mesolithic age man still roamed as a hunter, and although his artistic achievements were less impressive than formerly, he invented both metal and writing. The written word enabled mankind to compile information, and by passing it along to those who lived after him to pyramid it into what we call civilization. As men settled in groups, communication became more important, and both the picture and the written word were needed.

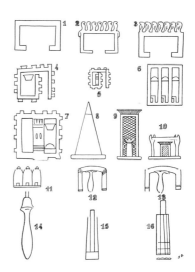

Fig. 1.1   Architectural Hieroglyphs

When man built simple structures he continued to use words, but when buildings became complicated and when it became necessary to explain the ideas to another person or to make a record of the building, the builder used a pictorial method. This gave not only a briefer description, but a more accurate one.

The pictorial method seems to have received strong encouragement from the erection of the great monuments of ancient Egypt. Here, in the Ancient Kingdom (4400–2466 B.C.), architectural hieroglyphs were invented (Fig. 1.1). During the Amarna Period (1375–1350 B.C.), a style of drawing combining plan and elevation was developed and used not only for the guidance of builders, but also as part of the mortuary art on the walls of the tombs of kings (Fig. 1.2). This pictorial type of drawing may be considered a distant relative of present-day delineation.

For actual construction, plans were drawn on papyrus (Fig. 1.3) or on limestone (Fig. 1.4). Both of the plans illustrated were drawn in several colors of ink to represent the various materials shown.

Fig. 1.2   "The Palace," Painted on Stucco

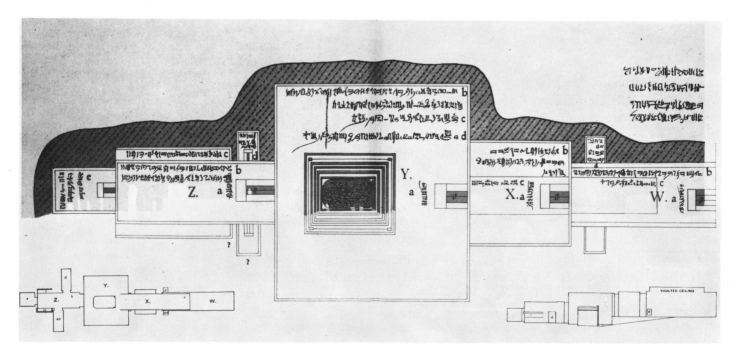

Fig. 1.3   Plan of the Tomb of Rameses IV, Painted on Papyrus

While this remarkable development was going on in Egypt, a similar development toward the pictorial was in progress in Babylonia and Assyria. Here earth, landscape, fields, and buildings were drawn on clay tablets with a pointed stick. Curved lines were avoided because they were difficult to draw in soft clay (Fig. 1.5).

Although there are many epigraphic and literary references to a developed system of architectural drawing in ancient Greece, none of these drawings have been found. This is probably because they were made on such perishable materials as whitened or waxed wood, lead or charcoal on wood, and pottery. Authorities who have studied the administration of the Greek temples explain that the choice of wood or marble depended on the importance of the document and the length of time it was to last. Architectural plans were evidently classified as temporary, and executed on wood.

The early Roman works were built by the Greeks. A Greek architect, for example, was imported for the construction of the temples of Jupiter and Juno, both of which were built in Rome in 146 B.C. But because the practical side of architecture appealed to the Romans, they soon undertook the work for themselves. Thermae, amphitheaters, basilicas, temples, aqueducts, bridges, tombs, palaces, and houses all testify to the ability the Romans eventually developed. There is little doubt that drawings must have been used in building these great works. Their very complexity and the perfection of the relation of parts are proof enough. Yet Rome, like Greece, left few drawings, and only record plans on marble, such as "The Marble Plan of Rome," Fig. 1.6, have survived.

Fig. 1.4
A Plan on Limestone of the Tomb of Rameses IX. Draftsman unknown

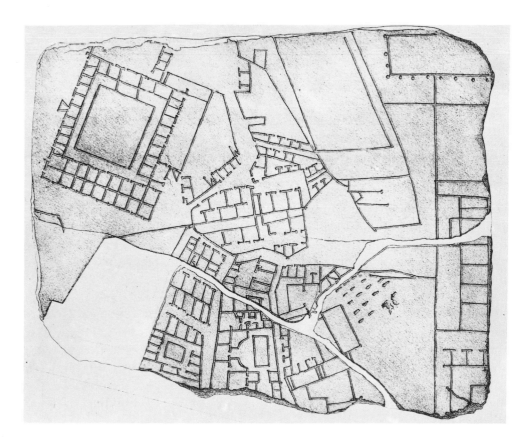

Fig. 1.5
Clay Tablet with Plan of Nippur

Fig. 1.6   The Marble Plan of Rome, Fragment No. 184

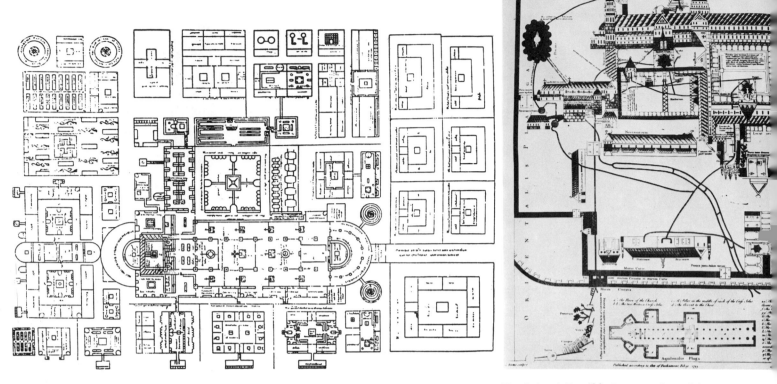

Fig. 1.7   The Plan of the Cloister of St. Gallen

Fig. 1.8   A Twelfth Century Plan of the Cathedral and Benedictine Monastery of Canterbury

Drawing in the Monasteries

The lack of pictorial architectural drawing (other than the plan drawings mentioned) extends to that period of time between the fall of Rome and the year 1000. What little drawing was done then was probably executed in monasteries, where the feeble flame of civilization was kept alive. The plan of the Cloister of St. Gallen (820 A.D.) shown in Fig. 1.7, a building on the shores of Lake Constance, in what is now Switzerland, is typical of this simple type of drawing. A later plan (Fig. 1.8)—this one quite pictorial—was produced sometime in the twelfth century by the Monk Eadwin. In this drawing the elevations are given a false perspective to help explain the form of the building.

Unfortunately, the period during which the monks built the great abbeys was marked by many construction failures, because the monks were unskilled in engineering calculations. As the abbeys grew richer, however, they began to employ lay-architects, or master masons. These men, with their groups of masons, rarely settled in communities, but usually wandered from job to job. The bonds of fellowship between the members of the masons' guild seem to have been strong, and gradually building returned to lay hands.

Of the many names of masons and master masons that have come down to us, one stands out—that of a Frenchman named Wilars de Honecort, who lived about 1250. Like most cultured men of his time, de Honecort traveled through France, from north to east, and across the entire German Empire. During these travels he recorded details of French cathedrals, making ink sketches in a vellum sketchbook that he kept for his own use and for the instruction of his pupils. Here we find plans, elevations, and even pseudo-perspectives (Fig. 1.9).

The tireless work of de Honecort and men like him eventually produced the great cathedrals of Europe. These were built from plan and elevation drawings, supplemented by details which were made on the site as the job progressed. During this period draftsmanship reached a high peak of perfection (Fig. 1.10). True, because the principles of descriptive geometry were not yet known (they were to be developed in 1794 by Monge) such oddities occur as the lack of foreshortening in circular windows in the splayed corners of towers, but in spite of these shortcomings the Gothic draftsman produced some beautiful drawings.

Because the master mason lived on the job for its duration (and sometimes the lives of three master masons were consumed in the building of one cathedral) he was able to visualize the end result of his conception without the help of a rendering. He therefore needed to make only working drawings, supplementing these with an occasional model. The beauty of the Gothic cathedrals of France and Germany testifies to the success of this system.

The Master Masons

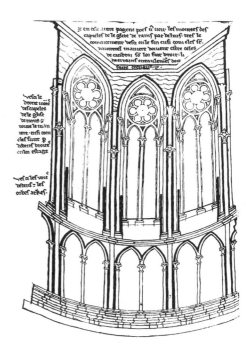

Fig. 1.9　The Cathedral at Rheims: Inside View of Choir Chapel

Fig. 1.10　Cologne Cathedral: Partial Elevation of Tower

Fig. 1.11
Sectional Perspective of St. Peter's,
Rome. Donato Bramante, draftsman

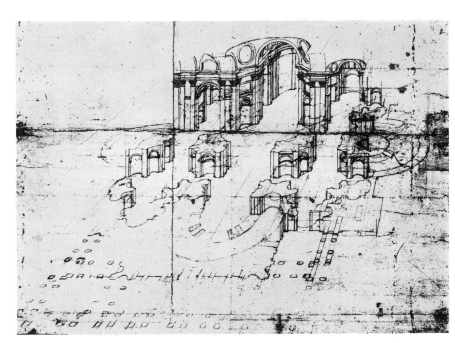

Fig. 1.12
Sectional Perspective of St. Peter's,
Rome. Baldassare Peruzzi, draftsman

Renaissance Rendering

Rendering as we know it was born during the Italian Renaissance. Italy, which had lain culturally dormant since the fall of Rome, suddenly began to stir. The discovery and publication in the fifteenth century of the Vitruvius Treatise on Architecture (written during the reign of Augustus) stimulated a new interest in classical antiquity and an upsurge in the activity of building. In Italy, where the Reformation did not take hold, and where comparatively few churches had been built during the Middle Ages, there was a revival on a grand scale of church as well as domestic architecture. It was in the building of these churches that the architects developed the principles of perspective and rendering.

Whereas the Gothic churches were constructed far from the influence of the Church of Rome, the architects of Italy had to work in constant consultation with the popes. As the heads of the Church were vitally interested in the appearance of the new buildings, it was necessary to make as many "pictures" of the proposed structures as possible. The stage had been set for the invention of scientific perspective by the painters of architectural subjects, who, although they had no rules, used "perspective by eye." Paolo Uccello, a Florentine, and Andrea Mantegna of Padua were among the first writers on the rules of perspective. Others, such as da Vinci, Michelangelo, Raphael, Titian, and Giulio Romano, followed. During the sixteenth century more elaborate books were written on the subject by Serlio and Vignola, and still later, in the seventeenth century, a thorough treatise on perspective was published by Pozzo.

The late fifteenth century Italian architects Bramante and Peruzzi (Figs. 1.11 and 1.12) were among the first to design in perspective.

Another great stimulus to the drawing of the Renaissance was the invention of paper. When Egyptian papyrus was brought to Europe it quickly became popular because it cost less than the animal skins then in use, and could be rolled. It continued to be used occasionally in Italy until the eleventh century, when parchment and cotton paper were introduced.

The Chinese are given credit[1] for developing the art of making paper from fibrous materials converted to pulp in water, and the earliest clearly dated paper shows the year 264. The Arabians introduced the art into Europe through Spain, and linen and hemp fiber came into use, as well as cotton. By the seventeenth century France was the center of the industry, shipping paper to Russia, Sweden, Denmark, Holland, Germany, and England. Both Holland and England perfected the process by the beginning of the nineteenth century.

While the Italian architects found paper still expensive and scarce, it was more abundant and easier to draw upon than any of the materials previously available; this fact encouraged experimentation, and therefore progress.

The printing press, together with the inventions of perspective and paper, made possible the exchange of architectural ideas through books. It was only a step from the linear perspectives of Bramante and Peruzzi to the development of the full picture, or the expression of form in perspective by the use of light and shade (Fig. 1.13).

At first the buildings were rendered without surroundings, either in perspective or in a false perspective type of elevation. Later, however, the buildings were represented in actual settings (Fig. 1.14). Here the values and scale of the surroundings not only located the church in its actual setting, but also complemented the main building in the picture.

[1] Munsell, Joel: *Chronology of the Art of Paper Making*, p. 5

Fig. 1.13 A Design for the Facade of St. Peter's, Rome. Michelangelo Buonarotti, draftsman

Fig. 1.14 Church Dedicated to St. Luke, Evangelist

CHIESA DEDICATA À S·LVCA EVANGELISTA ET A S·MARTINA V·M·DOVE FV L ANTICO TEMPIO DI MARTE IN CAMPO VACCINO.
Architettura del Caualier Pietro Berrettini da Cortona

Other Italian Renderings

While the architects of Italy had the Church as an important client, they were also commissioned to execute stage designs. These were, for the most part, drawn in perspective and shaded by use of water color washes (Fig. 1.15). Baldassare Peruzzi (1481–1537) was another architect who used a combination of perspective and shading with water color wash (Fig. 1.16). In addition, he sometimes worked in pen and ink over a preliminary red and/or brown or black charcoal sketch. Often he used brown or gray washes, and occasionally he employed bistre, a dark brown water color.

Another source of income for the architect in Italy lay in the great interest of the public for pictures of Roman ruins in imaginary compositions. The most skilled and prolific delineator of this type of rendering was Piranesi (1720–1778), whose works are still regarded as masterpieces of draftsmanship and composition. Figure 1.17, "Tempico Antico," illustrates his ability to "lead" the eye of the spectator to the vital portions of the drawing.

Fig. 1.15   Stage Design for *Il Ciro*, Filipo Juvara, draftsman

Early Delineation in France and Germany

Although delineation had developed in Italy during the fifteenth century, it was not until a century later that the architects of France became aware of these new developments. At first the French were timid in their efforts to use the new-found skills, but eventually they not only employed the rendered ground-level perspective, but also began to experiment with aerial

Fig. 1.16   Stage Design with Roman Buildings of Ancient Times. Baldassare Peruzzi, draftsman

Fig. 1.17   Tempico Antico, by Piranesi

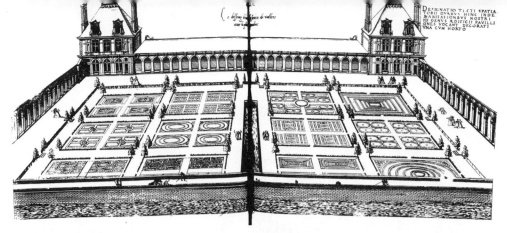

Fig. 1.18 An Aerial View, by Du Cerceau

Fig. 1.19 "L'Eglise du Monastere du Port-Royal," by le Pautre

perspectives. These were first drawn without surrounding land beyond the borders of the immediate plot of land (Fig. 1.18), but later were shown with complete surroundings. The French later began to study their buildings by the use of the rendered sectional perspective (Fig. 1.19).

Germany, where building was dominated by the master mason for several centuries, was slow to adopt the rendered perspective, and for the most part the architects still used the plan and elevation to study their buildings. Architects' training emphasized engineering, and the pictorial approach of the rendered perspective had no place. A few of the German Renaissance architects traveling in other countries, however, began to render elevations of their projects (Fig. 1.20).

Fig. 1.20 Entwurf für ein Warenlager. Andreas Gärtner, draftsman

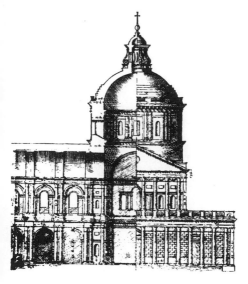

Fig. 1.22   St. Paul's, Covent Garden. Thomas Malton, designer

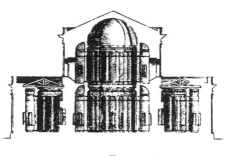

Fig. 1.21   Studies for a Church.
Inigo Jones, draftsman

Fig. 1.23   Two Cottage Designs. James Malton, draftsman

Early Delineation in England

Because England was so far away from Rome, it was the last country to be stimulated by the new movement, and English Renaissance drawings were linear in quality. Inigo Jones (1573–1652), who traveled in Italy and modeled his work after the Italian architects of the fifteenth and sixteenth centuries, rendered first in pen and line (Fig. 1.21) and later in line and pale wash. When the Grand Tour began, travelers brought back stories of the new type of architectural delineation from Italy, and this influenced the style.

The rendered elevation and the fully rendered ground perspective were soon added to the architect's presentation of plan, section, and elevation (Fig. 1.22). During this period James Malton published *An Essay on British Cottage Architecture*, complete with rendered elevations. Figure 1.23 shows two of the simpler designs, both rendered in water color. Other media used were pen and ink; wash used alone or with pen and ink; or water color used alone, with pencil, or with pen and ink.

Fig. 1.24 Long Leat in Wiltshire.
Jan Kip, draftsman

Additional stimulation to the art of architectural rendering was provided by a number of foreigners who came to England and were commissioned to make "views" of English buildings and landscapes. These were, for the most part, aerial perspectives (similar to those done in France) of such subjects as the king's palace, seats of the nobility and gentry, cathedrals, and public buildings (Fig. 1.24).

The end of the eighteenth century in Europe was a period of revolution, and also one of invention. The migration of architectural thought was hastened by improvements in travel and communication. In France, architectural education became formalized, and delineation was influenced accordingly. The École des Beaux Arts stressed beauty of delineation in the study of designs, while the École Polytechnique emphasized the simple engineering technique for architects primarily interested in construction. It was the École des Beaux Arts which influenced rendering most strongly and created the climate for the development of many of the advances in delineation in France.

The work of Charles Percier (1764–1838), one of the architects to Napoleon, provides an excellent cross section of delineation as it existed in France at the beginning of the nineteenth century. An examination of his drawings shows the use of most of the techniques and media known in his day, including the modern graphite pencil, which was invented in 1795 and soon replaced the sticks made from pulverized graphite, metallic lead, or metallic silver. Many of Percier's drawings were made in pencil washed with bistre. He also combined pencil with Chinese ink and used Chinese ink alone. Occasionally on the same drawing he combined pen and ink, Chinese ink, and water color. An example of his use of pen and ink is shown in Fig. 1.25.

Even more prolific, and certainly the greatest draftsman of nineteenth century France was Eugène Emmanuel Viollet-le-Duc (1814–1879), who consolidated and combined the various techniques of those who lived before him. One of his most realistic perspectives was the "Projet Academie Imperiale du Musique" (Fig. 1.26), which was made in a combination of pencil and water color. By careful manipulation of his brush so as to obtain

Nineteenth Century France

Fig. 1.25 Vue de l'Interieur de L'Eglise Notre Dame. Charles Percier, draftsman

Fig. 1.26 Projet Academie Imperiale du Musique. Viollet le Duc, draftsman

11

Fig. 1.27 Dekoration zur *Zauberflöte*.
Carl Friedrich Schinkel, draftsman

a certain amount of tonal variation and texture, by the accurate plotting of shades and shadows, the selection of an excellent viewpoint, and the use of dark values in the foreground and light values in the distance, he obtained an almost photographic quality. Since this rendering was made a short time after the invention of the camera (sometime between 1816 and 1829) it is obvious that his realistic style was an attempt to simulate the accuracy of the new instrument.

Nineteenth Century Germany and England

The same kind of photographic quality was obtained by Carl Friedrich Schinkel in Germany (1781–1841) in his "Dekoration zur 'Zauberflöte'" ("Design for 'The Magic Flute'"), Fig. 1.27. While this water color rendering illustrates his ability to obtain reality when he wished to do so, his pencil presentation "Packhofgebaude, Berlin" (Fig. 1.28) shows that he could, when he wished, present a much more simplified study. This simplification may have been a frank recognition of the simplicity of "modern" architecture, which was beginning to appear.

Fig. 1.28 Packhofgebaude, Berlin.
Carl Friedrich Schinkel, draftsman

Fig. 1.29   Preliminary Design of Fonthill Abbey. James Wyatt, draftsman

Fig. 1.30   Cottage Design for a
Single Labourer. Joseph Gandy, draftsman

Fig. 1.31   Design for Dunrobbin Castle. Sir Charles Barry, draftsman

This versatility is also evident in the renderings of nineteenth century England. James Wyatt (1746–1813) in his "Preliminary Design of Fonthill Abbey" (Fig. 1.29), shows the building standing starkly in late afternoon sunlight against the beautiful English countryside. Instead of describing the building in detail, this treatment emphasized the mood it was to have. During the same period numerous small cottage designs were done in a similar manner (Fig. 1.30).

A number of architects also began to explore the possibilities of the newly invented pencil. Sir Charles Barry, in his "Design for Dunrobbin Castle" (Fig. 1.31), seems to have understood the new medium better than most of his contemporaries, many of whom nearly covered the paper with graphite in their effort to show detail.

Delineation in America   European tradition has had a strong effect upon delineation in the United States. The numerous European architects who migrated to America brought with them the methods and techniques they had learned and practiced in their homelands. The architects who practiced here were either educated in Europe or trained in the United States under the English pupilage system. Group architectural training was first given in American schools of technology, and as early as 1860 was taught as part of the science of building. However, the Society of Beaux Arts Architects, formed in New York in 1894, helped to encourage a less mathematical approach to rendering. Gradually, as the American schools of architecture matured, they took the burden of education upon themselves. Today great numbers of students from various countries of the world now come to the United States to study architecture.

Rendering Today   Not only are the traditional materials, such as water color, pen and ink, etc., used in present day rendering, but new materials and media are constantly being invented, and the traditional media are constantly being improved. New kinds of pencils, inks, and papers are being offered, and they are relatively available and relatively inexpensive.

Looking back, it may be seen that the forces that affected the development of architectural rendering have been interwoven with the major developments that helped shape the civilizations of the world. The skills and techniques developed by architects since man first became interested in the pictorial aspects of architecture have been nurtured, then passed down to each succeeding generation. The line of development from the architectural hieroglyphs of the Ancient Kingdom of Egypt to today's renderings is a straight one, varying now and then, but always growing and developing toward a more versatile presentation.

This line of growth was made possible by many forces, some of them architectural, some not. Chief among them was the desire of all architects to bridge the gap between their own imaginations and those of other people who were not architects, to explain complicated thoughts in an uncomplicated manner. Today any subject matter may be pictured if the basic tools and a knowledge of techniques are at hand. Perspective, shades and shadows, and other techniques could be discovered only when someone provided the inspiration and the medium with which to draw. The ability to render may have lain dormant for centuries before paper appeared at the time of the Renaissance, yet could not be expressed. To this one invention alone we owe eternal gratitude. If the landscape painter gave the stimulus to the quest for reality, so did the inventor of the camera, but neither could have produced rendering as we know it. It took the endless patience of many architects, to experiment and to push into the unknown, as well as to try new media.

The Architect as Delineator   Every architect has no doubt felt the desire to know more about delineation, so that his clients may see their buildings as he has conceived them. Many architects have not had sufficient specialized training in rendering and hesitate to sketch because they lack information about materials and techniques. With the directions found in this book, it will require only a little effort and persistence for an architect to master the various techniques. Proficiency will come with practice.

The importance of rendering in architecture

MODERN CONSTRUCTION is complex, but what would it be like if instructions were by words alone? The answer is, of course, that a large building, such as a skyscraper, probably could not be built at all, while even the smallest building would require constant on-the-job direction by a resident architect. Since one architect could build only a few buildings during his lifetime, there simply would not be enough architects to go around. Available practitioners would be hired by the wealthy, and the middle and lower classes would be left literally out in the cold.

Drawing, then, is of great value, not only to the architect, but to all mankind in this complex society. But if our society has become complex, so has architectural drawing, and today few laymen can understand or "read" working drawings. Because of this, the architectural picture, or rendering, has become an important and indispensable part of today's practice. The picture is a bridge between the intellect of the client and that of the architect—a common meeting ground without hard-to-understand technicalities. Both of the two possible substitutes have proved inadequate: the model because it completely lacks human scale; the unrendered linear perspective because it neither describes materials and textures nor tells which areas are voids and which solids.

If the rendering is important as a means of communication between architect and client, it is doubly important to the architect himself, inasmuch as it is his means of visualizing the building and thereby eliminating flaws in the design.

The finished sketch usually represents an amalgamation as well as a refinement of the ideas of both owner and architect. The owner, when he is first interviewed, usually has many ideas of his own. These he describes to the architect verbally, or possibly by a rough sketch. Some of these ideas may be good, some not. In any case, they must be taken into consideration. Using his knowledge and skills, the architect tries to utilize the owner's ideas, and if possible to improve upon them. This is done by sketching. The pencil sketch is of mutual value to architect and owner because it can help to settle at an early stage any possible disagreements and misunderstandings about the design of the building. The architect himself, in order to "prove out" the design that has grown from the meeting of minds between himself and the owner, usually makes numerous freehand perspective sketches of the building from various points of view. These quick sketches enable him to eliminate flaws before they become part of the working drawings and are built. As a final guarantee that the design is acceptable to the owner, a finished rendering (the degree of finish will depend upon the size of the job) is made and shown to the owner before working drawings and specifications are begun.

Few owners will depend solely upon an architect's reputation in the design of a building, and nearly all will ask for some kind of picture of it before they will proceed. At the same time, few architects will use such poor judgment as to proceed with construction drawings before the owner has been shown what his structure will ultimately look like. Otherwise the owner may be painfully surprised at its final appearance. There are on record actual cases in which a client has refused to accept a building after its completion, and there is even a case in which a South American church building could not be used for years because the governing board would not consecrate it.

Renderings for Study   The rendering accomplishes a number of other things for the architect. It permits him, in one of the few approved ways, to "sell" the job to his client. Many a project has been abandoned in the sketch stage because the client was simply not inspired by a good rendering to want to build. The rendering also offers an early opportunity for determining textures and colors of materials. If these look well in the rendering, they will indeed be handsome in the finished building. The rendering is more than a pretty picture; it is a guide for actual construction.

Some clients will suggest colors and textures of materials, but if the client does not volunteer suggestions, the architect can either ask him for his ideas, or obtain them by observing the client's home, his clothing, and the color of his car. He should try to find out if there are colors and textures that the client dislikes, since these must be assiduously avoided. Finally, the architect must be sure to show accurately and honestly how the building will look in its actual surroundings. He must be particularly careful to show existing trees and bushes if they are to remain; the owner usually admires foliage on his property.

If the rendering is important in communicating with an individual client, it is doubly helpful in dealing with building committees, boards, or design juries. An adequate picture often serves as a strong point of agreement between groups of people (architects as well as laymen), since it provides an equal opportunity for each individual to see for himself what the final building will look like. It quickly evokes an approval and eliminates hours of haggling. On the other hand, if the design is poor, or if the rendering is too sketchy, "stunty," or badly drawn, a group, like an individual, will quickly react unfavorably. In the school of architecture, a poorly rendered design, or one presented in the graphic linear manner, gives the jury the impression that the student does not understand his own design, or is afraid of bringing out its bad points. There are exceptions to this, and rightly so, but for the most part an adequately rendered design problem will always compete favorably with the rest.

Once the rendering has been made and the design that it illustrates accepted, it becomes a useful tool to the owner. It is, together with sketch plans, a tangible thing with which to apply for a mortgage or other financial backing. Few lending institutions will advance money without a proper description of the project.

If the structure is being planned for a large organization, it is usually necessary for those in charge of the building program to obtain final approval from the president and board of the company before proceeding to the construction stage. Once such approval is obtained, they can turn the rendering over to an advertising department or agency, which will in turn stimulate public interest and justify the expenditure to the stockholders. Such a picture has definite prestige and advertising value to the company itself. Charitable institutions and churches can use such a drawing to raise funds for the proposed addition or new building.

There are times also when a rendering is needed to obtain approval by zoning boards, planning commissions, and other governmental bodies. Sometimes, if acceptance of a building depends upon public vote, thousands of copies of the rendering are made and distributed directly to the voters before election.

The rendering, then, is an indispensable, practical item for both the architect and owner. But it must be recognized that it also gives a great emotional satisfaction to the client, who usually has saved or planned for years before being able to proceed with his project. The rendering is visual evidence of his success, and it helps the architect to carry the owner's dreams toward reality.

Renderings and Financial Backing

Renderings and Prestige

Chapter 3

The magic of imagery

The Natural Setting

THE WORLD OF NATURE supplies an inexhaustible storehouse of inspiration to the delineator, who may be required at any time to portray in its setting a mountaintop ski lodge, a tropical house, or anything in between. He must have the ability to visualize scenes in brilliant sunlight or dull gray mist, according to the location and mood of the project at hand. He should be familiar with all kinds of trees and shrubbery, from the twisted, gnarled limber pine of the heights to the graceful spruce, fir, pine, elm, maple, and oak of the fertile hills and valleys. Skies are his property too, whether light, blue, and cheerful, or dark, gray, and forbidding. Many projects are built on bodies of water, so he must be able to simulate it, whether it is as small and placid as a street puddle, as peaceful as a lagoon, or as wild as the bubbling, rushing mountain stream. The renderer must be able to borrow the wild fragrant beauties of the deep wood, the quiet dignity of the well-mannered countryside, or the bustling excitement of the smoky city.

These are the raw materials of nature that provide inspiration and vocabulary for pictorial expression. Selected according to need and combined as desired, they provide colorful settings for the endless varieties of buildings to be rendered.

It would be helpful indeed if this great vocabulary could be memorized, but few of us can manage such feats. Instead, the average renderer studies the basic qualities and proportions of elements, such as trees, that he uses most often. If possible, he takes pictures of each site and renders from these, adding foliage or removing it as required. Finally, he draws upon the work of the photographer and usually keeps a file of pictures nearby for inspiration.

Selection of Elements

A great part of the success of any rendering depends upon the proper selection of these natural elements for the project at hand. A public building must, above all, appear dignified, and therefore should be rendered with a quiet, cloudless sky, and quiet surroundings. If color is used, it should be subtle.

A mausoleum might be rendered in much the same way, but with the introduction of weeping willow trees, whose bowed branches and trailing foliage suggest sorrow. A church is often pictured best in the oblique rays of early morning light, since it is usually used at that time. On the other hand, many buildings, by their very nature, should be rendered in a gay, bustling mood. Theaters, restaurants, motion picture houses, and bowling alleys are in this category. Here the spectator can be made to "feel" the excitement of the building by the use of fleecy clouds, large groups of scale figures, automobiles, and bright spots of color. Natural elements should be carefully selected for each project, with suitability ever in mind.

The world of nature supplies ideas for the setting of the rendered building, but what about the building itself? Illustrating it requires knowledge of a combination of sciences: perspective, shades and shadows, and the workings of light. If it is to be rendered in color, the principles of color theory must be observed, since they provide the renderer with certain simple rules, not only for the sophisticated use of color, but for the actual mixing of the pigments themselves. The subtle colors in a fine rendering are not accidental: they are the result of much study and experience. Most people (that is, all who are not color blind) can attain excellent results by the use of a few simple rules. The color-blind delineator (and there are a few) usually works in one color, or in black and white.

Finally, a facility in composition is vital to the renderer. Unless the various forms in a picture are composed properly, chaos will result.

Skills for Rendering Buildings

Use of all of the above sciences will provide a perspective in line and a color scheme if color is to be used. From this point forward, the skills required are those of the renderer. While the modern artist often works for abstract beauty alone, the architectural delineator seeks abstract beauty plus the illusion of reality.

Abstract beauty in an architectural picture is the result of conscious arrangement of the representational elements in the picture (such as building, foreground, background, trees, sky, and scale figures), so that they form a surface design that is pleasant to look at even if interest in the subject matter is disregarded for the moment. It is obtained by organizing the various components of the picture, such as lines, planes, lights, darks, movement, and color into a pleasing unified geometric pattern. This is done by making a number of preliminary charcoal or pencil sketches of the composition before the final rendering is begun.

Achieving Reality Plus Beauty

The technique—that is, the method used in the execution of a rendering—depends upon the medium to be used, the subject matter, and desired mood of the picture. Pointed media, such as the graphite pencil and pen and ink, lend themselves to the rendering of buildings with a lot of texture and small elements. The carbon pencil, smudge charcoal, pastels, water color, tempera, and the airbrush, all of which are "area" media (with the possible exception of the carbon pencil, which can be used as either a pointed or an area medium), are most suitable to rendering buildings with large, plain wall areas. Sometimes water color is combined with graphite pencil or with pen and ink.

It is an interesting fact that the average delineator specializes in one or two media. This limitation is sometimes due to the shortage of time available for rendering, or lack of time for experimentation. More often it is because of a lack of training in the use of other media. While few people attain

Choice of Medium

equal proficiency in all of the media, it is a good idea at least to try them all. This frequently leads one not only to discover that he likes a new medium better than the one he has been using, but that his degree of success is greater. Part of the enjoyment of teaching rendering lies in helping the student discover the medium to which he is psychologically best suited. Once he finds his medium, he becomes more sure of himself and his renderings begin to assume a professional appearance.

Refinement and Style   There are times when a quick sketch is sufficient, and others when a finished rendering is called for. The time element will always be with us. In all of the chapters on technique, the author has endeavored to describe both methods. It is earnestly hoped that the reader will not only try the methods described in this book, but will experiment with new media and techniques.

Finally a word about developing a style. Everyone in a primary class is taught to write the same way. Before long, however, each individual's writing begins to look different from anyone else's. Each adult's writing has characteristics all its own, and even the average bank teller can distinguish it from hundreds of thousands of others. It is the same with style in drawing or rendering. If a delineator copies the work of a professional renderer whose style he admires, little growth will manifest itself until he lays the model aside. He should look at the work of many men, analyze it, learn from it, and then try to use what he has learned in his own work. Competence comes with much patience, practice, and experience.

A *quick look at perspective*

THE DISCOVERY of perspective by the painters and architects of the fifteenth century gave them and all who lived after them a means of combining in one drawing width, depth, and height. Drawings made before that time were distorted and flat. For about four centuries the three-dimensional perspective was used by artist and architect alike, and many painters produced pictures of existing buildings and also worked along with architects to render in perspective buildings still on the drawing board. When the camera was invented early in the nineteenth century, the photographer quickly took the place of the artist who painted existing architecture. Artists began to seek new means of expression that the camera could not duplicate and found such expression in the cubists' use of a fourth dimension, in abstraction, dadaism, expressionism, fantasy, fauvism, and the like. Many artists, shunning realism, followed the new movement and no longer worked with architects.

Artists, Architects, and Perspective

The cubist, for instance, combined in one picture a number of different views of the same object from a number of stations, as if he were walking around the object. Architectural rendering, however, requires clarity and simplicity and could not utilize this concept. As no better method than the rendered scenic perspective has yet been invented for studying or illustrating architectural design, it is still universally used by architects, some of whom have become specialists in architectural rendering.

Most beginners do not realize the importance of making a proper perspective before they are actually ready to begin to render. There is no substitute for a thorough knowledge of all of the phases of perspective, which it is assumed the reader already has. The average student of perspective, however, is appalled, not only by its complexity, but also by the fact that very little is said by many authors to bridge the gap between the rules for constructing a linear perspective and the magical finished mental image which he intends to put on paper. Anyone who has studied perspective as a science can draw a finished perspective, but there is a difference between a soulless mechanical drawing of this kind and one which takes advantage of a few rules discovered by the professionals. One can learn about the rules of baseball by reading a book; playing it is another matter. So can the ren-

Rules Plus Experience

derer learn the basic rules of perspective, and apply them in an unintelligent way. Later, however, his experience teaches him that the selection of a viewpoint, for instance, must be made with great skill if he is to get the most out of his rendering. We have all had the sad experience, I am sure, of laboriously plotting the various required points for a perspective, only to discover after hours of work that the viewpoint selected did not show the building to its best advantage. If we were doing the job for ourselves we wasted several hours of our precious time. If we were employed by someone, it was hard to explain such an error to our employer.

Perspective as Indicator of Bad Design

What are the purposes for making a linear perspective? Certainly to provide a good, clean drawing which describes the shape of the building and gives a complete guide for the rendering. But even more than that, and more basically, the linear perspective shows, before we have spent a great deal of time at rendering, what the building is going to look like from various angles. If the proportions of our design are bad, this shortcoming will quickly manifest itself, and we will know immediately that we must redesign the sections of the building that do not look well. Unscrupulous persons have purposely drawn their perspectives so as to improve inferior designs. This approach is not only dishonest, but dangerous, since the eventual disillusionment can lead to all sorts of trouble.

Selection of Viewpoint

There is no substitute for a correct and honest perspective. In addition to its truthfulness, a perspective should be marked by its ability to make the building seem to "live"—to look exactly as it will when it is constructed. This means that the viewpoint must be a believable one, but not necessarily at the usual eye height. Sometimes it is better to take a viewpoint that is either higher or lower than eye level. The viewpoint should vary with the size and type of building.

The viewpoint, or "point-of-station," is the fundamental point of a perspective, since the position of every working point depends upon its selection. The "point-of-station" has a dual position; it appears in both plan and elevation. The position in plan decides the location of the vanishing points and measuring points. Its location in elevation determines the location of the horizon. A house designed for the top of a hill might be studied so that the spectator seems to be looking up at it from the bottom of the hill. This means that he would select a viewpoint at the elevation of the bottom of the hill. On the other hand, if the house is perched on the edge of a cliff, a viewpoint at the bottom of the hill would show too much of the underside of the building. Here a bird's-eye view, with the eye level above the level of the house, would probably provide the best picture.

The viewpoint for a house with a body of water in the foreground must be chosen to show enough water for interesting reflections. The viewpoint for a tall building, such as a church or other towerlike structure, or perhaps a skyscraper, should be taken quite low so that the inspiring height of the building will manifest itself most clearly. On the other hand, if a bird's-eye view of such a building is required, the viewpoint should be taken high enough to show the whole building and all its interesting setbacks. Large trees, rocks, or other identifying landmarks should be carefully located in the pencil perspective to help the client visualize the actual site with the building in place.

Sometimes it will be found that for large complexes of buildings, such as industrial establishments, it is impossible to obtain a truly descriptive view without resorting to an aerial perspective, as well as one or more ground level views. In selecting the viewpoint for aerial perspectives, several rules must be observed and then modified by experience. To begin with, too high an eye level will show too much of the roof area and too little of the wall areas. If the building complex is made up of groups of buildings which are located at various angles on the plot, the point of view must be taken so that none of the buildings are shown in too foreshortened or oblique a manner. It is quite usual in selecting a point of view for such a project to include not only all of the buildings, but the driveways, walkways, parking areas, and surrounding areas such as farmland, forest, water, or adjoining buildings. Note also that in aerial perspectives of low buildings glazed areas are completely transparent, and therefore floors, furniture, and other interior furnishings that can be seen must be completely and accurately constructed before the rendering is begun.

Aerial Perspective

The viewpoint may frequently be selected in order to show the approaches to a building and to point out the main entrance. It is well to indicate outstanding trees and bushes, and other important characteristics of the site, in order that the spectator can quickly orient himself. In a normal ground view it is, of course, necessary to show these as well as such other local color as scale figures, automobiles, buses, or trucks. For industrial plants, railroad cars should be shown.

The most interesting ground level perspective is the one that shows two sides of a building, with one side dominating. If the project at hand happens to be a city building with only one facade showing, the greatest interest can be obtained by taking the viewpoint to the left or right of the center of the building. A great many delineators, particularly on projects which have one "best" elevation, construct their perspectives so that this is the only one that can be seen. Architectural photographers, too, seem to make this mistake.

Details and Dominating Facades

There are a few general guides which should be followed in making a perspective, and although most of them are mentioned in books specifically devoted to the subject, it is worthwhile repeating them here:

1. The location of the station point will determine the location of the vanishing points and measuring points. Angle "C," created by projections between the point-of-station and the limits of the building, should not be more than 60 degrees. Some authorities even say that it should not be greater than 45 degrees, since a wider angle than this will distort the view of the building. In any case, the station point should be in the center of the visual cone (Fig. 4.1).

2. A line between the point-of-station and the corner of the building which intersects the picture plane at "A" should bisect this angle "C." The picture plane should be perpendicular to the line of vision, "SA."

3. The point-of-station in plan should be such that more of one side of the building, obviously the most important side, should be shown. The fact that one side is foreshortened more perceptibly than the other gives a pleasing contrast to the perspective.

General Rules for Mechanical Perspectives

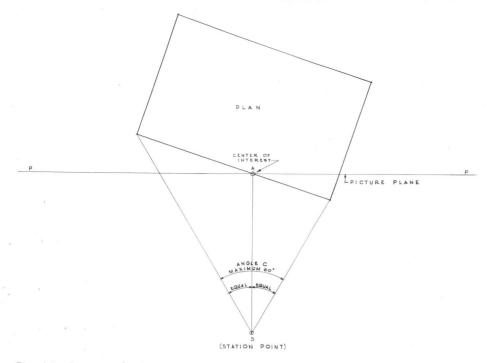

Fig. 4.1   Locating the Station Point

4. Avoid a dead center vanishing point in a one-point perspective. A viewpoint either left or right of center will invariably give a better looking perspective.

5. In ground level perspectives, it is well to keep the horizon line low. This will enable you to limit the amount of foreground, at least on a flat site, and to concentrate attention on the building itself. It is difficult to arrive at a definite rule for the height of the foreground; however, an analysis of the work of successful renderers will show that this distance is usually limited to one-third of the height of the sheet, at the very most. It may in fact be considerably less, and can vary from one-seventh to one-third the height of the sheet.

Of course, if the building is on a hill, or if there is something important to be shown in the foreground, such as a reflecting pool, the height of such foreground may be more than one-third the height of the picture.

6. If, after the rendering has been begun, the foreground appears to be massive in relation to the rest of the picture, it may be vignetted—that is, made smaller by stopping it at an irregular line before it reaches the mat line (Fig. 4.2).

7. When making a perspective of a long, low building, it is frequently desirable, instead of locating the picture plane at a corner of the building, to move it so that it bisects the elevation at a point approximately one-third the length of the building from the point closest to the point of view. This enlarges the perspective and keeps it from looking too long and low.

8. In order to locate the point-of-station properly, care should be taken not to place it too near the building, since the vanishing and measuring points will be too close together and distortion will result. On the other hand, if it is located too far away from the building, considerable detail will be lost.

A good rule for locating the point-of-station in an aerial perspective is to limit the distance between the ground line and point-of-station to one-half the distance between the station point and the nearest part of the building.

Fig. 4.2   Vignetting the Foreground (See also Fig. 15.11)

9. The backgrounds of aerial perspectives, particularly when they are very complicated and encompass vast areas, are not usually constructed, but are drawn by eye.

10. In the mechanical layout of circular forms, such as lighting fixtures or tables in interior perspectives, those at the sides of the drawing usually acquire a distorted appearance. Here it is best to take liberties and draw the ellipses without distortion by using a horizontal axis as the center line of each ellipse.

11. To avoid distortion in the perspective of a circular building, lay out the perspective through the center of the circle.

Perspective Charts and Perspective Scales

For those who prefer a less mathematical method of constructing perspectives, there are perspective charts. These consist of perspective grids which have been laid out for different perspective conditions. A set of such charts consists of perspective grids for a number of desired types of perspectives. The architect simply fastens the desired chart to his board, lays a piece of tracing paper over it, and using each grid section as a module related to the scale of his perspective, determines his horizontal and vertical dimensions over the grids below.

While the use of grid charts obviates the necessity for a large drawing board, and certainly cuts down the amount of brainwork and patience required in the construction of a perspective, it should be recognized that perspective charts cannot be made for every desired condition. In addition, if the design of the building is slightly changed, it is much easier to go back to a constructed perspective to make the corrections than to try to make the corrections over a perspective chart. There are many cases when an architect will find both perspective charts and perspective scales useful.

Perspective by Approximation

Delineators are always looking for short cuts to help to reduce the amount of time required for making line perspectives. Some merely lay out the main lines of the building and then locate doors, windows, and other detail by eye. Others, like Vincent Furno, use (on ground perspectives only) either of the two methods illustrated in Fig. 4.3A and 4.3B, in which the main lines and a number of perspective guide lines are used as a basis for perspective by eye.

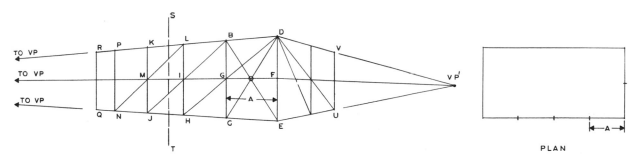

Fig. 4.3A   Perspective by Approximation: Method No. 1

1. Draw a freehand sketch of the building as you want to see it.

2. Place another piece of tracing paper over the rough sketch and extend lines to obtain vanishing points VP and VP[1].

3. Assuming the long facade has four equal divisions (this number will, of course, vary), lay out distance "A" in perspective by eye, and draw a

Method No. 1

vertical, "B-C," thereby creating a square (or rectangle, as the case may be) in perspective.

4. Draw diagonals BE and CD.

5. Divide DE in halves.

6. Draw a line through FO, and extend it past the left end of the long facade.

7. Draw a line through DG, continuing it until it strikes the base line of the building at H.

8. To create the second square or rectangle in the perspective, draw a perpendicular through H.

9. Draw a line through BI to J.

10. Draw a vertical JK, thus creating a third square in perspective.

11. Draw line LMN.

12. Draw vertical NP, thus creating the fourth square or rectangle in the perspective.

13. Erase area PRQN, which is extra building length. The long facade represented by DENP is now in approximately correct perspective.

14. To complete the perspective, lay out all horizontal distances by eye in reference to the four equal squares or rectangles.

15. To lay out heights, slide your scale left and right, holding it vertically, until you find the point at which the height of the building scales correctly, say at ST. Scale all vertical dimensions on it, and vanish all heights left and right as required.

16. Depths of reveals, etc., are laid out along EU and projected to their proper locations in perspective.

17. Complete the perspective on the short facade by following the same method described above.

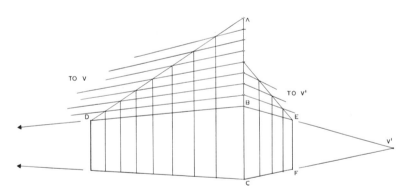

Fig. 4.3B   Perspective by Approximation: Method No. 2

Method No. 2   1. Draw a freehand sketch of the building as you want to see it.

2. Place another piece of tracing paper over the rough sketch and extend the horizontal lines of the building to vanishing points V and V^1.

3. Assuming you want to keep the length of your building as you have sketched it, refer to Fig. 4.3B and proceed with Steps 4–10.

4. Extend line CB vertically to A. (Length BA can be made equal to BC, or can be greater in length for ease of scaling.) If the long elevation of the building divides itself into, say, 30 equal parts, BA can be laid out in 30 equal increments at a convenient scale, such as $\frac{1}{4}$ in./1 ft.

5. Draw a line between A and D.

6. Draw a line from each point between A and B to V.

7. Draw vertical lines from the intersections of the vanishing lines drawn in Step 6 and line AD.

8. You now have 30 equal spaces laid out in perspective, and horizontal distances can be laid out by eye in relation to them.

9. The same method can be used to lay out increments on side BEFC.

10. Heights and depths of reveals can be laid out as described for Fig. 4.3A.

Great care must be exerted in transferring the perspective from the original construction—which is usually on tracing paper—to the paper upon which the rendering will be made. If the completed perspective itself turns out to be either too large or too small for the final picture, it can easily be increased or decreased in size by having it photostated and its dimensions changed in the process. In fairness to your photostat operator, however, you should note on the perspective the actual dimension—length or height—that you would like him to make the print. If photostat facilities are not readily available, the perspective may be enlarged or diminished by the use of a planograph, proportional divider, or other means. The photostat, however, saves many hours of drafting.

There are a number of ways of "transferring" the perspective from either the original perspective drawing or the photostat to the rendering paper. The best of these, and the one which will give you the cleanest line drawing, is done as follows:

Trace the perspective on a sheet of good rag bond tracing paper, using an "F" or "H" pencil. After it has been traced from the original drawing, carefully roll and file the original in a safe place. It represents many hours' work and you may need it again. One of the saddest events that the author can remember happened when he was a young draftsman—the destruction of a complicated perspective tracing by his boss's dog, Dinty. The office wasn't the same for weeks.

Turn this new tracing upside down and trace every line through on the back of the tracing paper. You are now ready to transfer the drawing to your rendering paper. Look at the charcoal or pencil study that you have made showing the location of the building in the picture, and, using this as a guide, locate the perspective in the proper place. Fasten the tracing down tightly with tape or thumb tacks and then, with a sharp 2-H or 3-H pencil, trace every line so that the pressure of the pencil will transfer the graphite to the sheet below. If you press too hard, you will not only tear the tracing paper, but you will indent the rendering paper and damage it so that it may be useless for rendering.

After the transfer has been made, strengthen the drawing on your rendering paper so that you have a clear, clean, complete drawing to work with. This process may be used exactly for renderings in graphite pencil, pen and ink, water color, tempera, and airbrush.

However, the final transfer for carbon pencil, lithograph pencil, pastels, and smudge charcoal is best accomplished by inserting a large sheet of carbon paper, face down, between the tracing and the rendering paper. The process is then completed as before, and any strengthening of lines should be done with a carbon pencil. The use of carbon and carbon pencil is necessary in the above-mentioned media, as these media will not "take" over graphite pencil, which is a slippery medium.

Use of Colored Paper   If colored paper is being used for the rendering, it will be found that white carbon paper is desirable, allowing all the transferred lines to be easily seen.

A simple pencil (graphite or carbon) line drawing on the rendering paper will suffice for the various pencil media, pen and ink, smudge charcoal, water color, tempera, and pastels. For rendering in Chinese ink—in which much sponging is done—it is best to make a dilute ink line drawing on cold pressed paper and then to erase all pencil lines.

When you have reached this point, if your schedule permits, it is well to put the drawing aside for a while, as the mechanical process of the work that you have just completed conflicts sharply with the more creative mental attitude required for the actual rendering.

Chapter 5

Some rules of composition

Rules, Practice, and Beauty

THE BEAUTY of a finished rendering skillfully done frequently astounds the novice. He is likely to assume that the delineator is some sort of genius who can make beautiful pictures without any great effort, and he may be right. But most delineators (and even most geniuses) must learn the basic rules and methods when they first begin to study rendering. Not that some do not learn faster than others, but all must learn the basic rules, and consciously practice them before they can acquire skill. One must toddle before he walks, and walk before he runs. Many an architect, not understanding this, and not realizing that renderings are executed by the use of a definite series of steps, has given up, believing that he has no talent for this art. The author can say unequivocally that *anyone* can learn to render if he has the patience, and *wants* to learn all of the related arts such as composition.

Arranging lines, masses, and color into an harmonious whole is an important phase of producing a satisfactory rendering. All of the beauty of the building, as well as the beauties of nature, such as skies, trees, grass plots, and bushes; and the scale-giving elements, such as people and automobiles, can be incorporated into a homogeneous whole which is pleasant to look at, or they can be an inept, irritating collection of elements which will not please the eye. Neither the architect nor the layman will know *why* the rendering is not pleasant to look at—but both will know that it is not.

The three basic elements of composition may be called unity, emphasis, and balance. Let us first examine the principle of unity.

Unity

The various parts of a picture must be united in a skillfully ordered arrangement. The whole picture should be composed around the building, which is the center of interest. The building should occupy the greatest portion of the picture, so that it looks important and demands attention. Remember that the owner is interested first in the building, and second in the landscape and sky around it. The landscape around a building should be attractive, but only insofar as it complements the structure. The most magnificent sky, if it occupies too much of the picture, or demands too much attention, will detract from the building, and the building will lose importance. If the building is more horizontal than vertical, the composition should be a horizontal one. If, on the other hand, it is more vertical, a vertical composi-

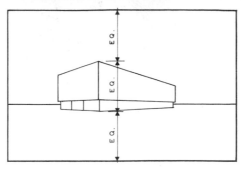
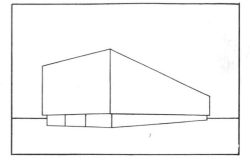

A. Wrong   B. Right

Fig. 5.2   Locating the Building in the Picture

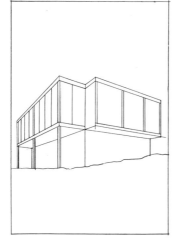

A. Wrong

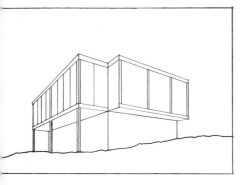

B. Right

Fig. 5.1   Fitting the Problem
to the Paper

The Illusion of Distance

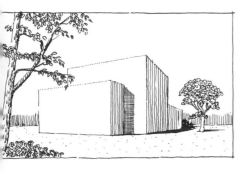

Fig. 5.3   The Perspective
of Trees

tion is called for. If this simple principle is followed, the shape of the building and the shape of the sheet of paper will complement each other and there will not be too much or too little sky area or entourage (Fig. 5.1).

When the size of the building and its proper relation to the shape of the paper have been decided, a number of charcoal or soft pencil studies can be made on tracing paper, showing surrounding elements such as roadways, walkways, trees, bushes; and other elements such as scale figures and automobiles in foreground, middleground, and background.

If the view is from the normal eye level, try locating the horizon line fairly low on the sheet so that the foreground is quite foreshortened. Remember that the distance between the bottom of the picture and the bottom of the building should never be the same as the height of the building itself, and that neither of these should be the same as the height of the sky. See Fig. 5.2.

In these studies, try consciously to connect all of the elements of the picture in a meaningful manner; perhaps by value, or color, or perspective movement. Keep the pattern simple, but also keep it from being monotonous. Eliminate all detail in these early studies; the detail will fall into its proper place if the main elements are first properly located. In placing trees, make one of them dominant—higher and more detailed than the rest. Make one side of your composition richer by the use of tree groupings, but not so much richer that the opposite side will appear flat. In showing trees, experiment by using them in groups; a single tree usually has a lonesome look and is not important in itself. If there are trees on the site which will be located between the point of vision and the building, draw them so that they will not obscure the building itself or parts thereof. Leave the lower branches bare.

One of the best ways to create the illusion of distance in a picture is to make the trees and bushes in the foreground tallest, those in the mid-distance slightly shorter, and those in the distance shortest. Those in the foreground will be quite detailed; individual leaves and the tree structure will be seen very plainly, so these must be accurately detailed. Those in the mid-distance will be lighter in value and less detailed, while those in the distance will merely be shown in mass and may be quite light. See Fig. 5.3. Remembering that a final effect of restfulness and repose is desired, avoid a perspective of landscape in which one or more of the elements (such as a row of trees) seems to run out of the picture. See Fig. 5.4. If the site is such that this cannot be avoided, take the liberty of showing a dark tree of a type different from those on the site astride the row of trees that seem to run out of the picture. Make this tree higher so that it definitely "cuts" the perspective movement. See Fig. 5.5.

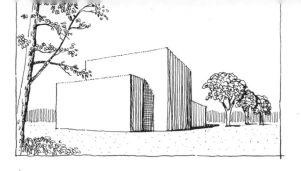
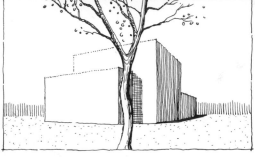

A
B

Fig. 5.4   Tree Arrangements to Avoid

In rendering a building which is curved in plan or elevation, trees with straight trunks should be used in front of and near it (Fig. 5.6A). If, on the other hand, the building is long and rectilinear, its appearance can be softened by using groups of bending trees—such as birches—to cut the harsh lines of the building and to keep it from seeming to "float." These trees should be located at a point which is roughly a third of the length of the building (Fig. 5.6B). If trees such as these are not on the site, it is usually safe to show them, and to suggest to the owner that they be included in the landscaping program.

The arrangement of trees in a rendering may be accomplished in numerous ways. A few of these are shown in Fig. 5.6; analysis of the various illustrations throughout this book will reveal many others.

Bushes should be shown (and planted) in groups placed so that they soften the lines of the building, and lead the eye to the center of interest, usually the entrance. See Fig. 5.7. If there are hills or mountains in the background looming above the height of the building, centering one of them

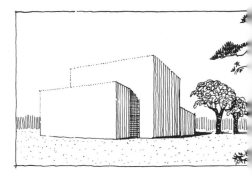

Fig. 5.5   Stopping Perspective Movement with a Different Tree Type

Fig. 5.6   Complementing the Design with Trees

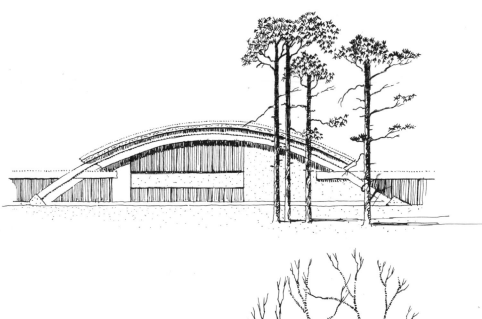

A

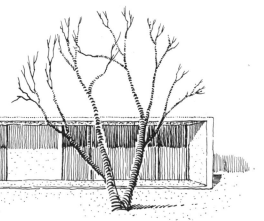

B

Fig. 5.7 Locating the Center of Interest with Bushes

in the picture behind the building will make the rendering monotonous and uninteresting, and should be avoided. The highest peak can be located off to one side, and all of the lower ranges placed so that they lead up to the highest mountain. Ranges of mountains should never be drawn parallel to each other; instead, the eye should be led from the low ranges in the foreground to the highest range in the background by the use of a zig-zag arrangement of mountaintops.

Emphasis

We mentioned earlier in the chapter that the building must be the most important element in the composition. It must receive the greatest emphasis, not only by means of size, but also by value. When we have completed a rendering, it must be easily "read," or understood, at a glance. This means that the building itself must be complemented by the use of value and color in the surroundings.

Having selected a source for the sunlight, we already know which side of the building will be in light and which in shade. Obviously, in order to make the building appear to be three-dimensional, the light side should have dark areas next to it for contrast. On the other hand, those parts of the building which are dark because they are in shade should have light values next to them so that they stand out to best advantage as shown in Fig. 5.8. A light sky, for instance, is often used behind that side of the building which is dark, and a dark sky behind those areas which are light, so that the building does not seem to "float" in the sky. Using dark against light and light against dark is a safe rule to follow. The rendering is intended to express the forms of the architecture, and value comparisons should be arranged accordingly.

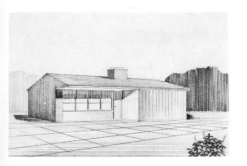

Fig. 5.8 Use of Contrast

Value Studies

There are a number of basic approaches which are worth considering in making value studies. The first of these, and probably the most usual, is (as described in the chapter on light) an arrangement showing elements in the foreground as darkest and those in the distance as lightest, with gradations between. A number of variations to this scheme are possible:

1. Gray foreground, light building and mid-distance, and dark background.
2. Light foreground, dark building, and gray background.
3. Light foreground, gray building, and dark background.
4. Dark foreground, light building, and gray background.
5. Light foreground, dark building, and light background.

All of these are illustrated in Fig. 5.9, "Basic Value Arrangements."

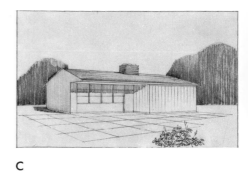

A   B   C

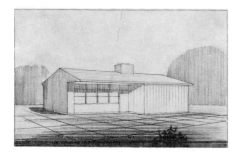

D   E

Fig. 5.9   Basic Value Arrangements

No matter which of these arrangements is used, it is well to throw a dark shadow on the ground in the foreground, whether from trees or from a building behind the spectator, so that the building will seem to recede into the distance. If, when the rough value study has been completed, the building or parts of it appear indistinct, putting some "gray" or dark trees immediately behind the structure will help it to stand out.

Emphasis Within the Building

We have already established the fact that the building should occupy the major position in the rendering, and by so doing capture greatest emphasis. In addition, there should be emphasis within the building itself. This may be at an entrance, at a door, or at some other important part of the building. Emphasis on parts of the structure can be achieved by great value comparison. For example, the wall area around an entrance may be quite light, while the entrance itself may have very dark shadows. A whole section of a building may be emphasized by rendering it lightly with a dark background or with dark trees next to it. Once the part of the building to be emphasized has been decided, the rest of the building should be deliberately de-emphasized, possibly by value comparisons less strong than those at the focal point, or by showing greatest detail near the center of interest and gradually reducing surrounding detail as its distance from the center increases. See Fig. 5.10.

Fig. 5.10   Locating the Center of Interest

An entrance may be emphasized in other ways: a roadway, for instance, may curve from the foreground of the rendering to the entrance, thus leading the eye to it. Such a roadway may be lined with shrubbery or trees. Groups of figures may be located strategically so that the eye is led from a group in the foreground to others on the walkways, and still others near the entrance. Truck docks, carports, or garages may be "pointed out" by showing automobiles or trucks in or near them.

When color is used, vital parts of a building may be emphasized with bright colors, and less important parts of the building "played down" by the use of more subdued colors.

To emphasize the height of a building it is well to use a low point of view, i.e., near the ground, since this will diminish the height of the foreground and make the building seem high by comparison.

Balance

Once a dominant center of interest has been established, all other parts of the composition should be arranged around it so that each part receives its proper relative emphasis. The sections should be united by values which are neither too light nor too dark to hold them together. For instance, a dark foreground and a gray background will not hold together if a white streak of paper separates them. Such a situation may be remedied by joining them together with parallel ground areas which gradually diminish in value from the dark foreground to the light background. These areas may be tonal or color variations of earth, lawn, fields, shrubs, ground shadows, etc.

Tone Balance

It is well to assess the value study as you work upon it. Pin it on a tackboard and analyze it critically from a distance. You must be your severest critic. You may discover during these analyses that one part of the rendering has become much darker than the rest, and the composition seems to be out of balance. Or a very dark shadow, or dark trees on one side of the rendering, may seem to weigh it down so that the other side seems to "float." This situation can be remedied by lightening the side which is too dark, drawing some darker objects, such as trees or shadows, on the opposite side of the sheet, or both. It should be remembered that a small dark area will balance a much larger "gray" area.

Occasionally you may find that no matter how hard you try, your composition contains too much sky. Showing a group of leafy tree branches which hang into the sky area from a tree located behind the spectator will improve the composition. In addition to correcting a sky that is too large, tree branches such as these usually help to provide a dark framework for the picture. See Fig. 5.11, "Framing the Picture with Tree Branches."

A good way to check the balance of a composition and keep the building the major item of importance is to make sure that the area the building occupies is not equaled by either the area of the foreground or the area of the sky.

Fig. 5.11   Framing the Picture with Tree Branches

Abstracting the Composition

The beginner invariably tries to show too much in a composition. He may indicate too much of the lawn, too many cars in a parking space, too much detail in the foliage, and so on. He may profitably borrow from the modern artist, such as Matisse, who begins by drawing or painting a detailed picture and gradually, in successive sketches, simplifies it, each time leaving out a detail which is not absolutely necessary for the purpose of identification. Architecturally this means that in the value study stage we should deliberately leave out, or erase, parts of a lawn that has become too large, shrubbery which has become overpowering, parts of a stone indication that looks monotonous because there is too much of it, clouds that seem to detract from the building itself, and detail in general. The student sometimes considers this an ironical bit of advice on the ground that if a small amount of a thing is good, a large amount is better. However, as he becomes more proficient at rendering he too eliminates unnecessary details.

Chapter 6

A *study of light*

PERHAPS IN NO OTHER ERA have buildings been glazed in so many different ways. Often glass is used in small openings; sometimes it is used in large areas. Occasionally glass is used as the major part of the facade. Many times exterior elements such as low walls and gardens project themselves through the glass and into the interior. The manner in which glass is rendered depends upon its size and location in a given building. While Lever House, for instance, has transparent panes as part of what has been called the cultivated elegance of the decorator architecture,[1] other buildings have curtain walls, and still others have sash which are playfully sized and located in the manner termed "brutal expression" ("the hard, dissident articulation of the individual parts of the building"[2]).

But another element enters into the appearance of glass in a rendering. When heat-absorbing or glare-reducing glass is used, or when the sash are set deep in an exterior wall, the window openings will appear to be somewhat dark and of a bronze, gray, or green cast, according to the type of glass used. Occasionally a building will be designed so that its outer walls are of mirrored-type glass, which appears as a mirror when viewed from a brightly lighted side and is transparent to the viewer on the darker opposite side. When clear glass is used in large openings, the delineator must, in an exterior view, show the furniture, furnishings, walls, floor and ceiling, interior planting, and any other objects in the design as if the glass wall were not there (Plate VII). Of course, the extent of the interior that may be seen will depend upon the depth of interior spaces, the angle of the perspective, and the amount of sunlight that can reach the interior, as well as upon the interior illumination. In any event, such a view is always interesting since it shows a "living" building and draws the eye into important parts of the structure. Sometimes it is desirable to show reflections of trees, clouds, or buildings as well (Fig. 18.27). An interior view, on the other hand, should wherever possible permit the observer to look outside (Fig. 15.13).

[1] *Encyclopaedia of Modern Architecture,* General Editor, Gerd Hatje, London: Thames & Hudson, p. 24.
[2] *Ibid.*

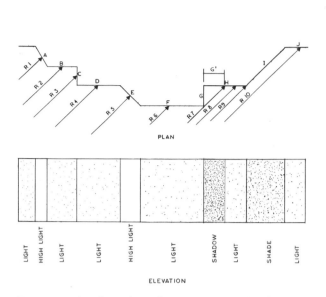

Fig. 6.1   Sketch 1: The Relative Intensity of Light in Plan

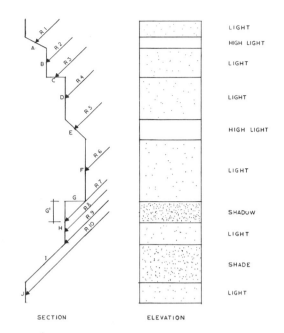

Sketch 2: Light in Elevation

What rules are available to the architect who wishes to make such a rendering? There is the science of perspective, and that of shades and shadows. Neither of these need be presented in detail here, since there are books which adequately handle these subjects—as sciences. Few books on shades and shadows, however, go into the subtleties of light and reflected light for the renderer. Since these are of the utmost importance in expressing the exterior-interior view, and certainly as important as the basic rules themselves, it seems worthwhile to examine them at some length.

Selection of Light Source

It is usual to assume a conventional light source for a rendering. This, as we will all remember, is at an angle of 45 degrees from the left and 45 degrees from above. However, it must be realized that this is only a convention, and that while a design might look well with such 45-degree shadows cast upon it, as at noontime, the same design may not look well with shadows cast by an early morning or late afternoon sun at an angle of perhaps 20 degrees with the ground line. Therefore, it is well to study a design with several different light conditions before making a rendering.

If the conventional light source is at all suspect, perhaps it would be well to think out your problem even further before laying out your shadows. Some buildings, by the very nature of their use, might look better at one time of the day than at another. A church, for instance, is used most during the early morning hours (Plate XIII) when the sun's rays are still quite low. A dwelling is seen at all hours; therefore almost any light condition may be assumed. And yet, it may be located in a shady spot where it may rarely receive the direct rays of the sun, and where the most prevalent light might be reflected upon it. If the client bought the property because of its shade trees, he will not be impressed with a house shown in bright sunlight. A skyscraper may be so large that several different kinds of light will bear upon it at the same time (Plate XII). Also, it may have cloud shadows on part of it. There is even a distinct possibility that the building would look best at night, or at dusk, as in Plate XI. Some renderers use no shades or shadows at all. The selection of a light source, then, must always be thought out very carefully before a rendering is made. It is best to study all possibilities and make sure that the building will look well in any possible light condition, and then select the one most appropriate for the presentation.

Assuming that a daylight view has been chosen and that the 45-degree shades and shadows have been mechanically laid out, a value study may be made in charcoal or soft pencil on tracing paper placed over the perspective. The lightest values (other than the white of the paper) will be the *highlights* on pitched areas which receive the light rays most directly (see Fig. 6.1, Sketch 1). The *lights,* which are the next lightest values, will be the glancing rays that fall on the vertical surfaces of the building, or on horizontal planes. Now turn Sketch 1 so that Plane A is at the top, and view it as a section (Sketch 2). The undersides of planes with angles of 45 degrees or less to the horizontal will be in *shade* and will be dark in value. Those dark areas cast by projections of the building or other objects interfering with the light rays are called *shadows* and are the darkest of all values. The darkest shadows are cast by edges of surfaces receiving the most direct light.

Whether viewed as plan or section, it is assumed that all of the light rays are parallel with each other, and that the rays shown in Sketches 1 and 2 of Fig. 6.1 are typical ones, selected for ease of illustration. Ray R^5 strikes surface "E" perpendicularly; therefore surface "E" will be in highlight. Ray R^1, which strikes surface "A" at a nearly perpendicular angle, therefore would be in light and would be almost as light as the highlight. Rays R^2, R^3, R^4, R^6, R^8, and R^{10} all strike their respective planes at an angle of 45 degrees; therefore, Planes B, C, D, F, H, and J, are all in light. No direct rays strike surface "G" or "I"; therefore these planes are in shade. That portion of

Making a Value Study

Fig. 6.2   The Workings of Reflected Light

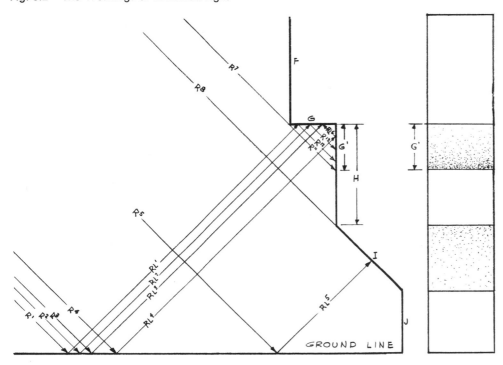

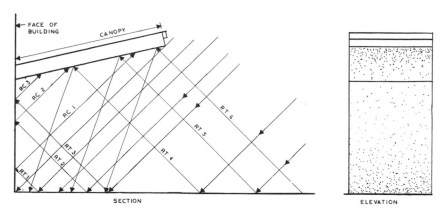

Fig. 6.3   Reflected Light on a Tilted Canopy

surface "H" marked G^1 will be in shadow, cast by the edge formed by the intersection of "F" and "G."

Figure 6.1, Sketch 2, also shows how light appears in elevation when its relative intensity is determined by the above principles.

Reflected Light

It must be remembered that light rays "bounce" from place to place, and in so doing modify shadows such as G^1 in Fig. 6.2. Let us examine the course of several such rays that ricochet from the ground in section. Ray RL^1, bounding upward at an angle of 45 degrees, strikes Plane "G" near its outer edge, then rebounds at an angle of 90 degrees to the bottom of Shadow G^1. Ray RL^3 acts in the same way, falling into Shadow G^1, near its top. The intensity of light diminishes according to the distance it travels. Ray $RL^3 + RL^6$, being shorter than Ray $RL^1 + R^{12}$, will be the brighter of the two. Therefore, Shadow G^1 will be graded by reflected light, with its lower part being darkest and its upper part lightest.

Shade, as on the underside of a sloping canopy, is also modified by reflected light (Fig. 6.3). Ray RT^1 bounds up from the ground, rebounds from the building, as RC^1, and strikes the underside of the canopy near its outer edge. Ray RC^3 does the same thing as RC^1, but travels a much longer distance from the face of the building. Therefore, the underside of the canopy, although in shade, will be graded from light at the face of the building to dark at the outer edge of the canopy.

When light rays strike a large pane of glass, they pass through it and ricochet inside the room (Fig. 6.4). Since Ray RT^3 travels a longer distance than Ray RT^1, the ceiling will be darkest at the partition. These same rays, bounding farther than the ceiling, will strike the rear partition in such a manner that Ray RT^3 travels farther than RT^1. Therefore the partition will be lightest near the floor and darkest near the ceiling.

Double Gradation

Figure 6.5 illustrates double gradation in reflected light. A series of rays typified by Ray R^1, casts a shadow "X" on wall "Y." Reflected rays RL^1, RL^2, and RL^3 bound off the ground and into the shade side of pier "A," then rebound into shadow "X." Since reflected ray RR^3 is shorter than reflected ray RR^1, the shadow will be graded from light at the pier to dark at its outer edge. The shadow, however, will also receive reflected rays, typified by RL^4, RL^5, and RL^6, which bounce off the ground in a line perpendicular to

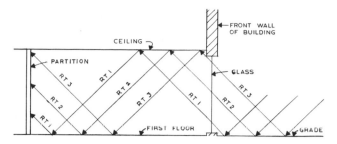

Fig. 6.4   Reflected Light Passing Through Glass

the wall on which the shadow falls. Since reflected ray "A" is shorter than reflected ray "C" (in section), it is obvious that the shadow will be graded from light at the bottom to dark at the top.

If an elevation is in sunlight, normal shadows will be cast by the direct rays of the sun at 45 degrees, and from the left, as in the left-hand portion of the plan (marked "A") in Fig. 6.6. If, however, the same elevation is entirely in shade, it may be assumed that reflected light, bounding from the ground in the reverse direction, will strike the facade from the right side, as in Fig. 6.5. Thus, if there is a horizontal projection near the ground (see section), it will throw a reverse shadow on the face of the building (see elevation, portion B) which may be plotted in a manner similar to that used for ordinary shadows. In the same way, back light throws shadows on the left and top sides of window muntins and mullions which are in shade, rather than to the right and bottom of these projections as when they are bathed in direct sunshine.

A problem which must be met with immediately in making a rendering is that which has to do with the relative values of parallel planes. Considering

Reflected Shadows

Light and Air

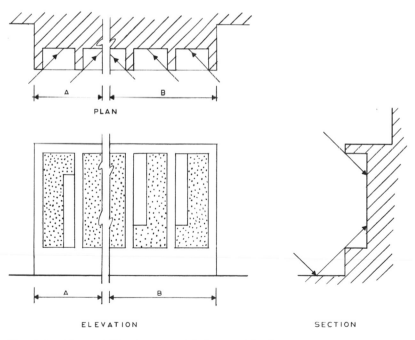

Fig. 6.6   Normal Shadows and Reflected Shadows

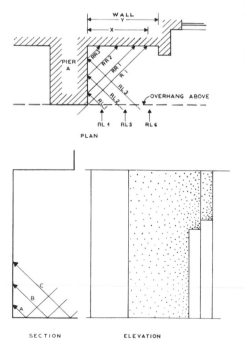

Fig. 6.5   Reflected Light in Elevation: Shadows

that all walls of the hypothetical plan in Fig. 6.1, Sketch 2, are of the same material—say limestone—which would be the lightest? To solve this problem, try to remember your last vacation in a mountainous area. If you will recall, the mountain that you stood upon always looked darker to you than a mountain in the distance. This was so because air—all air—has substance, and therefore the ability to filter light and affect vision. The more air between the spectator and an object in the distance, the lighter that object will seem. If we adopt this rule as a convention in rendering, then it follows that in Fig. 6.1, Sketch 2, Wall "F" will be darkest, and Walls "B" and "J" lightest, with Walls "H" and "D" ranging between.

Light and Glass

The presence of glass in large areas of a perspective presents certain problems to the renderer. If there is a sheet of glass between the spectator and an object, the value of the object will be lightened somewhat. If there are two sheets of glass, the object will be lightened even more, and so on.

But glass presents other problems. For instance, the renderer must have rules regarding glare. The presence of glare is easy to determine if the following rules are remembered: When the spectator is directly opposite a glass area, at his own level, a small glass opening will appear dark, but a large glass area will be transparent. If he is either above or below the glass area, the glass will be in glare. For example, if he is standing at ground level and is looking at a high building with a facade of glass, the glass will be darkest at the level of his eyes and will become increasingly lighter as he looks upward, with the greatest glare at the top of the building.

Similarly, if he stands in front of a glass facade, the glass directly in front of him will appear to be darkest, while that at the ends of the building will be lightest, with the greatest glare at the ends of the building.

Theories and Observation

Keep these rules constantly in mind. Observe the theories at work every day on actual structures as you walk along the street. Notice in particular that the vagaries of light and the presence of atmosphere cause constant change in value and color in every wall surface, under every projection. Become aware of the differences in value and color of the many pieces of each building material, such as stone. Remember that no two things in nature are exactly alike. Notice that the texture and color of different pieces of the same material are affected in different ways by age and time of day. Also, as the sun becomes bright or dull, the same building will take on a hundred different degrees of brightness—sometimes within the space of a minute. When you have absorbed these phenomena, and the general rules set down in this chapter, you will be in a position to develop your own conventions for rendering light and shade under any condition. From then on practice the application of these conventions and thereby avoid the deadly mechanical type of rendering which is the sign of the amateur.

Color—fact and theory

UNTIL QUITE RECENTLY, color reproduction for books and magazines was of poor quality. It has always been expensive, and therefore less widely used than the black and white printing processes. People have come to accept black and white in pictures as reality instead of merely an abstraction of reality, which it really is. Yet the delineator usually finds that a rendering in color has a much greater appeal than one in black and white.

A rendering in color brings to mind real things and similar scenes that the spectator has experienced. Color enables the delineator to identify variations and textures in a rendering much more fully, and correspondingly helps the spectator to understand the message that the rendering is meant to convey. To prove the difference in the amount of appeal, it is only necessary to hang two skillfully drawn renderings of the same subject side by side —one in black and white, the other in color. Invariably the eye will go first to the one rendered in color, and only after this has been fully observed will it go to the black and white presentation.

Many theories have been advanced to explain color. Most agree that objects themselves do not have color, but that color is caused by their relative ability to absorb light rays. Because objects do not absorb the same quantity of light at each wave length, different colors are produced. When light strikes the object itself, it penetrates the surface somewhat. The amount of penetration and absorption depends upon the texture of the object. If an object absorbs all colors except red, red rays are reflected to the eye and we call the object red. White light is a mixture of all colors. These may be seen when sunlight, striking the curved surfaces of raindrops, is spread into a rainbow. The same effect may be obtained by causing a narrow beam of light to pass through a glass prism (Fig. 7.1).

White surfaces reflect all colors, absorbing none. Black, on the other hand, represents a complete lack of light and color. Black surfaces do not reflect colors, but absorb them instead.

These basic facts are only a small part of the body of fascinating information about color and light amassed by men of science, especially those in the fields of optics and photography. But practical application of

Color and Light

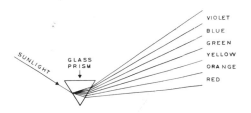

Fig. 7.1   Refraction of Light Through a Glass Prism

color by delineators and others who work with pigments must follow a slightly different path. For the purpose of this discussion we shall refer to color as not merely reflection, but as an entity of itself, with its own properties.

Properties of Color

Color may be described as having three outstanding properties: hue, value, and intensity. *Hue* means the name of the color, such as blue, which differentiates it from another color, such as green. *Value* designates the brightness of a color: that is, whether it is a light blue or dark blue. *Intensity,* or *chroma,* denotes the extent to which the hue is free from any white constituent. The temperature of a color has no physical basis, but blue-greens, and blue-violets, which seem to recede, are considered cool colors; and reds, red-oranges, and red-violets, which seem to advance, are considered warm colors.

Effects of Types of Light

Since color may be thought of as reflected light, it should be recognized that the kind of light that falls upon the object will affect its appearance. A color that appears to be bluish-green when viewed in daylight, will look yellowish-green in incandescent light. Under daylight fluorescent lighting—which does not contain all of the colors of the spectrum—the same color will appear to be completely blue. Because of this phenomenon the delineator should work by daylight whenever possible and should also arrange to show the rendering to all interested parties in the same light, so as to insure color constancy.

If the light in which a rendering is to be shown is important, so are the surroundings, since any bright or garish wall colors near the presentation will vitally affect the appearance of the colors in the picture. The best surroundings are those of a neutral tone.

Effect of Surroundings on Color

There are certain other phenomena which should be kept in mind in selecting colors for a rendering. An area of a picture rendered in a bright color will seem larger than it actually is, because a bright color is more stimulating to the nerves of the retina of the eye than a grayed hue. A white area enclosed by a darker area appears to swell in dimension. If the same color is used in several different parts of a picture, it may appear to be different in hue because of the different colors that surround it. An area painted yellow will seem larger than one painted orange, and an orange area will seem larger than one painted red. Invariably a blue area will seem larger than a black one.

The fact that colors look different in different surroundings has led to many a disappointment where colors were selected for decoration with no thought of their eventual neighboring colors. Many a beautiful vase has been purchased because it looked magnificent in a carefully prepared display in a store, only to become just an extraneous item when it was placed in incompatible surroundings in the home. This phenomenon is also responsible for the fact that women frequently are disappointed outside the store in dresses that were displayed under ideal conditions.

In rendering, colors of deep value will seem to be heavier than pale colors, and can cause an imbalance in a picture if too much of the deep color is used on one side. Finally, it should be remembered that light colors, or tints, always look brighter if they are viewed against a black background, while dark hues usually seem more dramatic against a white background.

If a room is painted with one of the cool colors, the apparent size of the room will be increased. If one of the warm colors is used, the room will seem to be smaller. Bright colors such as yellow-oranges, yellows, and yellow-greens, have a luminous quality and should be used to lighten an otherwise dark room.

It is probably well at this point to mention that colors affect people psychologically. Blue, for instance, reduces mental excitability, and therefore helps one to concentrate. It is both cooling and sedative, but cannot be used indiscriminately, as too much of it will produce melancholia. These qualities were discovered during the Middle Ages, and are partly responsible for the use of so much blue in the stained glass windows in the great cathedrals. Green is also cooling, and acts as an opiate. Yellow is cheery and stimulating and draws attention. Red is exciting and stimulates the brain; purple is sedative and soothing. Brown is restful and warming but should be combined with orange, yellow, or gold, because it can be depressing if used alone. Gray suggests cold and like brown it is depressing unless combined with a livelier color. White, on the other hand, is cheering and reflects sunlight, particularly when used with red, yellow, or orange.

Psychological Effects of Color

Man has always been interested in color, and has surrounded himself with it. Men of the Magdalenian period painted animals in color on the walls of their caves. During the earliest ages in Egypt, color was used in religious rites and clothing, as well as in architecture. Temples were marked off in zones by colors in Mesopotamia and Asia, while in Greece, polychromy developed to a high art, and red, blue, green, yellow, purple, white, brown, and black were used. During the Middle Ages color was used as a stimulus to emotion. However, during the Renaissance, color—at least in architecture—seems for a while to have been lost. This was probably due to the fact that although ample mention of the architecture of Ancient Rome was made by Vitruvius, no mention was made of the use of color. In addition, some doctrines of the Reformation forbade adornment with color.

Color in Human History

As the world of science developed, an increasing amount of attention was given to the secrets of color and their relation to mankind. Robert Boyle discovered in the seventeenth century that red, yellow, and blue came from white light by reflection and refraction. Sir Isaac Newton, while trying to solve the problems of the telescope in 1666, noticed the refraction and dispersion of light through a prism. He discovered that all color is contained in sunlight, and that when a beam of light passes through a prism, the direction of the light waves is changed so that the violet waves, for example, are bent more sharply than red, and a rainbow results. See Fig. 7.1. Having obtained this information, Newton then formed the first of all chromatic circles by bending these colors, pulling the red and violet ends around, and separating them with purple.

Chromatic Circles and Solids

Johann Wolfgang von Goethe (1749–1823), the German poet, also dabbled in color, producing his own color wheel. See Fig. 7.2.

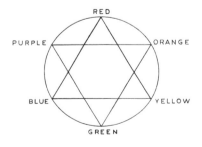

Fig. 7.2 Goethe's Color Wheel

The Munsell System of Color

In the United States today the best known and most widely used system of color standardization is that invented by Albert H. Munsell. He became greatly interested in the practical application of color, and was disturbed by the fact that the popular names for colors do not describe them adequately for professional purposes. They are named after flowers or plants, such as violet, indigo, old rose, primrose; after fruits, such as peach, pomegranate, grape, avocado, plum, etc.; or places, such as French blue, Naples yellow, or Prussian blue. Others are named after actual persons, such as Davy's gray or Hooker's Green.[1]

Essentially, the Munsell system consists of an orderly arrangement of colors in the shape of a three-dimensional color solid roughly spherical in shape. See Plate I. It is based on a color circle of 10 major hues, made up of five *principal hues* (red, yellow, green, blue, and purple), and five *intermediate hues* (yellow-red, green-yellow, blue-green, purple-blue, and red-purple). All of the 10 major hues, which appear to be about equidistant to the spectator, are number 5 of a group of 10 numbers. Therefore, the whole hue circle is composed of 100 hues. A scale of reflectances, or *values*, as they are known in the Munsell system, extends like a core through the center of the hue circle. A supposedly perfect white, having 100 per cent reflectance, located at the apex of the value scale, is numbered 10. At the bottom, a supposedly perfect black, (0 per cent reflectance) is numbered 0. Nine graduated value steps connect these poles.

Radiating from this scale of values, or central core, are the increments of saturation (called *chroma* in the Munsell system). These, too, seem to be about equidistant to the spectator. The numbers of these increments vary from 0, at neutral gray to as high as 16, according to the amount of saturation produced by a given hue at a given value level. Since colors vary in chroma or saturation, some colors extend farther from the neutral axis than others, and the solid is therefore not symmetrical. Pure red, with a chroma of 14, for instance, extends farther than blue-green, with a chroma of only 6.

Munsell Notation

Through an intricate system of notation, each hue is described by a letter, which locates it on the 100-step equator; a number from 1 to 9, to give its value; and another number to locate it in relation to the neutral axis.

With this information it is possible to describe exactly any given hue and to locate its place in the color solid. Furthermore, as Munsell stated,[2] one can "select one familiar color, and study what others will combine with it to please the eye," by the use of three typical paths: one vertical, with rapid change of value, another lateral, with rapid change of hue; and a third inward, through the neutral center, to seek out the opposite color field. All other paths are combined by two or three of these typical directions in the color solid.

Possibly because this selective process is so complicated, the Munsell system is not generally used by artists or delineators. It is a splendid, methodical way of standardizing, categorizing, and identifying colors, and

---

[1] As Munsell has said: "Can we imagine musical tones called lark, canary, crow, cat, dog, or mouse, because they bear some distant resemblance to the cries of those animals?"

[2] *A Color Notation* by A. H. Munsell, p. 87.

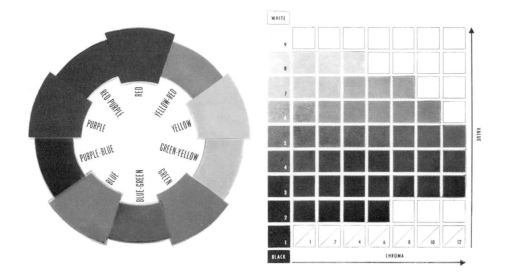

Hue circle (left) shows the principal hues, each of which is No. 5 of a family of ten adjoining hues. The chart at right shows all the variations in value and chroma for 5PB; the gray scale shows the steps between theoretical black and theoretical white. The color tree (below) illustrates the three-dimensional relationship of hue, value, and chroma. (Illustrations by Allcolor Company, Inc.; reproduced with permission from the Kodak Data Book *Color as Seen and Photographed.*)

Plate I

The Munsell color system

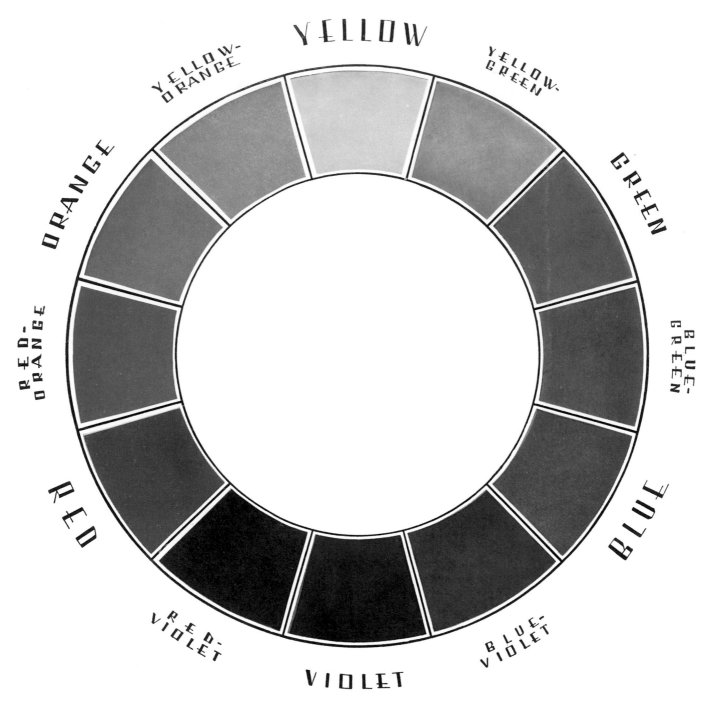

Plate II

Twelve-hue
color wheel

the *Munsell Book of Color* now provides the method accepted by the American Standards Association for the identification of color.

While on the one hand the various parts of the Munsell system are made up of *hue, value,* and *chroma,* the Ostwald system, also in use, concerns itself with *hue, black,* and *white.* The Ostwald solid (Fig. 7.3A) is in the form of a double cone rather than a sphere. In this system there are 24 hues around the equator, and eight value steps from white at the top, or north pole, to black at the bottom, or south pole.

If the solid were to be cut in half vertically, the resulting section would be diamond shaped, as in Fig. 7.3B. Each side (left and right) of the diamond would form a triangle. All the colors in the left one would, for instance, be derived from Hue 20 (green) and those in the right triangle from Hue 8 (red). Hues 20 and 8 are complements, since they appear opposite each other on the hue circle. The entire solid is, of course, made up of 12 sections such as this.

The Ostwald Color System

Fig. 7.3A   Ostwald Color Solid

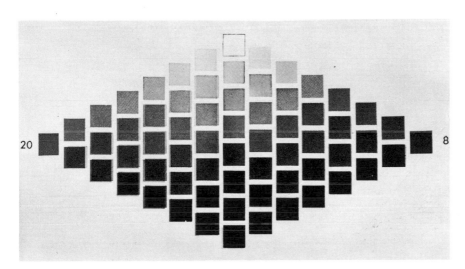

Fig. 7.3B   Vertical Section Through the Ostwald Color Solid

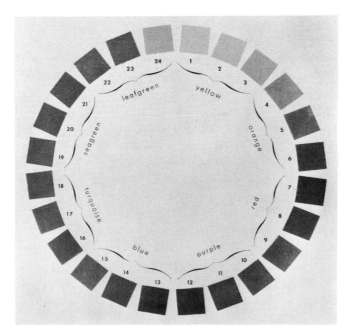

Fig. 7.4A   Hues Around the Equator

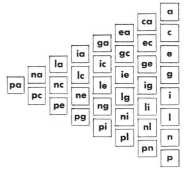

Fig. 7.4B   One-Half of the Vertical Section Through the Ostwald Color Solid, Showing the Color Notation

Since each section is made up of 56 colors, the complete solid contains 672 chromatic colors, plus the eight steps of the gray scale. In each color triangle, these vertical scales parallel to black and white (the isochromes) are equal in purity. Those colors parallel to a line between pure color and white (the isotones) in the top portion of the cone, contain an equal amount of black. Those scales parallel to a line between pure color and black (the isotints in the bottom) have equal white content. It may be seen from this description that the Ostwald system is based upon the assumption that all colors may be mixed from combinations of pure hue, white, and black.

Ostwald Notation

Combinations of various numbers and letters make up the Ostwald color notations. The hues, all full colors (free of white and black) numbered from 1 to 24, are arranged in groups of three, and these are called yellow, orange, red, purple, blue, turquoise, sea green, and leaf green. The gray scale is lettered from "A" for white at the top, to "P" for black, at the bottom. Two of these letters are always required: the first indicates that the color contains the same amount of white as the gray of the gray scale (Fig. 7.5), in which the series ends. The second letter indicates that the color contains the same amount of black as the gray of the gray scale in which the series ends.

In other words, any two *letters* will specify the amount of white and black of a color in terms of the gray scale. Any *number* from 1 to 24 specifies hue, and is written at the beginning of the notation like this: 22 PA.

Like the Munsell system, the Ostwald color solid may be used for the selection of color harmonies. These are located according to geometric relationships within the various parts of the solid itself.[1] But this more or less mathematical system has not been accepted for general use by either artists or delineators, possibly because of its very complexity, and also because it is impossible with black and white paint pigments to obtain the colors in the Ostwald Color Solid.

Black and white paints, instead of evenly lightening or darkening a given hue, change it. White, because it contains blue, "chalks" a hue, while black (which also contains blue) sullies it. If one attempts, for instance, to gray yellow by the addition of black, the result is green. So, while it is well for artists to know the Ostwald system, it cannot be used to advantage by those who work with paint pigments.

It is interesting to note that the colors of the Munsell system seem to lend themselves best to the development of standards in packaging and other manufactured products in general, while the colors of the Ostwald system have been used to a great extent by manufacturers of interior and exterior wall paints.

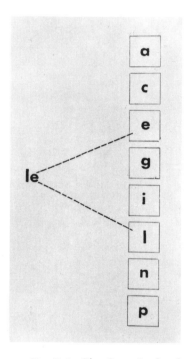

Fig. 7.5 The Gray Scale of the Ostwald Color Solid

Differences Between Light and Pigment

Unfortunately, the same laws do not apply to colors in light and colors in pigment. Physicists generally believe that red, green, and blue-violet are the true primaries. It is impossible, however, to obtain a full intensity yellow with such a pigment mixture. Therefore, the color wheel that uses red, yellow, and blue as its primaries, while not agreeing with the theories of the

[1] Egbert Jacobson, *Basic Color*, Part II, pp. 56–108.

physicists, is most satisfactory for the use of the artist. While a large variety of colors can be obtained by mixing these three primaries—red, yellow, and blue—in order to produce as wide a range of colors as possible, the primaries would have to include a magenta red and a blue-green instead of a blue. These are the primaries of printing rules. In other words, the artist or delineator simply cannot make a perfect chromatic circle with his pigment as can the printer, with his more nearly perfect inks. The qualities of the pigments themselves, and a knowledge of the way that they mix and react with each other, are the important elements to the delineator, and these enable him to produce sufficiently well and with foreseeable perfection any architectural picture required.

From a practical standpoint, the delineator will find the simple color wheel (Plate II) of great assistance in determining color schemes and harmony. Neither the Munsell nor the Ostwald color solid is easy or inexpensive to make, and since the color wheel provides the delineator with a simple, yet adequate, means of determining color schemes and color harmonies, it seems obvious that this is the tool to use. Although the color wheel shown in Plate II contains 12 colors, it can also be made with 18. In order to make such a color wheel, the following procedure may be used:

Making a Color Wheel

On a sheet of 140-lb cold-pressed stretched paper (stretched as in Chapter 14) or 140-lb cold-pressed illustration board, draw a circle 10 in. in diameter. Using the same center, draw an inner circle 6 in. in diameter. The ring between the two circles should then be divided into 12 parts, making each segment 30 degrees. In order to keep the colors from running together, a space of about $\frac{1}{16}$ in. should separate each segment from the next.

After the pencil drawing has been completed the following materials should be assembled:

1. Water colors (half tubes):
   a. Cadmium yellow pale
   b. Vermilion
   c. Alizarin crimson
   d. French ultramarine blue
   e. Cobalt blue
   f. Hooker's green
2. A small bucket or other container for water
3. A No. 4 water color brush
4. Six wash pans (white)
5. Several white blotters

Before applying washes of color, examine the 12-hue color wheel shown in Plate II and notice that the primary colors (yellow, red, and blue) are located at the third points of the color wheel. Write these names lightly outside the segments in which they are to appear, and then identify the colors for the other segments in the same manner. The secondaries are located halfway between the primaries, and the tertiaries between the primaries and secondaries. The primary colors are so called because by mixing paints of these three hues, theoretically, at least, all other hues may be obtained. In actual practice, because of the limitations of pigments, this is not so.

The colors for the 12 segments of the color circle may be purchased from any art materials shop. Grumbacher's colors are excellent for this purpose. But if you prefer to use the colors of the palette suggested by the author later in this chapter, the mixing should proceed as follows:

Primary colors: Following are suggested pigments for the mixing of primary colors:

> *Yellow*—Cadmium yellow pale
> *Red*—Rose madder or alizarin crimson
> *Blue*—Cobalt blue with a small amount of French ultramarine blue.

Secondary colors: Each of the secondary colors—green, violet, and orange —is located halfway between two of the primary colors. Green is thus between yellow and blue, violet between red and blue, and orange halfway between red and yellow. Following are the suggested pigments for obtaining the secondary colors:

> *Green*—Hooker's green with a small amount of cadmium yellow added.
> *Violet*—A combination of the proper amounts of the red and blue used
> for the primary colors.
> *Orange*—Vermilion with a small amount of cadmium yellow in it.

Tertiaries: The tertiaries, the colors situated between the primaries and secondaries on the color wheel, are mixed as follows:

> *Yellow-green*—Some of the yellow and some of the green previously
> mixed.
> *Blue-green*—Some of the blue and some of the green previously mixed.
> *Blue-violet*—Some of the blue and some of the violet previously mixed.
> *Red-violet*—Some of the red and some of the violet previously mixed.
> *Red-orange*—Some of the red and some of the orange previously mixed.

These cannot be mixed in equal amounts because of the differences in strength between the various pigments. Before applying any of the colors to the color wheel, and in order to insure that the color is correct, it is well to place a sample on a piece of paper, let it dry, and then compare with the colors in Plate II.

The 18-hue Color Wheel
To make a chromatic circle with 18 hues instead of 12, proceed in the manner described above until you have developed the primary and secondary colors. To obtain the tertiaries, of which there will be two instead of one between each primary and secondary, proceed as follows:

The tertiary immediately to the right of the yellow primary will be yellow-yellow-green, followed by green-yellow-green. Between green and blue will be the tertiary green-blue-green, with blue-green-blue on its right.

The tertiaries between violet and blue will, of course, become violet-blue-violet, and blue-violet-blue. The tertiaries between violet and red will be violet-red-violet and red-violet-red. Those between orange and yellow will be orange-yellow-orange and yellow-orange-yellow.

Use of the Color Wheel
The color wheel is a means not alone for studying color, but also for locating harmonies. To begin with, it is a constant reminder of the relationship of colors one to another. This is a basic arrangement, each element of which can always be found in the same position. It provides simple color categories into which all pigment names must fall. It also provides a visual vocabulary of basic colors from which tints and shades may be made.

As in the study of color in light, the rules for color harmony by the use of pigments are based on personal taste (that is, the personal taste of most people). The rules set down here will be found to relate closely to the rules that nature seems to use in her colors. We seldom see colors used in full intensity in the world around us, and where intense hues occur, they are usually in small amounts. Greens in nature are not harsh, but are soft, grayed, yellow greens. The skies above us usually have very pale hues. Since the average person's mind is attuned to the world about him, he can accept such subtleties more readily than the harshness of loud, clashing colors.

Color Schemes

It should be recognized at the outset that good color schemes are made of only a few colors, properly selected, mixed, and blended. The difference between good art, such as that found in the great museums of the world, and calendar art, can be explained to a great extent by this phenomenon. The professional artist uses a few colors with many shades of these colors, while the amateur is inclined to use a great many more colors than he needs for the problem. At once he provides himself with more problems than he can handle, and introduces so many conflicting notes that his work becomes unpleasant to behold.

One Color with Black, White, or Gray

The simplest of all schemes is that in which one color is used with black, white or gray. The average book (without the dust jacket) is an example of this kind of color scheme.

The Monochromatic Scheme

The monochromatic color scheme, which can be very sophisticated, is one in which many shades of a single color are used. Of course, not all colors will lend themselves to a monochromatic scheme, simply because the lighter colors cannot achieve deep enough tones for emphasis. This automatically eliminates yellow, orange, and pale green.

The Analogous Scheme

The analogous color scheme permits the use of colors which adjoin each other on the color wheel (Plate II), such as yellow, yellow-green, and green, or red, red-orange, and orange. These colors are not necessarily used in their pure form in various parts of the picture, but are mixed together in varying amounts so that numerous shades may be made out of the few colors used. It is usual for one of the colors in such a scheme to predominate in a picture; that is, to be used in a larger area than the rest.

Analogous Plus Complementary Accent

One of the most common color schemes consists of a series of analogous colors, plus a complementary accent, i.e., a color on the opposite side of the wheel to the center of the analogous run. For example, a scheme that uses yellow-orange, orange, and yellow-green could be combined with violet. By mixing these colors together in various amounts it will be found that the complementary accent (violet) will "gray" and soften the three analogous colors, deepen them for the darker tones, and at the same time complement them.

Complementary Scheme

For a simple complementary scheme, two colors opposite each other on the color wheel—such as blue-violet and yellow-orange—are used. Neither of these need be used in pure form, but literally hundreds of shades may be obtained by blending them together in varying amounts.

An interesting aspect of complements is the way they affect each other. In pure form they actually complement each other; each has the quality of making the other look better by its proximity. But as they are mixed together, they modify each other to a point where they finally form a neutral gray. It should be noted, however, that the neutral gray obtained by mixing different sets of complements will vary; sometimes a mousey gray occurs, and at other times a warm, brownish-gray.

Grays can be formed by mixing two complements, such as red and green, yellow and violet, orange and blue, or red-orange and blue-green. A tie-score is as unsatisfactory in rendering as in a ball game, and since completely neutral grays seem to have no color at all, they are to be avoided or used very sparingly. In other words, use more of one complement than the other so that the resultant mixture will appear to contain more of one color than the other.

Another interesting phenomenon is that colors that appear in neither pigment sometimes appear when two complements are mixed. With certain proportions of yellow and violet, a rust color will appear. A little color experimentation will illustrate this point. Mix the various complementary colors together in pairs and watch what happens to each color as it is blended with its complement.

Near or Split Complements A split complement takes the form of a "Y" on the color wheel, with one arm of the "Y" pointing, for instance, to yellow-orange, the other arm to yellow-green, and the stem of the "Y" pointing to violet. For example, the scheme could be composed of violet, plus two colors, one each side of the direct complement, which in this case is not used. This resembles the complementary scheme, but provides a slightly wider range of colors and shades.

Triads Another excellent color scheme may be obtained by the mixture of triads; that is, three colors located at the third points of the color wheel. This combination provides a wide range of hues, shades, and tints. A fact to be kept in mind regarding the last three color schemes is that different kinds of colors and great variations may be obtained by varying the pigments that are used. In other words, the three different sets of orange and blue complements can be obtained by using three different kinds of blue in your palette, such as cobalt, French ultramarine, or cerulean. A red and green complementary color scheme permits the use of either Hooker's green or emerald green. A yellow-violet complementary color scheme can be carried out with either cadmium yellow pale or yellow ochre.

Browns are a mixture of orange with blue, green, or gray; while grays result from mixtures of three primary or two complementary colors. The type of gray—warm or cool—can be mixed to suit.

Colored Papers No discussion of color would be complete without mention of colored charcoal and pastel papers. These are available at any art materials store in a number of shades of gray, brown, yellow, green, orange, and red. (See Chapter 10, on carbon pencil rendering.) The last two colors may be quickly eliminated, since colors as bright as these are usually not suitable for renderings. Generally speaking, the more delicately tinted papers—cool brown, warm or cool gray, pale yellow, or pale green—are easier to work on, but there are times when the darker papers are required. A good rule to remember is that the delicately tinted papers lend themselves to transparent washes, either of water color or of body color of a thin or medium consistency, while the darker papers give sharper contrasts when these are desired, or when thick body color (tempera) is to be used.

As mentioned earlier, a sophisticated color scheme is usually the result not only of careful selection of the scheme and of the proper use of colors in proper areas, but also nearly always of mixing together for each part of the painting all of the colors of your color scheme in varying amounts.

There are two kinds of color schemes in general: the first in which the colors of nature are used, such as a blue sky, green grass, etc.; and the other in which these colors are modified. An example might be a blue monochromatic color scheme where all the shades and tints are blue. Again, in the analogous color scheme yellow, yellow-green, and green, it is obvious that the sky cannot be blue, so it is likely to become a pale shade of green. The interesting fact about the use of such a stylized color scheme is that the eye will readily accept grass which is not green or a sky which is not blue, because the result is often more dramatic than if the usual colors were used. In addition, skies in nature are rarely pure blue, but are likely at any time at all to contain green, yellow, orange, or gray. In similar fashion—and this can be observed at almost any time of the year except perhaps in spring —lawns, trees, and bushes are not bright green at all, but are a mixture of subdued gray-green, yellow-green, orange-green, etc.

The renderer who recognizes these phenomena produces a much more realistic rendering than the amateur who uses pure hues. No two things in nature are exactly alike, and the variations that the delineator can include in his colors in things natural give him a great variety.

Helpful Hints for Mixing Colors

Values and Color Choice

A successful rendering cannot be made without first determining the values of the various parts of the picture. Without contrast, even subtle colors do not show off to good advantage. Before proceeding with the application of any color, a value study must be made. Be sure that the colors you use are suitable. Bright red, for instance, would not give the desired effect in the rendering of a mausoleum, nor does it usually appear to be correct when used alone in a sky. The color chosen must be able to produce a deep value if one is desired. The colors that are used in such incidental items as scale figures and automobiles must be mixed to complement the colors in the building being rendered, and should not draw attention to themselves by their brightness or garishness.

The Color Study

It is well to make a color study before beginning work on the final rendering. After selecting the several colors that you intend to use, which fall into one of the categories described above, put a little of each of the pigments on a piece of illustration board or paper similar to that upon which you are going to render. The possible range of this color combination can be ascertained in a few minutes by simply dabbling in these colors with a wet brush. For instance, if a scheme such as red, yellow, and blue is to be used, and you have decided upon cadmium yellow pale, cobalt blue, and alizarin crimson, you can quickly learn by mixing them together in varying amounts that you can obtain anything from pure yellow, red, or blue, to grayish blues, reds, or yellows, warm browns, tans, and grayish tans. This is an enjoyable process which reveals all of the potentialities and limitations of your colors. After this freehand color and value study you are thoroughly prepared—at least in knowledge of color—to begin rendering.

Palettes   Before modern science discovered artificial ways of making them, paints were very rare, hard to obtain, and very expensive. Most artists made their own paints from earths such as the ochres, umbers, and siennas; from minerals like copper, lead, or iron, or from mixtures of burned wood and the blood of animals. Other items, such as burned teeth and shinbones of animals, were crushed and roasted. The soot of certain oils, burnt ivory, the ink-bag of the cuttlefish, tiny snails, the roots, sap, and leaves of flowers and trees, berries, and the husks of nuts were also used. The processes of manufacture were secret and were passed from one generation to the next.

Ancient Greek literature speaks of the use of four colors: white, yellow, red, and black. The works of those times show a number of other shades that were obtained by mixing combinations of these four. During the Renaissance, only a few colors were used, and this limited palette consisted of red, yellow, blue, and black (and many shades thereof). The Impressionists, who won acclaim in Paris before 1886, used intense blues, greens, reds, and purples. They renounced the use of black, reveled in strong and varied color, and were always conscious of the effect of light on colors.

Modern pigments are manufactured from a variety of substances, and it is a most intricate process. Earths such as the ochres, siennas, and umbers are used in the natural form or roasted. Animal materials, such as insects, provide certain colors. Stones, such as slate, are utilized, as well as the roots of plants, gum resins, and vegetables. Such metals as aluminum, cobalt, potassium, cadmium, copper, zinc, and iron play a part in the manufacture of pigments, as do charcoal, coal tar, and soot from certain oils. Many combinations are the result of a chemical reaction between a basic metal and another element such as oxygen, sulphur, chlorine, or arsenic. Since there are so many possible chemical combinations, there are literally hundreds of different pigments available. One manufacturer alone (Winsor & Newton, Inc.) advertises 151 pigments.

Purchase of Paints   When shopping for paints, therefore, it is well to have a good idea of what you want to buy before you go to the art materials store. The author uses the following palette for water color, and recommends it because it permits the mixture of just about every hue, shade, or tint that the delineator needs:

Yellows
Cadmium yellow pale
Yellow ochre
Oranges
Cadmium orange
Vermilion
Reds
Alizarin crimson or rose madder

Blues
French ultramarine blue
Cobalt blue
Cerulean blue
Greens
Hooker's green dark
Emerald green

There are many possible palette variations, and each delineator or artist uses his own, usually obtained from someone else or from experience. Examples of these, selected at random, follow:

Yellows
Aureolin
Cadmium yellow (deep)
Indian yellow
Chrome yellow (pale)
Yellow ochre
Blues
French ultramarine blue
Cobalt blue
Cerulean blue
Antwerp blue

Oranges
Vermilion
Venetian red
Carmine
Red
Indian red
Green
Emerald green

Yellows
Cadmium yellow (deep)
Yellow ochre
Oranges
Cadmium orange
Vermilion
Reds
Alizarin crimson

Blues
French ultramarine blue
Cobalt blue
Cerulean blue
Brown
Vandyke brown
Earth color
Burnt sienna

Yellows
Cadmium yellow
Aureolin
Cadmium lemon
Oranges
Vermilion
Cadmium orange
Reds
Alizarin crimson
Blues
French ultramarine blue
Cobalt blue
Winsor blue

Greens
Hooker's green No. 2
Grays
Davy's gray (warm tone)
Payne's gray (cool tone)
Brownish gray
Sepia
Earth colors
Raw sienna
Burnt sienna
Raw umber
Burnt umber

From these palettes, and from experience, the reader will discover that a number of pigments, such as those in the palette below, are basic and widely used:

Yellows
Cadmium yellow (pale or deep)
Yellow ochre
Aureolin
Oranges
Vermilion
Cadmium orange
Reds
Alizarin crimson
Rose madder

Blues
French ultramarine blue
Cobalt blue
Cerulean blue
Green
Emerald green

Whatever colors you add to these will depend upon personal taste and experience. Half the fun of being a delineator lies in the contemplation of a color you have not tried that lies temptingly in the showcase.

Qualities of Water Color Pigments

Generally, all water colors fall into the following categories:

Those that make clear, transparent washes are cadmium yellow, cadmium orange, alizarin crimson, rose madder, cobalt blue, and Hooker's green.

Those that make "granulated" washes which give a mottled effect include yellow ochre, vermilion, French ultramarine blue, cerulean blue, and emerald green.

Granulation occurs whether the color is applied in washes or by direct painting, and is not lessened by mixture with other pigments. This quality is advantageous in the painting of certain types of skies, trees, and building materials, and gives effects that can be obtained in no other way. More will be said about this in Chapter 14, which deals with water color rendering.

One final word about water colors. The best that are available are Winsor & Newton's Artist's Colors. They are predictable; that is, are always exactly the same, no matter when or where you purchase them. They are sold in full tubes and half tubes. The author suggests using the half tubes, since whole tubes will sometimes dry out before they are used. Winsor & Newton's Student Colors are fair, but not nearly so true or predictable as the Artist's Colors. A number of other brands are also available, but not always predictable, and this is a quality to be sought in pigments for rendering.

The best water colors are expensive. They vary in price according to the color, but one tube of an expensive pigment will usually last as long as several tubes of a less expensive water color, because less is required for any specific job. The expensive pigment is stronger, and because it is predictable in both color and reaction it will never surprise the artist unpleasantly. The less expensive colors simply do not possess these qualities. One other reason for using good pigments: they are relatively permanent. True, some colors are more permanent than others, even in Winsor & Newton's Artist's line, but most of the less expensive paints fade and change color with time.

Basic equipment and the general approach to rendering

ONE OF THE MOST ENJOYABLE aspects of any new venture is the preparation for it, and the variety of enticingly packaged materials makes a visit to an art materials store a thrill in itself. The beginner, unfortunately, sometimes wastes time and money by purchasing the wrong materials and supplies. Only after a period of trial and error does he discover that he must replace them with others better suited to his needs. The purpose of this chapter is to give information regarding basic equipment that will be required by those who wish to render. Specific equipment for special techniques will be listed separately in each chapter according to medium.

Drawing Boards

The largest and most important piece of equipment to be selected is the drawing board, and the delineator owes it to himself to buy the board best suited to his needs—one that will minimize the physical problems of handling materials and equipment, and enable him to concentrate on the creative side of his work.

Portable Boards

The simplest and least expensive of all drawing boards is the portable board without cleats (Fig. 8.1). These boards are usually manufactured in basswood, with a pinewood frame and a basswood laminated surface, or with a basswood core and a basswood laminated surface. The less expensive boards do not always have straight and true hardwood edges, and must be equipped with a metal "straightedge."

Sizes of portable boards vary with the manufacturer and the materials used, but in general the sizes (in inches) are as follows:

12 x 17	20 x 26
16 x 21	23 x 31
18 x 24	24 x 36
20 x 24½	31 x 42

The author recommends that practice renderings be made at a picture size of 14 x 21 in. Since this picture size will be placed in the middle of a sheet which should be at least 2½ in. larger all around, the 23 x 31 board is recommended.

There are boards on the market equipped with parallel rules (or T-squares) which are arranged so that they cannot be easily removed. While

Fig. 8.1 Drawing Board Without Cleats

these are practical for drafting, they are not to be recommended for the renderer, as his T-square is frequently used in many positions.

The portable drawing board can be placed on any suitable table available and blocked up to a tilting position by the use of 2 x 4 in. blocks easily obtained at any lumber yard.

Portable Drawing Boards with Cleats

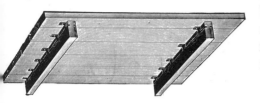

Fig. 8.2   Drawing Board with Cleats

There are also portable drawing boards made with narrow strips of wood such as basswood, joined together by tongue and groove, and held by two hardwood ledges attached to the underside near the edges (Fig. 8.2). These boards are much heavier and sturdier than the ones previously described, and may either be placed on a table or supported by wooden horses, either flat or tilting. They are available in approximately the following sizes (in inches):

24 x 32	38 x 72
31 x 42	44 x 72
38 x 48	44 x 84
38 x 60	50 x 84
44 x 60	

The architect who has sufficient space for a fairly large board can purchase a 3 x 7 ft flush wood door and support this on a pair of horses. The surface is true and smooth and this arrangement is both economical and adequate.

Tilt Drafting Tables

Fig. 8.3   Tilt-Top Drafting Table

Tilt drafting tables are made with a frame of hardwood, pinewood drawing board top and hardwood edges (Fig. 8.3). By the use of a semicircular arc arrangement, they may be adjusted to any desired angle and can also be varied in height. Some of these boards are equipped with a strip of hardwood which is fastened to the front edge of the board and held away from it about ½ in. by wooden clips. When a drawing larger than the board is being made, the lower portion of it, which will not fit on the board, can be protected by passing it between the wooden strip and the lower edge of the board itself, rolling it, then tacking it under the board. The wooden strip, which lies between the draftsman and the paper, protects the drawing from damage by abrasion.

This type of board is available in the following approximate sizes (in inches):

31 x 42
38 x 48
38 x 60

For general purposes, the 38 x 48 in. drawing table is most satisfactory.

Drafting Tables with Drawers

Several different types of drafting tables with or without storage space are available of both wood and steel (Fig. 8.4).[1] These usually have four vertical supporting legs but are also made with fixed bases. They may be equipped with a tool drawer and/or a file drawer. The tops of these tables are usually of wood but some may be obtained in a combination of steel, honeycomb, and vinyl sandwich construction. The tops are adjustable to

[1] Courtesy of Stacor Corp., Newark, N.J. 07114.

almost any height desired. Some representative sizes (in inches) are given below:

Steel base

37½ x 50
37½ x 60
37½ x 72
43½ x 72

As certain processes used in the various types of rendering, particularly those using wet media, are somewhat destructive, and also since it is necessary sometimes to remove the drawing board from the drafting table for sponging or appraisal, it is necessary to use a separate portable drafting board (without cleats) on top of a drafting table. The drafting table remains flat and the drawing board is brought to the desired tilt by the use of 2- x 4-in. blocks. The use of a portable drawing board also protects the surface of the permanent drafting table and saves it for drafting.

Fig. 8.4   Drafting Tables

Several different types of stools and chairs are available for renderers. (Fig. 8.5). Some are made of wood, others of metal. Some of the metal stools are adjustable and are equipped with backs.

The simple wooden stool, which comes in 24-in. and 30-in. heights, with a 14-in. round seat, is most useful to the delineator. Metal stools are made in 28-in. and 30-in. heights, while the adjustable type can be varied from 22 to 28 in., from 26 to 32 in., or from 27 to 33 in. A good rule of thumb in determining the height of the stool is to select one that will provide a space of 5 in. between the seat of the stool and the underside of the drawing board.

Drafting Stools

The second most useful piece of equipment is a reference table, where drawings connected with the project at hand may be kept. An excellent place for this table, which should be as large as possible, and which may be a drawing board, a drafting table, or a flush door on horses, is immediately behind the renderer, although it will also be useful if it occupies a position at his side.

A small cabinet—say 30 in. high, with a top 18 by 24 in., and placed on casters—will be found useful for storage of materials. This may be placed conveniently at one side, so that pigments and other supplies are within easy reach. The top should be large enough to hold water colors, brushes, water pail, etc. Some delineators devote half of the top of the cabinet to colored pigments, the other half to black and white pigments. By using such a cabinet, the artist can keep pigments and water at a safe distance from the drawing.

Fig. 8.5   Drafting Stools

Tack Board

A tack board of wood, cork, or other material upon which drawings may be fastened with thumbtacks is a very necessary item of equipment for the delineator. If possible this should be placed on a wall behind the drawing board, so that charcoal studies, color studies, and other reference material may be fastened to it and be constantly available. While this can be as large as space will permit, a good rule of thumb is to make it the same size as the drafting table, perhaps 38 x 54 in.

Files
Drawing files are made in both wood and metal, and are usually available in sections of drawers which are either 2 in. or 3½ in. deep. Wooden files (Fig. 8.6) are made in a number of sizes as follows:

Inside dimensions of drawer (in.)	Maximum drawing size (in.)
25 x 38	24 x 36
32 x 42¾	30 x 42
37½ x 50	36 x 48

These files are made in groups of from two to five drawers which can be stacked to any desired height, on a base.

Steel sectional drawing files (Fig. 8.7) are made in slightly different sizes:

Inside dimensions of drawer (in.)	Maximum drawing size (in.)
26 x 37	24 x 36
32 x 43	30 x 42
38 x 50	36 x 48

Like the wooden files, these may be purchased in groups and stacked.

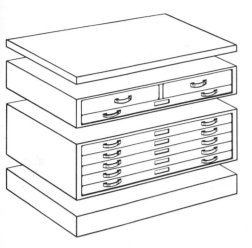

Fig. 8.6   Wooden Drawing Files

Fig. 8.7   Steel Sectional Drawing Files

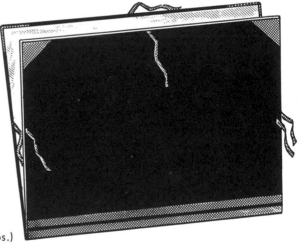

Fig. 8.8   Sketch Portfolio
(Courtesy Arthur Brown and Bros.)

Temporary Storage
If there are not enough drawings and renderings to require files, it is advisable to store them in an artist's portfolio of the proper size (Fig. 8.8). These are readily available at art materials stores, or can be made of cardboard and gummed paper. A portfolio will keep drawings clean and will prevent damage by abrasion as well as the fading of colors.

Placing Equipment
While it is not always possible to have optimum conditions, the delineator should select a quiet spot where he is out of general circulation, since his work demands a great deal of concentration and privacy. If possible, the drawing table should be placed next to a window, so that natural light will pass over the left shoulder. The location should be as free as possible from dust, splashing water, paint, and other destructive elements.

For artificial light, a three-tube fluorescent fixture about 48 in. long is most desirable. This fixture should be supplied with warm white lamps, which are best for mixing colors because they give light containing most of the colors of the spectrum. Daylight bulbs should not be used. A light neutral color such as beige, with a high reflectance quality, is a good choice for the walls.

Besides furnishing his studio, the renderer must equip himself intelligently with the more portable tools of his trade: T-squares, triangles, scales, curves, and drafting instruments, to begin with. Paints, brushes, and papers are described under each of the media discussed in the later chapters of this book.

Drafting Equipment

The least expensive T-squares are made entirely of wood, but those made of maple lined with transparent plastic edges (Fig. 8.9A) are more desirable because the transparent edges permit the renderer to see what is immediately below the section of the drawing he is working on. T-squares are available in lengths from 18 in. to 60 in., in 6-in. increments. It is advisable that the square be as long as your drawing board is wide, but no longer, since an overlapping T-square is easily knocked off by passers-by.

T-squares

Adjustable T-squares: T-squares that are adjustable to required angles are also available (Fig. 8.9B). These come in the various lengths described above.

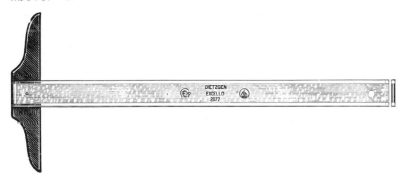

Fig. 8.9A   Maple T-Square with Transparent Plastic Edges   (Courtesy Eugene Dietzgen Co.)

Fig. 8.9B   T-Square with Adjustable Head   (Courtesy Eugene Dietzgen Co.)

The renderer will need at last two transparent plastic triangles, one 30–60 degrees, and the other 45 degrees. They are available in various sizes from 4 in. to 18 in. A 12-in., 30 to 60-degree triangle and a 10-in., 45-degree triangle are adequate for general use. They should be equipped with finger lifts.

Triangles

If the budget will allow additional expenditure, an 18-in., 60-degree triangle and an 8-in. adjustable triangle that indicates the angles from 45 to 90 degrees may also be purchased.

Scales   A 12-in., four-bevel architect's scale (Fig. 8.10), with numbers marked in white for scales of ⅛, ¼, ⅜, ½, ¾, 1, 1½, and 3 in. to the foot, is required by the renderer. In addition, a 6-ft folding carpenter's rule, marked off in feet and inches, is desirable for measuring distances greater than one foot. Like other drafting instruments, these should be made by a reputable manufacturer to insure accuracy.

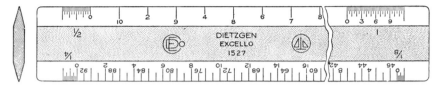

Fig. 8.10   Four-Bevel Architect's Scale   (Courtesy Eugene Dietzgen Co.)

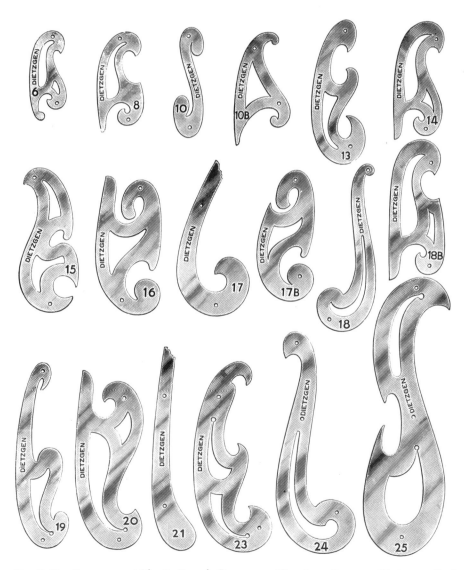

Fig. 8.11   Transparent Plastic French Curves   (Courtesy Eugene Dietzgen Co.)

Although some of the curves that must be drawn by the renderer are made freehand, there are a number of devices which permit their mechanical plotting. Among these are:

French curves, which are made of plastic and which come in various sizes and designs (Fig. 8.11)

Adjustable curve rules, which have a flexible ruling edge attached to a flexible spiral spring (Fig. 8.12)

Splines, which consist of a plastic edge and weights which hold the plastic edge at the desired curve (Fig. 8.13)

Transparent plastic railroad curves (Fig. 8.14)

Transparent plastic ship curves (Fig. 8.15)

For the beginner, several French curves, plus an adjustable curve rule, will meet nearly every situation.

Sets of drafting instruments come in various sizes and degrees of completeness, from the smallest, which usually contain a large compass and a large divider, to the more complete sets containing many instruments that the

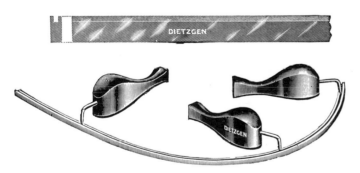

Fig. 8.12   Adjustable Curve Rules   (Courtesy Eugene Dietzgen Co.)

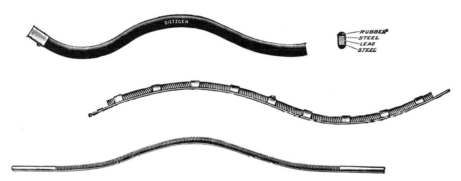

Fig. 8.13   Splines   (Courtesy Eugene Dietzgen Co.)

Fig. 8.14   Transparent Plastic Railroad Curves   (Courtesy Eugene Dietzgen Co.)

Fig. 8.15 Transparent Plastic
Copenhagen Ship Curves

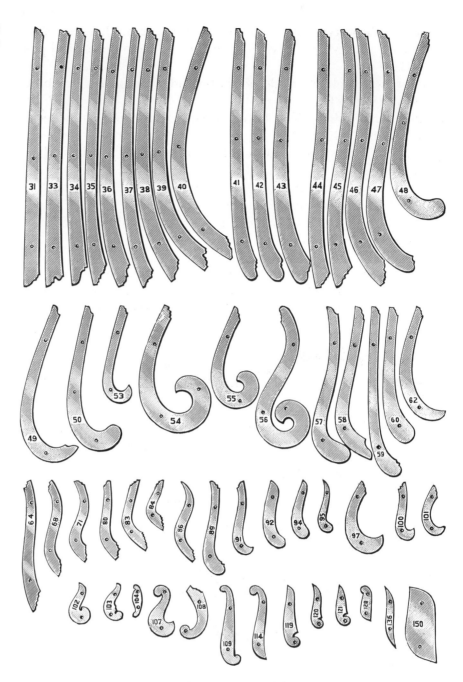

delineator does not use. It is desirable for the beginner to learn to use all of the instruments, but as he becomes experienced, he will find that he can dispense with many of them, relying on his compasses and scale, as well as on judgment by eye.

An adequate set of instruments should contain the following items:
Large dividers and extension
Large compass with extension
Bow compass and bow divider
Large and small ruling pens
Drop compass with both pencil and ink attachments
Small screw driver for adjusting instruments
Container for spare parts such as points and screws.

In addition, as the budget allows, it is well to add a set of proportional dividers.

Pencils

A complete description of pencils will be found in Chapter 10. The renderer however, will require certain pencils for the preparation of any rendering, and these should include the following: 2-H, H, and HB. Some draftsmen prefer refill holders and leads, which save the time required for sharpening wooden pencils.

Pencil Pointers

There are a number of mechanical pointers available, such as Keuffel and Esser's pencil lead pointer (Fig. 8.16), which are easy to use and are clean. These provide good, sharp, conical points for general drafting. However, a sandpaper block or file should be acquired for making the specially shaped points that are occasionally required.

Erasers

The delineator will need pink pearl (soft), ruby (firm), and art gum erasers for his work. In addition, there will be times when he will need a glass eraser or a sharp knife or razor blade for errors that are unusually difficult to remove.

Erasing shields: An inexpensive metal erasing shield with openings of various sizes and shapes will also be found helpful to protect parts of the drawing around an erasure.

Fixative: There are a number of different kinds of fixative. Charcoal fixative, which usually is amber in color, has a tendency to stain. Pastel fixative, which is colorless, can be used for "fixing" pencil, charcoal, or pastel work. In addition there are a number of plastic fixatives, such as Krylon, which are of the acrylic family. One of the finer acrylic fixatives is called "peppermint" and actually has a peppermint odor. Some fixative is sold in bottles and must be sprayed on with the use of an atomizer from a distance of four or five feet. Others are obtainable in pressurized cans which produce a fine mist on the drawing. Of the two, the canned spray is the safer and certainly requires less work than spraying by atomizer.

The desk brush, an indispensable piece of equipment, is used for keeping the board clean of erasure crumbs, dust, and dirt. This type of brush has a flat handle about ½ in. thick and comes in various sizes. It has soft flexible bristles about 2 in. long.

Diminishing glass: A diminishing glass is useful for assaying the rendering during its progress.

Fig. 8.16 Pencil Lead Pointer

Drafting tape and thumbtacks: Thumbtacks are used for fastening backing paper to the drawing board, while drafting tape is used for fastening other paper to the backing sheet. Tape does not interfere with drafting instruments as they are moved across the board, and, unlike thumbtacks, does not permanently damage backing paper or the board itself.

Backing paper: Several different kinds of paper can be used for covering the slight roughness, or grain, of the wooden drawing board. The most commonly used are: buff detail paper; plastic coated paper, which is relatively waterproof; and tracing paper.

Tracing paper: For rough sketching, an inexpensive thin yellow tracing paper is desirable. This comes in rolls 36 in. or 48 in. wide, and can be cut by the supplier into such workable widths as 12 or 18 in.

A good white rag bond tracing paper is needed for the preparation of the perspective drawing and for charcoal and color studies. This is also available in rolls 36 or 48 in. wide, and can be cut to desired widths.

Cleaning drawing instruments: Instruments which are constantly used are bound to collect dust, graphite, or paint. They are best cleaned with a cleaning fluid, such as carbon tetrachloride, and a clean cloth. Soap and water are to be avoided, because they remove the finish on instruments such as T-squares and cause them to warp.

General Approach to Rendering

At the outset, it should be recognized that there are many ways of making a rendering, and the final result will depend upon such diverse factors as a man's training, the amount of experience he has had, and the time available for producing the rendering. It should be made clear at this time, however, that there is a difference between a sketch—which is usually no more than a rough study for a rendering—and a finished presentation, which is the result of a preconceived and well-executed plan of procedure. One can see examples of both the quick "arty" sketch and the finished rendering in various books and magazines.

The Sketch

The success of a spontaneous sketch depends upon the skill of the renderer and his experience, as well as upon his emotional status at the time the rendering is done. The "arty" sketch, which looks as if it had been accomplished in a very short time, may possibly be the twelfth or thirteenth of a whole series. A noncreative period will show itself in a rendering of this type, and since there is no way of predicting when such a period will appear, the architect must have a system that will produce a guaranteed result whenever he needs it. He must know when he begins a rendering that it will be finished in good fashion at a definite time. Insofar as possible, it is the purpose of this book to provide in the following chapters on technique a method of procedure which will satisfy the architect's requirements and which, if followed, will produce desired results.

Subjects for Practice

One's own designs are ideal for rendering practice, but these are not always available, numerous enough, or suited to the medium to be tried. Where, then, if the renderer has no design of his own, does he seek a subject? The architectural magazines are filled with photographs of the latest designs, some by famous architects, and these can be enlarged to any desired size (14 x 21 in. is an ideal picture size) by means of the photostat or pantograph. After enlargement, the building can be traced on tracing paper (the design modified if desired), and the photograph put aside, since the values and light source obtained by the photographer are usually not so good as the delineator can get in his value study. The photographer seeks one effect, embodying stark contrasts which blot out much detail; the delineator another, in which all parts of the building design are expressed with the utmost clarity and honesty.

As for the building's surroundings, these can be changed or modified. Trees and bushes can be added or taken away, walks and roadways can be modified, or the building can be placed in an entirely different (and perhaps more inspiring) setting. A country house can become a seaside house; a building in a stark setting can be relocated in a verdant one, and so on. The amount of magic he uses in transporting the building is entirely up to the delineator. He can do exactly as he wishes while practicing and no one can say nay!

One cannot begin a rendering without proper investigation of the project and proper preparation. The sight of a clean sheet of paper, whether it is for a letter or a rendering, is sometimes appalling simply because one is afraid to spoil it. However, a clever writer knows that he must write and then rewrite his letter, and makes a draft before attempting the final copy So, too, the clever delineator realizes that there are many problems to be decided before he attempts to work on his final sheet of paper, and makes preliminary studies.

The Value Study

A study in value is the best way to begin your preliminary investigation, whether the rendering is to be in black and white or in color. In a black and white rendering there will be no contrast if the values are not correct, and in a color rendering the colors will not look well if the values are not right. The value study is usually drawn on tracing paper which has been placed over the perspective line drawing on the illustration board below. It is usually drawn in charcoal or soft pencil. The author personally prefers a medium grade of charcoal, because changes may be made more easily in this medium than with pencil. Modifications and erasures may be made with the fingers, with a chamois, or with a kneaded eraser.

The value study should never require more than 10 or 15 minutes. It should be a spontaneous *impression* of the final picture, and not an attempt at a finished result (Fig. 8.17). A short piece of charcoal, perhaps 1 in. or 1½ in. long, is ideal for this purpose. One should leave out all but the essential elements of the picture, and details should be "indicated" or suggested. Such items as roof rafters, boards, shingles, and other details that would

Fig. 8.17 Typical Charcoal Value Study

take a long time to draw should be omitted. A few of these may be quickly drawn in to tell all that is necessary about the detail. At this phase of the rendering one is interested in determining answers to the large problems and not the details.

Several value studies may be made before the renderer is satisfied that he has obtained the maximum success in planning the following:

1. Light source.
2. Proper relationship of values in building, sky, trees, bushes and scale figures.
3. The location of the focal point of the picture.
4. The location, character, and amount of entourage, such as buildings, background, walkways, roadways, trees, bushes, scale figures, automobiles, plots of grass, shadows, and bodies of water.
5. The size of the building in relation to the total picture. (See Chapter 5.)
6. The quality of the sky: clear or clouded, flat or domed.
7. Expression of building design through use of contrast:
    a. The building may be made light, with dark surroundings.
    b. The building may be relatively dark with light surroundings.
    c. The walls may be light and the roof dark.
    d. The walls may be dark and the roof light.
    e. The sky may be darker than the building, or lighter than the building.

When the value study shows a satisfactory arrangement and composition, as well as a pleasant relationship of values, fixative should be blown on and the drawing fastened to the tack board. Then it can be assayed again from a distance before the next step is begun.

The Color Study

For renderings that are to be made in color—such as water color, tempera, or pastels—it is also necessary to make a color study (Fig. 14.22). This may be done in a manner similar to the value study by using pastels on tracing paper, water color on tracing paper or on water color paper, or perhaps tempera on either tracing or water color paper. While it would seem that water color or tempera might seep through tracing paper and damage the illustration board below, this will not happen if a good heavy grade of tracing paper is used. The paper will buckle, but the paint will not seep through.

The color study, like the value study, helps one to decide a number of things before the final rendering is begun. The palette must first be chosen, and upon this decision depends much of the final appearance of the rendering. The guesswork must be removed from the selection of colors for each portion of the building, and each part of the surrounding area, including the sky. The color study provides a knowledge of the way that the various colors will combine and gives a quick idea of the final appearance of the rendering.

Realistic or Conventional Colors

The selection of the palette will depend to a great extent upon your client. Some people prefer the colors of nature as they see them—blue sky, green grass, green foliage. Others enjoy a slightly more sophisticated taste and would be appalled if you gave them natural colors. Members of this group are more likely to appreciate the off-tones and shades obtained by mixing together the several colors of a limited palette. They prefer to see anything but a blue sky and will be more satisfied with such tones as gray, green, blue-green, yellow, orange, etc. The grass in such a rendering may take such colors as gray-green, orange, yellow, brown, or even blue (in a monochromatic scheme).

Another problem that can be solved at the time of the color study is that of the selection of the actual pigments of your palette in relation to the color scheme that you have selected. There may be limitation of palette if one must show the actual color of a material in the building, such as limestone, brick, or wood. The color of limestone, for instance, is made of the following pigments: cobalt blue; alizarin crimson; yellow ochre. This means that these three colors must be included in your palette.

An additional problem is the choice between clear or granulating pigments. If there are building colors and textures to be indicated that require the pebbly appearance that can be obtained by the use of granulated pigments, this must be taken into consideration, as discussed in Chapter 7.

Using the palette suggested in Chapter 7, and looking at the color wheel, the following color schemes can be selected:

Monochromatic
French ultramarine blue, or
Cobalt blue, or
Hooker's green

Analogous
1. Cadmium orange
   Cadmium yellow, pale
   Emerald green
2. Emerald green
   Hooker's green
   French ultramarine blue

3. Alizarin crimson
   Vermilion
   Cadmium orange

Analogous plus complementary accent
1. Cadmium orange
   Cadmium yellow, pale
   Emerald green
   French ultramarine blue
2. Emerald green
   Hooker's green
   French ultramarine blue
   Alizarin crimson

3. Alizarin crimson
   Vermilion
   Cadmium orange
   Cobalt blue
4. French ultramarine blue
   Cadmium orange
   Cadmium yellow pale
   Vermilion

Complementary schemes
1. Alizarin crimson
   Hooker's green
2. Vermilion
   Cobalt blue
3. Vermilion
   French ultramarine blue

4. Cadmium orange
   French ultramarine blue
5. Yellow ochre
   French ultramarine blue

Split complementary schemes

1. Alizarin crimson or rose madder
   Emerald green
   Hooker's green
2. Hooker's green
   Alizarin crimson or rose madder
   Vermilion
3. French ultramarine blue
   Vermilion
   Cadmium yellow pale

4. Cobalt blue
   Vermilion
   Yellow ochre
5. French ultramarine blue
   Hooker's green
   Vermilion
6. French ultramarine blue
   Emerald green
   Alizarin crimson

Triads

1. Yellow ochre
   Cobalt blue
   Alizarin crimson or rose madder
2. Cadmium yellow pale
   Cobalt blue
   Alizarin crimson or rose madder

3. Cadmium yellow pale
   French ultramarine blue
   Alizarin crimson or rose madder
4. Emerald green
   French ultramarine blue
   Vermilion

Color Experimentation

After the actual pigments have been selected for the job at hand, and even before the color study is made, the colors, shades, and tints that the chosen combination will produce should be investigated. This can be done by putting a small amount of each pigment on a piece of heavy white paper, or illustration board, then drawing the several colors together in varying amounts with a wet brush. If you are using alizarin crimson, for instance, with yellow ochre and cobalt blue, you will discover that not only can you get pure red, yellow, and blue, but by careful mixing you can achieve browns, purples, mauves, and gray-greens. If you are working in water color, lighter shades and tints can be obtained by the use of more or less water. If, on the other hand, you are working in tempera, with the colors described in Chapter 7, you will find that the colors may be lightened or darkened by the addition of white or black. If, after experimenting with the colors that you have selected, you find that you cannot mix a color that you absolutely need, select a new palette and color scheme and go through the same process until you are sure that you can produce the color required.

The Finished Rendering

Having completed the value and color studies, you are well prepared to begin the final rendering. You will meet problems that you did not anticipate and that you have not yet settled, but these will be few and minor. It should be remembered that the end result will be a combination of the correct values of the value study and the colors of the color study, and that the final rendering will be an interpretation and improvement on these preliminary studies. If the preliminary studies look well, the final rendering will be successful. If there are basic errors in the preliminary studies, they will show themselves clearly in the final rendering.

The actual technique for making a rendering is described in complete detail in the various following chapters on techniques, but the method for appraising renderings is common to all and can be discussed here. Often the delineator is so close to the problem that he cannot see its basic mistakes. Sometimes he will become so absorbed in each detail that he will not realize that there is something basically wrong with the problem as a whole. The author cannot stress too strongly the importance of systematically checking oneself by looking at the drawing at various stages from a distance. If the drawing board is too heavy to lift, stand on top of a fixed (not revolving) stool and look down upon it. If the drawing board is light enough to move, stand it against the wall and look at it from a distance of 10 or even 15 ft. If you have a diminishing glass, you may leave the drawing in its original position and see the whole picture through the glass. During these periods—which are also valuable as moments of relaxation—compare the values with those in your preliminary studies. Any basic differences will quickly manifest themselves and should be noted so they can be corrected immediately. Even when the rendering is finished and the values and colors seem correct, look at it again with a critical eye to see if there are any changes or additions to be made, then make these while you are standing away from the board in a direct, fresh, manner. This procedure will sometimes suggest the perfect note to bring your rendering to life.

Matting

While great care should be taken during the making of the rendering to keep the edges reasonably square and clean, the addition of a mat seems to "clean up" the edges. It also acts as a foil for values and colors in the rendering itself. Generally speaking, the width of the mat should vary according to the size of the rendering. A general rule for a 14 x 21 in. picture, for instance, is to make the sides and top of the mat 2½ in. and the bottom of the mat 3½ in. wide.

As for the color of the mat, there are many to choose from; some are listed below.[1]

Antiques

Charcoal	Fabric white	Dove gray	Off white
Slate	Brilliant white	Pearl gray	Autumn brown
Light gray	Crimson	T.V. gray	Cream
Dark blue	Ivory	Heather gray	Warm gray
Canary	Dark green	Heather blue	Pastel gray
Maroon	Ivy	Heather green	Sea foam
Super white			

The above are available in 32- x 40-in. size. In addition, brilliant white, ivory, and off white are also available in 30- x 40-in. size.

Tones

Black	Horizon blue	Turquoise	Saffron
Chestnut	Autumn gold	Deep coral	Pumpkin
Rose	Olive	Mint	Bayberry
Avocado	Pussy willow	Terre verte	Cocoa
Tan	Caribbean blue	Meadow green	Terra cotta
Aquamarine	Stone gray	French blue	Gobelin blue
Ecru	Flamingo pink	Peacock	

The above are available in 32- x 40-in. size, while black is also available in 30- x 40-in. size.

[1] Courtesy Charles T. Bainbridge's Sons, Brooklyn, N.Y.

Gold

Pebble finish   Size 32 x 40 in.
Smooth finish

Pebble finish

Single Thickness:	*Double Thickness:*
Off white and white	Off white and white
Cream and white	Cream and white
T.V. gray and white	T.V. gray and white
Light gray and white	Light gray and white
Warm gray and white	Warm gray and white

Cream and white and warm gray and white, single thickness also available in 22- x 28-in. and 28- x 44-in. sizes.

Single and double thicknesses available in sizes 16 x 20 in., 20 x 30 in., 30 x 40 in. and 32 x 40 in.

Special deluxe qualities are available when required, as well as extra large sizes up to 30 x 60 in.

Burlap covered mat board, 32 x 40 in.

White	Raven black	Russet
Eggshell	Chinese red	Colonial yellow
Natural	Taupe	Minton yellow
Brown tweed	Oak brown	Brass
Antique gold	Golden brown	Arbor green
Jade	Colonial blue	

Linen covered mat board, 32 x 40 in.

White	Sage	Fern
Natural	Celery	Geranium
Gray	Jet black	Eggshell
Cinnamon	Daffodil	

Silk covered mat board, 32 x 40 in.

Alice blue	Pearl	Nile
Raspberry	Corn	Platinum
Chamois	White	Eggshell
Ecru	Sand	Black

Moire covered mat board, 32 x 40 in.

White	Lemon	Rust
Beige	Shell pink	April green
Peach	Dresden blue	Moire black
Melon	Cerise	Colonial green

Grass cloth covered mat board, 32 x 40 in.

Natural	Bamboo	Forest
Sandalwood	Beachwood	Green gold
Eggshell	Driftwood	Rattan

Velour covered mat board, 32 x 40 in.

Nubian black	Willow green	Rich gold
Bronze	Warm russet	Ice blue
Dark green	Cool blue	

In addition, a special Museum Mounting Board, all rag, is available in various sizes and plies in solid ivory and solid white.

Care should be taken in the selection of the mat since the wrong texture or color will distract from the color balance of the picture or overwhelm the values of a black and white rendering. Remember that the eye is drawn to bright colors, and they may take attention away from the rendering itself. A good rule is to use white, cream, buff, or eggshell, either matte, pebbled, or linen finish, and to beware of the brighter colors, at least for a while.

An inexpensive mat can be made for your own use from kid finish Bristol board which comes in 1, 2, or 3 plies, 23 x 39 in. However, in order to show the rendering at its best to anyone else, it is advisable to use mat board.

After the picture size has been drawn upon the mat itself, assuming that you are using mat board, the opening should be cut with a bevelled edge, which gives the mat an appearance of greater depth and provides an interesting surrounding shadow line for the rendering.

Cutting the Mat

Information is given in the various chapters on the technique for "fixing" renderings which require this process. If the presentation is to be framed and glazed after it is matted, it will not need further protection. If, on the other hand, it is not to be framed and it will be handled by a number of people, it is wise to cover the face of it with a sheet of transparent plastic material, which may be obtained in varying sizes from any art materials store. This should be of sufficient thickness so that it will not buckle from dampness or handling and can be fastened at the back of the rendering with drafting tape.

Protecting the Finished Rendering

The moments following the completion of a rendering are usually quite hectic, and the temptation to deliver the original drawing without first having had it photographed is pretty strong. But once it leaves your hands, it is hard to get it back, and so, at all costs, it should be snapped before delivery. The photographer should be one who specializes in this work—it is a specialty—and the rendering should be photographed in his studio, where he can control all the conditions, thereby keeping straight lines true, and use his large view camera that can take an 8- x 10-in. negative. With a negative of this size almost any size print can be made with maximum clarity.

Photographing the Rendering

The photographer is armed with four different kinds of black and white and color films for photographing these types of architectural subjects:

1. Line drawings.

2. Black and white drawings with halftones (such as pencil renderings).

3. Colored renderings that are to be photographed in black and white.

4. Colored renderings that are to be photographed in color.

Black and white line drawings photograph most clearly if no washes are used on the drawing, since a special film, No. 1 above, that is sensitive only to jet black and pure white is used for line drawings. If shadings are required, they can be achieved either by the use of Zip-A-Tone (with dots) or by hatching with a fine pen.

Photographs can be made any size or shape, but for economy's sake, choice should be limited to the standard sizes (in inches) listed below:

8 x 10	20 x 24
11 x 14	30 x 40
14 x 17	40 x 60
16 x 20	

These sizes are the same for black and white or color.

If the photographs are to be reproduced, glossy prints should be ordered, since the smooth surface preserves even the finest details of a picture. As a matter of fact, mat and pebbled finishes are used to subdue detail. (Remember the mat finishes used by portrait photographers.) For presentation-type enlargements, prints should be ordered on a mat surface (pebble grain).

Color Photographs

As mentioned above, photographs in color are available in the same sizes as in black and white. They are, of course, more expensive than black and white. To keep costs down and still retain a color record, some delineators prefer 35 mm. transparencies. If the job warrants the purchase of color prints, a color negative should be made.

It frequently happens that the period of time for photographing a rendering is minimal and the rendering can only be in the hands of the photographer for a short time. The most expeditious way of handling the photography of a rendering is to deal with a photographer who specializes in this work. If an appointment is made in advance, the photograph can be taken in ten or fifteen minutes.

When pressed for time, the photographer makes use of a color standard which consists of the primary colors of the Kodak Type C process. The colors of the Type C color control patches (which are printed on a strip of cardboard) have been selected as representative of those colors commonly used in photographic reproduction and are black, three-color (brown), white, cyan, violet, magenta, primary red, yellow, and green. When the rendering is photographed, the color standard (commonly known as the color control patch) is attached to the background near the rendering so that the same light falls on both the rendering and the color standard. When the color prints are made, the perfect color match is achieved in the rendering by matching the color standard, without the presence of the original rendering. (For black and white reproduction, the gray scale is used in the same manner as the color standard.)

The Color Transparency

If the rendering is to be reproduced in color in a magazine or a book, a color transparency is required. Such a transparency should be taken directly from the original rendering.

Mounting Photographs

If the photograph is for reproduction, a mounting is not required. However, if it is to be part of a presentation, a mounting will keep it from curling and will improve its appearance. All good architectural photographers have a dry mounting press, heated by electricity. In this pressure-under-heat process, a sheet of transparent dry mounting tissue is placed between the print and the mounting material and the three pieces are placed in the hot press. When the print is removed from the press, the material cools and the mounting is achieved.[1]

[1] Information on photography courtesy of Gil Amiaga, architectural photographer.

Rendering the entourage

THE BUILDING ITSELF is the major element in the completion of a rendering, yet it cannot stand alone. Surrounding it, according to its location, are trees, bushes, grass, roadways and walkways, adjoining buildings, scale figures, water, automobiles, trucks, trains, airplanes, and above all, a sky. Since each is an important part of the total abstract composition of a rendering, and since even the layman can detect poorly drawn or poorly located surrounding elements, each item should be rendered with the greatest of skill. If this is done, the entourage can complement the building and lead the spectator's eye to a desired focal point. If, on the other hand, the entourage is drawn unskillfully and located without plan, a spectator will be unimpressed with the rendering. Therefore, a detailed examination of the elements that go to make up the entourage of the average rendering seems worth while.

Trees and Bushes

The lives of men have long been enriched by the trees of the earth. Few of us realize how much we depend upon the tree. We use it for shade, and for protection against the elements. Wood is used for the building of houses and ships, in the manufacture of furniture, for the tanning of leather, for fuel, for medicine, and for the making of hundreds of other objects closely related to our daily lives. But the affection that man holds for trees goes further than the utilitarian. Trees are things of beauty and symbols of abundance, and man has learned to use them to enhance his surroundings and thereby establish his close connection with nature. They are an inseparable part of his life.

Importance of Trees

Trees help to identify the setting of a building in a general way, since particular species are associated with definite parts of the country. Some grow only near water, others in flat areas, while still others grow only in mountainous areas. To show a tree that cannot possibly grow on the site might invite embarrassing questions. It is wise to use the correct trees and draw them moderately well, particularly as regards shape and proportion. The client will be impressed with them and with the entire rendering.

The exact methods for drawing trees are discussed in the chapters on the various techniques, but before any method for rendering can be evolved or used, the structure of the tree itself must be thoroughly understood. The novice who does not understand this invariably produces a lollipop stick with a series of cottonlike balls stuck to it and calls this a tree. The more experienced delineator constructs the entire framework of the tree first and then applies foliage to it, remembering that each foliage mass must be supported by a part of the tree structure. Also, the root system of a tree is as much a part of it as the portion above ground, and the trunk rises not only from the ground itself, but from a series of roots, some of which appear above ground, particularly in soil that has been eroded. To show these roots gradually disappearing into the ground is to indicate a well-supported tree.

The diameter and height of the trunk itself will vary according to the age and species of the tree. So will the type of structure. Some trees, such as the white willow, start to divide into large branches close to the ground; others, like the elm, begin to divide higher; while still others, like the Virginia pine, have one trunk for the entire height of the tree. The general shape of the tree also varies with the species. The poplar, for instance, fits into a high, narrow oval. Most oaks fit into a circle, while the apple tree fits into a low, flat oval. The general shape, outline, texture, branch arrangement, and bark are sufficient to identify the species. The rest we leave with the botanist.

Obviously, a great deal of information about trees, particularly those in a given location, can be memorized. Those not often used are difficult to remember, however, and so it is well to keep a complete file of tree photographs and sketches for use in delineating buildings in areas outside your normal theater of operations.

Where possible, a set of photographs of trees on the site under consideration should be made. If the owner is fond of the trees and plans to keep them, he will expect to see them faithfully duplicated.

Basic Methods for Trees

Three basic methods are used for rendering trees. These are:

1. By drawing the structure of the tree alone, or with a few small bits of foliage;

2. By drawing the tree structure, then applying foliage masses upon it, with parts of the tree structure showing in the spaces between the foliage masses;

3. By lightly drawing the shape of the tree, painting the foliage in simple, relatively flat masses, then painting the trunks and a few branches to support the foliage. This is applicable to Chinese ink and water color rendering only.

Most renderers agree that trees should be suggested by simple means. If the tree is believable in shape and structure, little else needs to be done to make it three-dimensional. Therefore, the best way to practice basic forms of trees is by drawing or painting them in silhouette (Fig. 9.1), and by drawing their skeleton alone (Fig. 9.2).

Note: Include the following trees:

Elm—American white	Beech—120 ft max. height
White oak—max. height 150 ft	Shagbark hickory—max. height 140 ft
Black oak—max. height 150 ft	Black walnut
Scarlet oak—max. height 150 ft	White pine—max. height 250 ft
Live oak	Limber pine

Willow
Poplar
Sycamore—max. height 150 ft
White ash
Maple
White birch
Dogwood
Black locust

Red spruce
White spruce—max. height 150 ft
Balsam fir—60 ft height
White fir—275 ft height
Eastern red cedar—50 ft max. height
Western red cedar—200 ft max.
    height
Palm tree

Fig. 9.1   Trees in Silhouette

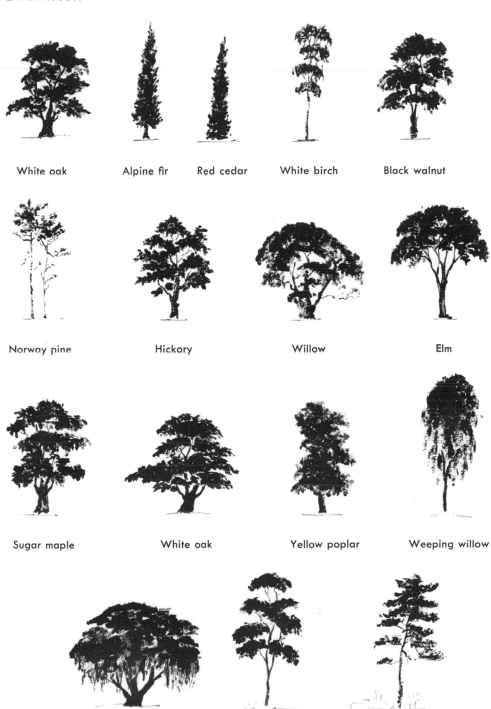

White oak   Alpine fir   Red cedar   White birch   Black walnut

Norway pine   Hickory   Willow   Elm

Sugar maple   White oak   Yellow poplar   Weeping willow

Live oak   Honey locust   Long-leaf pine

Fig. 9.2   Trees in Skeleton Form

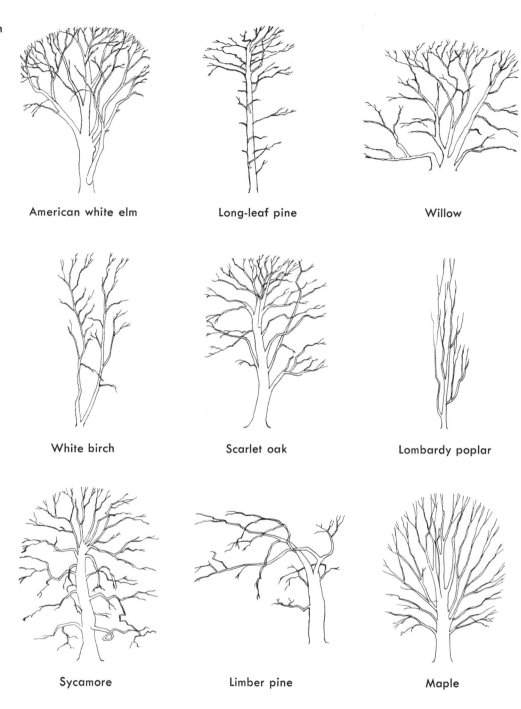

American white elm   Long-leaf pine   Willow

White birch   Scarlet oak   Lombardy poplar

Sycamore   Limber pine   Maple

The renderer will benefit from painting these trees in silhouette, using a small brush and a jar of dark showcard color or ink. The tree skeletons should be drawn with a sharp pencil. In drawing the skeleton remember that it needs to be complete not only in proportion, but also structurally, that is, each branch must spring in a believable way from the trunk, each smaller branch must spring in turn from the larger branches, and a sufficient number of twigs must be shown to make the structure seem complete. A good general rule for determining the diameter of each branch is this: The sum total of the sectional area of all the branches at any point should be slightly less than the cross-sectional area of the trunk or branch from which they spring.

Dark trees should be used behind light building masses, while light trees should be used behind dark masses. Trees located in front of a dark building or tree masses are usually left light, while those located in front of a light surface are usually made dark.

Remember that trees in a perspective will diminish in size according to their distance from the eye of the spectator. Those in the foreground will be large and the leaves may be quite detailed. Those in the mid-distance may be generalized and lighter, while those in the distance may consist of nothing more than flat planes with a few trunks and branches. These will be lightest.

Rarely is one tree used alone, because one tree, like one scale figure, has a lonesome appearance. It is best to use a number of trees, relatively close together (Fig. 9.3). After the charcoal study is made, it should be examined to make sure that the trees do not hide the design. This is a good time also to decide just how complete and textural the trees should be in order to complement and not compete with the architecture. They should be believable in size, shape, and location, and finally, all the trees and bushes but those most important in the composition should be eliminated. Also, make sure that one tree or tree mass is higher than all the rest, to establish a dominant note.

Fig. 9.3   Tree Groupings

Design for an Industrial Plant
Architects: Kempa and Schwartz
rendered by Robert Schwartz

The texture of trunks and branches will vary with the kind of tree being shown, but if it is kept in mind that each portion of the tree structure is round in section, it will be easy to render it intelligently. The source of light should be kept in mind. In sunlight, even though the value of the tree itself may be dark, parts of the structure may be rendered as light as the paper itself. In shade and in shadow, the values may be very dark. It is permissible to take liberties in selecting the values of the structure throughout the tree, showing light branches against dark foliage masses, or dark branches and twigs against light foliage masses. Accents such as shadows, cast by branches or foliage upon branches and trunks below, should be drawn around the members upon which they fall, as shown in Fig. 9.4.

Fig. 9.4   Details of Trees and Flowers

Rendering Foliage

The actual method for rendering foliage in each medium is discussed in the appropriate chapter. Generally speaking, however, the foliage should not be applied until a correct structure has been drawn. Obviously, foliage may be placed only where it can be supported by branches or twigs.

Trees and Shadows on the Ground

The shadow of a tree on the ground will, of course, depend upon the shape of the tree and the source of light. The length of the shadow can be determined if its height is known. Simply draw (in section) a ray of light from the top edge of the tree to the ground. The average tree is made up of spherical or partially spherical forms, and the shadow in turn is made up of intersecting ellipses and partial ellipses (Fig. 9.5, Sketch 1). When these are constructed, it will be found that small light areas, irregular in shape, are left between the shadows of the small ellipses. When the intersecting elliptical shadows are joined, and the shadow of the tree skeleton is made a part of the shadow, a believable shadow results (Fig. 9.5, Sketch 2).

Sketch 1

Sketch 2

Fig. 9.5   Construction of Tree Shadows on the Ground

The casting of a tree shadow should be done with care; it must be quite foreshortened or it will appear not to "lie down" upon the ground. The value of the shadow upon the ground will vary with the material upon which it falls. A shadow on grass will be darker, for instance, than on a light path. Tree shadows are an important means of showing rises and falls in terrain, flights of steps, and other changes in level. See Fig. 9.6. If they fall upon the building itself, they should not be deep in value, since deep shadows camouflage rather than express the form of the structure.

Fig. 9.6   Tree Shadows Used to Indicate Changes in Level

Grass Areas

Any grass area shows a wide deviation in value, color, or both, throughout its plot. Variations in tone are due to several factors, including difference of light, showing through of the soil beneath, variation in the natural color of the grass itself, and shadows upon the grass. While the actual execution of the grass will depend upon the technique in which it is rendered, there are several different methods of approach.

The first is to apply a graded wash, starting with light in the background and changing to dark in the foreground, using horizontal strokes. The second method is to use the same kind of wash, but to introduce light and dark variations as the wash is run. The white of the paper (or its color) should be allowed to show through the wash in a number of spots in order to obtain a light, effervescent appearance. Generally speaking, grass areas should have a sunny appearance so that shadows falling upon them need not be too dark.

Fig. 9.7   Building Reflected
in Wet Roadway
(See also Plate IV)

If the grass areas look uninteresting and unfinished after they have been completed by the above method, they may be stippled or stroked with short, vertical strokes, relatively close together. These are usually slightly darker than the base tone. If the rendering is in color, a graded wash, as described above, may first be applied, then another wash, slightly darker, may be run over the first, care being taken to let a good deal of the first wash appear through the second. Additional interest may sometimes be obtained in grass areas by sandpapering sections which lack interest, particularly if rough-textured paper is used.

Roadways and Walkways

Roads and walks are usually kept light in value, but should be varied in tone. After the base tone is put on the paper, additional interest can be given them by the use of lighter and darker streaks which simulate tire marks, shadows, etc. Expansion joints should be lightly shown in order to help provide scale. If the building is relatively placid in appearance and seems to need a "lift," it is sometimes desirable to assume that the walkways and roadways are wet, and show reflections of the building in them (Fig. 9.7).

Surrounding Buildings

The problem of how to render surrounding buildings is easily solved if they are kept indistinct and uninteresting. They should do no more than frame the building and locate it in time and space—in other words, identify the neighborhood. They should be definitely lighter or darker than the building being rendered, and may be made either way according to the values required to make the new building stand out. It is also usual to draw or paint them rather loosely in a less precise manner than the subject. If the rendering is in color, the same palette used for the building itself should be used for mixing the colors for the surrounding buildings.

Fig. 9.8   Sky Used to Frame the Composition
(See also Fig. 10.12)

Fig. 9.9   Clouds Used to Add
Interest (See also Fig. 13.9)

Skies

Like the other accoutrements, the sky exists only to complement the building. Too often the novice gets so interested in the sky that it becomes an end in itself and the result is that the owner is more interested in the sky than in the building. The author has attended meetings during which the

Fig. 9.10 Reflections in Placid Water (See also Plate XV)

client was so delighted with a beautiful sky that it was almost impossible to get him to discuss the design of the building itself. Sometimes it is unnecessary to draw or paint a sky at all, but if one is required, or desired, it should be kept relatively simple.

A cloudless sky can be domed by grading it from light at the horizon to dark at the top of the picture, or vice versa. The texture of a sky, or the clouds in it, may be arranged to perform a function. If the perspective of the building is so sudden that it seems to run off the sheet, clouds or the texture of the sky itself may be arranged to counter this motion (Fig. 9.8).

As a general rule, the type of sky required will depend upon the building itself. If the building is complicated and has a dynamic quality, a quiet sky is best. On the other hand, if the building is placid and unexciting, or lacks movement, a sky with plenty of clouds and variations in tone or color should be used (Fig. 9.9).

There are, of course, many different kinds of clouds, and the various types may be seen in books specifically related to the subject. An analysis of actual clouds will reveal that generally they are less round than one might think. Many have edges which are rectilinear or almost straight. No two cloud areas will be alike. In drawing them, care must be taken that they do not acquire the appearance of faces, animals, or geometric forms. They should not be made overly conspicuous.

There will be occasions when the delineator will be tempted to render either a sunrise or sunset, but these should be strictly avoided; the results obtained are greatly outweighed by the problems involved and created.

Water and Reflections

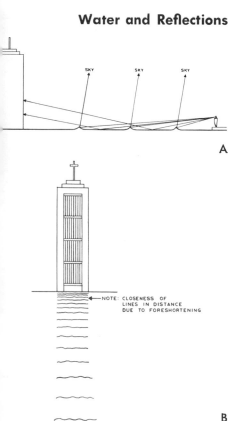

Fig. 9.11 Reflections in Rippled Water

In rendering water, the delineator must first decide whether it is to be made placid, slightly rippled, or rough. If it is to be placid, the reflection will look very much like the building itself, but it will be in an inverted position (Fig. 9.10). On the other hand, if the water is rippled or rough, the depth of the reflection will vary according to the roughness of the water; the height of the building will be greater in the water than in actuality because of the reflection of the building in waves far in front of the building itself (Fig. 9.11 A and B).

The principles of reflection may best be understood by examining a building located on water (Fig. 9.12, Sketch 1). In this sketch, the building is resting at the same level as the water and its reflection is exactly the height of the building itself. The height of each corner of the tower is reproduced beneath the level of the water, and the ends of these lines are then joined.

When a building does not rise from the water, but is located a short distance back from the water's edge, the reflection is determined by dropping true heights from the base of the building, as above, imagining that the water extends to the foundations of the structure itself. See Fig. 9.12, Sketch 2.

If the building is raised above the water, as in Fig. 9.12, Sketch 3, its reflection will begin as far below the surface of the water as the bottom of the building is located above the surface of the water. In a domed building, the depth of the reflection below the horizontal axis of the dome will be the same as the height of the building above the axis (Sketch 4). The reflection of any odd-shaped object lying in the water or at the water's edge will generally follow the same rule.

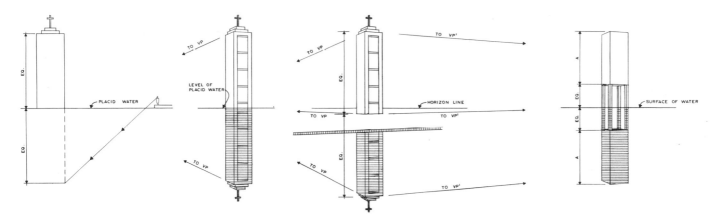

Fig. 9.12   Sketch 1: Reflection
             of a Building at Water Level
             When Water Is Placid

Sketch 2: Reflection of a Building
Back of the Water's Edge

Sketch 3: Reflection of
a Building Raised above Water Level

The same principles used for determining reflections in placid water, with the building located on the water itself, are used in plotting the reflection of a room in a mirror at one end. Any point in the reflection will be located as far "back" of the surface of the mirror as it is actually located in front of the mirror in the room. Constructed in perspective, the room will look exactly the same in reflection as in reality. It will, of course, be reversed.

To draw the reflection of a tilted object one must first drop a perpendicular from its top extremity. The distance from its top to the water line will be the same as the distance from the water line to the end of the object in reflection on a perpendicular line. See Fig. 9.12, Sketch 5.

For most purposes it is wise not to make the reflection appear mathematically conceived, but rather casual. Usually the water can be assumed to be slightly rippled, enough, that is, to deform at least slightly the line of the building in the reflection. The height of the building will be elongated.

The various lights and darks reflected in such a body of water will appear wavy (Fig. 9.10) broken by streaks of light or dark. It is usual to permit the white of the paper to appear in such a reflection in generous amounts, usually in a horizontal way, to simulate the roughness of the water. Reflections of buildings, tree trunks, etc. can be shown vertically, or at an angle if they are actually tilted (Fig. 9.12). The very indistinctness of the outline of a building reflected in slightly rippled water adds a great deal of charm, and the eye is more likely to accept such a reflection than one that is too distinct. This is particularly true of the reflection of tree masses in water. Often the tops of the trees in a reflection are permitted to be hazier and less distinct in outline than the trees themselves.

One final word: water should be either lighter or darker than surrounding elements. As to value and color, it should be remembered that the color of the water is made up of the color of the sky that is being reflected in it, the color of the water itself, the color of the bottom on which it rests, the color of buildings and of trees or other objects around the water. If the rendering is in color, the colors of the building reflected in the water area will be modified by all of these, with perhaps an occasional small spot of true building or sky color in the reflection. While there will be times when rough water needs to be shown, the waves and reflections in it tend to attract too much attention to themselves.

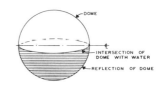

Sketch 4: Reflection of a Domed
Building

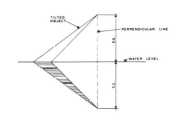

Sketch 5: Reflection of a Tilted
Object

As to the general gradation of water—where it should be dark and where light—the following rules should be remembered: Water will be light wherever it can reflect the bright value or color of the sky. If the sky is dark, the water will be dark. If the body of water is large, it usually is light in the distance, since the light sky at the horizon is reflected there; and dark in the foreground, where the darker value or color of the sky above is reflected. In addition, water is usually shown dark when smooth, and light when rough, because of the refraction of light by the many small waves.

Reflections of buildings in wet streets, as mentioned previously, are sometimes helpful in adding interest to an otherwise over-quiet rendering. If a wet street is used, the same principles hold true as for a building on a placid body of water, with the addition, of course, of the reflection of scale figures and perhaps automobiles. In night renderings, the reflections of lighted glass areas are graded so that they are brightest near the base of the building and gradually diminish in intensity toward the bottom of the picture.

Scale Figures   Most renderings include scale figures. If the structure is to be used by great numbers of people, groups may be shown, but no matter how many figures are indicated, they should be located so as to draw the spectator's eye to a focal point—usually the entrance to the building. This may be done by drawing a few figures in the foreground at large scale, a few more to the left or right in the mid-distance, and several more near the entrance itself (Fig. 9.13). If figures are distributed indiscriminately, the eye will travel back and forth between them a number of times before it locates the focal point of the picture.

Because styles in clothing change rather rapidly, extreme styles should be avoided. Very short or extremely long dresses for female figures, or wide shoulders in male figures, quickly date a rendering. Facetious figures may be fun in school, but have no place on the professional rendering. The figures on the many renderings in this book are seriously drawn, but not too detailed.

Fig. 9.13   Use of Scale Figures (See also Fig. 20.24)

Trucks and trains may be drawn if their presence helps to explain the uses to which the building is to be put, and to give it scale. Neither changes too rapidly in style. Automobiles and airplanes, however, do change in style so rapidly that their presence dates a building—often before a year has passed. It must be remembered that a rendering is part of a general presentation. Sometimes approval for construction is quickly obtained, but on other occasions, as with government buildings, approval may not be forthcoming for a number of years. If a rendering with automobiles or airplanes on it is shown to a committee for final consideration several years after it has been drawn, the committee is likely to draw the conclusion that the building design, like the automobiles or airplanes, is already out of style. It is well either to omit such embellishments or to draw them in such a general way that their style is not very obvious.

Renderings of industrial establishments frequently require the indication of trains. Locomotives rarely need to be shown. Freight cars may be indicated on sidings, but if too many are shown, they will tend to distract the viewer's attention from the building. If a locomotive must be shown, do not indicate smoke or steam issuing from it, as this attracts attention away from the building.

Automobiles, Trucks, Trains, and Airplanes

Nautical scenes invariably require the indication of various kinds of boats, and since these are not so quickly outdated as automobiles, they may be shown in greater detail. As a matter of fact, groups of boats often create a very pleasing pattern.

Boats

Pencil rendering

The Graphite Pencil— Where Did It Come From?

THE GRAPHITE PENCIL as we know it is not a very old instrument. Its predecessor the lead pencil, however, is mentioned in Egyptian history and supposedly was used for making preliminary lines which were then drawn over with brush and ink. Use of lead continued into Elizabethan times, although it was far from satisfactory as a marking or writing tool. After the famous Borrowdale Graphite Mine was discovered in Cumberland in the sixteenth century, pencils were made of pulverized graphite cemented into solid blocks, but even these were not practical.

The difficulty of using blocks and sticks for writing and drawing was overcome in 1795 when N. J. Conté first made pencils by grinding graphite with certain clays, pressing the compound into sticks, and firing it in a kiln. The demand for graphite was so great that its use was restricted at the time of James I in order to preserve the supply, and the mines were used for only a few weeks of the year. For the rest of the year they were flooded.

Types of Lead

Our common "lead" pencils are really made of graphite and China clay. The current supply of graphite comes from Ceylon or Mexico, while the clay which is mixed with the graphite comes from Central Bavaria. Generally speaking, there are four different types of "lead":

1. Ceramic lead—used for drawing and writing pencils.
2. Colored lead—made of a paste of metal cellulose wax and pigments —and not baked because the heat would destroy the color.
3. Soluble or indelible lead—which contains aniline dyes.
4. Wax crayons.

For the ceramic lead, the graphite in its crude form is first purified and broken down into minute particles. Similarly, the clay is pulverized, washed, and purified. When it is combined with the graphite, the resultant mixture is a fine powder. The preparations of clay and graphite vary, depending upon the degree of softness or hardness required. The more graphite, the softer and blacker the "lead" will be. The more China clay, the harder and lighter (in value) the pencil will be.

After the powder of graphite and China clay has been made, water and certain chemicals are added to it and it is mixed under pressure. Sometimes wax is added for smoothness. The resultant mass is then compressed under tremendous pressure and forced through a die to emerge as a soft, solid "lead," of pencil length. These leads are soft and unusable—almost the consistency of spaghetti—until they are put into grooves in boards and tempered by baking at 2000°F or more. This lead is then encased between two pieces of aromatic cedar wood, grooved to make a depression for it. The halves are fastened together by vinyl resin, clamped, and heated at a low temperature. The individual pencils are then cut to size, sandpapered, and lacquered with six to ten coats. The ends are sliced clean, and the name and grade stamped on the side with a hot dye. Although the Bureau of Standards in Washington has tried to standardize the grades of pencil, the grades still differ according to manufacturer.

Equipment Required

Pencils are graded from hard to soft, as follows:
  H indicates hard
  F indicates firm
  B indicates soft

The grades available are 9-H (hardest), 8-H, 7-H, 6-H, 5-H, 4-H, 3-H, 2-H and H, F, HB, 2-B, 3-B, 4-B, 5-B and 6-B. Of these, the soft pencils are best suited for freehand sketching and rendering, although some papers require harder pencils than others. There are two schools of thought on this: some delineators prefer to use only one or two of the softer pencils, such as 2-B and 4-B, while others prefer the effect obtained by varying the pencils according to the paper used. Coarse papers, such as Canson and Mongolfier, demand relatively hard pencils such as HB, F, and 2-H, while the layout is made with even a harder pencil. The reason for using harder or softer pencils according to the quality of the paper lies in the fact that paper is made of a weblike mass of interlaced fibers. When a pencil is passed over these fibers, it is worn down by the file action of the paper, which holds its particles in slight concavities. The rougher the paper, the more readily this file action occurs. The smoother the paper, the less the file action and the softer the pencil required.

Extremely rough paper, such as the Canson and Mongolfier, is usually satisfactory for a large drawing and unsatisfactory for a small one, since it is difficult to draw fine detail upon it. Medium rough surfaced paper, such as kid finish Bristol board, Strathmore paper, or rag bond tracing paper, is best for general work, while pencil sketch pad paper is fine for small studies.

Choice of Subject

Almost any subject can be rendered with the graphite pencil. It must be remembered, however, that the pencil is a relatively pointed medium, and therefore is best suited for buildings with small detail and least suitable for those with large, plain areas.

Preparing the Pencil

There are several basic ways of preparing the pencil for rendering, but before the point can be made ready for any of these, about ⅜ in. of the wood must be bared with a knife at the end opposite the grade mark. After this has been done, it must be decided how the pencil is to be used: as a penlike point, as a broad stroke (at an angle of about 45 degrees), as a very broad stroke (by holding it at an angle of as little as 20 degrees with the

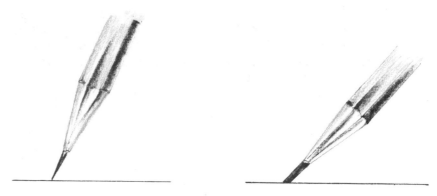

Conical Point
Bare ⅜ in. of graphite and form conical point on sandpaper block.

Broad Stroke
Make point conical; then form flat surface by stroking it across a piece of scrap paper.

Chisel Point
Step 1: Bare ⅜ in. graphite.
Step 2: Flatten both sides of point on sandpaper block.
Step 3: Flatten bottom of chisel to desired angle.

Fig. 10.1 Ways of preparing the graphite pencil

Very Broad Stroke
Bare ⅜ in. graphite and flatten lower side on sandpaper block.

horizontal) as a chisel, or as a pencil wash (obtained by holding the side of the pencil practically flat with the paper). See Fig. 10.1.

No matter what point is desired, it can be worn to the desired shape by the use of a sandpaper block or fine file. After this, it should be smoothed down on a piece of scratch paper and wiped with a cloth to remove any loose graphite. For quick identification, some delineators prefer to mark the various grades they are using with notches or cut-in rings, or with grades painted on all sides of the pencil. No matter how they are marked, time and effort can be saved by keeping the pencils in order, either on the drawing board or in the hand. For practice, sharpen five Grade B pencils in the ways described above and make five different sets of practice strokes as indicated in Fig. 10.2, using kid finish Bristol board.

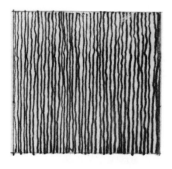

1

2

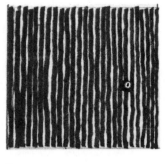

3

4

1. Penlike strokes made with conical point
2. Conical point held flat and moved lightly back and forth across paper
3. Broad strokes
4. Very broad strokes, made with pencil held at 20-degree angle (or less) with paper
5. Chisel point strokes

Note: A pencil can be used in many ways. Try them all and see which you like best.

Make these practice strokes carefully, deliberately, and as beautifully as possible. Each stroke should abut the next, with perhaps a small amount of white between them. Try building up values not only by strokes of even pressure, but by varying hand pressure (Fig. 10.3), as follows:

5

Fig. 10.2 Practice Strokes

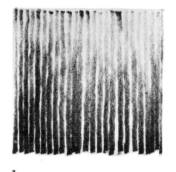

1

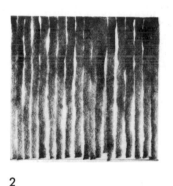

2

3

4

Fig. 10.3 Strokes Made by Varying Hand Pressure

1. Begin with light pressure and end with heavy.
2. Begin with heavy pressure and end with light.
3. Curve strokes by bearing down on one side of the pencil point more than the other.
4. Grade by use of graduated pressure or by building graded values with the side of the pencil.

Further exercises utilizing various grades of pencils will now be helpful. Remember that each stroke on a final rendering should be clean and concise, without fuzzy edges or a fuzzy texture. The pencil chosen will vary according to the value desired. An HB or F pencil will give a sharp, clean stroke on the light side of a building, while a 2-B or 3-B pencil will give a similar clean, but darker, stroke on the shade side.

Practicing Materials and Textures

Fig. 10.4   Relation of Dark Mass to Pattern

Methods of Indicating Textures

Before beginning a final rendering it is a good idea to practice various parts of it on the same paper that is to be used for the final rendering, and at the same scale. Since each person's individual style will differ, only general suggestions for technique can be given here, but no matter what the technique, one major premise must be kept in mind: The renderer should not attempt to capture the realism of a photograph, or the drawing will be monotonous and lack interest and life. There will be occasions when more or less contrast than a normal photograph will be required, but more important, the light and dark masses of the sketch must be manipulated so that they form a pleasing composition. If the normal pattern of light and dark is followed, the picture may become complicated and trite. Generally speaking, the major effect of such a picture pattern will be determined by the dark mass, and all other parts of the pattern must be related to it. Compare Fig. 10.4, "Relation of dark mass to pattern," with a similar final rendering, Fig. 10.19. Care must be taken in the indication of subordinate parts of the picture to fit them into the predetermined general pattern; otherwise camouflage, instead of clarity, will result. Similarly, if completely accurate rendering of local color and detail results in spottiness, these should be subordinated. Remember that the form of the building must be easily understood when the rendering is finished.

Roof shingles: Cover the roof area with strokes parallel to the ridge pole and with others parallel to the pitch of the roof (Fig. 10.5, Sketch 1, a & b). These can be drawn in relatively short strokes, leaving plenty of light between them and between groups of strokes. When this has been done, shingle butts and joints between shingles can be drawn over the base wash in wavy, varying lines, using a pointed pencil. Purposely avoid drawing too many of these, particularly those joints between shingles. The base washes will vary in intensity according to the local color of the shingles to be used. For a white roof, for instance, no general value need be laid down first.

Tile roof: Follow the same procedure for flat shingles, except that the edges of the tile, like the single butts for flat shingles, should be drawn with the sharp point of the pencil (Fig. 10.5, Sketch 2, a & b).

Wall shingles: To render shingles in sunlight, give the wall a "wash" similar to that described for roof shingles. To render them in shade, render each shingle separately, using vertical strokes, leaving the vertical joints white. Then draw in dark, wavy lines under some of the shingle butts (Fig. 10.5, Sketch 3, a & b).

Siding or clapboards: Draw the joint lines lightly, then put a light wash with perhaps an H or F pencil upon the entire area, varying it so that it is lighter here and darker there. Draw slightly wavy, freehand shadows under the butts and at the joints. Vary these in intensity and leave some of them out in order to avoid monotony (Fig. 10.5, Sketch 4).

Flush boards: These can be rendered in a way similar to that for siding or clapboards. The joints between the boards should be kept thin, and can be drawn in with a T-square and a sharp-edged pencil, using a wiping motion to avoid monotony (Fig. 10.5, Sketch 5).

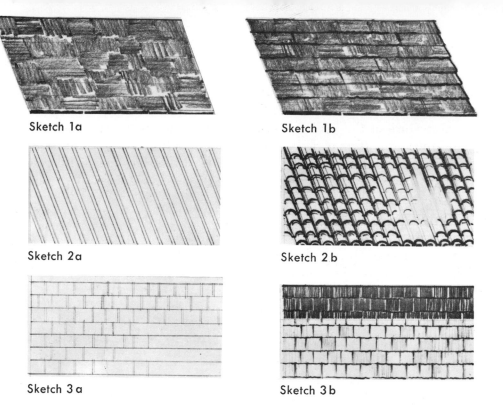

Sketch 1a

Sketch 1b

Sketch 2a

Sketch 2b

Sketch 3a

Sketch 3b

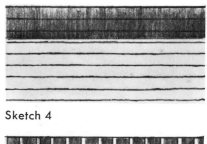

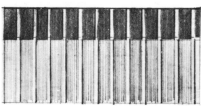

Sketch 4

Sketch 5

Fig. 10.5   Textures: Shingles, Tiles, Clapboards

Stucco or Cement

The value of stucco or cement will depend upon its actual local color as well as on the way that it will fit in with the total pictorial composition. It should be remembered that even white stucco will have a light gray quality in shade. If any value is given to the stucco in sunlight, it should be done with an H or 2-H pencil. Sometimes it is best not to put a wash on the light side at all, but to indicate texture by use of dots made with a fairly hard pencil (Fig. 10.6, Sketch 1).

Stone

Cut stone: Cut stones, such as limestone or granite, are rendered in a manner similar to stucco, except, of course, that joints must be indicated. If the entire wall is covered with joints they will be monotonous; therefore eliminate many of them, assuming that they are "washed out" by bright light in certain areas (Fig. 10.6, Sketch 5).

Fieldstone: Draw the pattern of fieldstone with a sharply pointed B pencil. Remember that its local color will vary from very light to medium dark, and therefore each stone must be rendered separately. Try using vertical

Fig. 10.6   Textures: Stucco, Stone, Brick

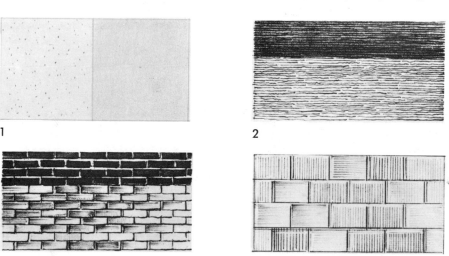

1

2

3

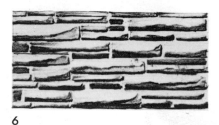

4

5

6

lines in order to express the verticality of the wall. Generally speaking, it is advisable not to render all stones, but only enough for the adequate expression of the texture of the wall. In most cases this means the stones at the edges, and top and bottom of the walls. A pleasing pattern can be formed by leaving streaks of white running in the direction of the sun's rays, with perhaps an occasional stone or joint breaking into this area (Fig. 10.6, Sketch 6).

Brick
There are two ways of rendering brick in pencil, according to the scale of the drawing. In both cases the brick joints should first be drawn in lightly. For a small scale—say ⅛ in. = 1 ft—a general wash, varying in intensity, should first be put upon the wall surface. Remember to leave plenty of light areas. The brick joints can then be put in with slightly wavy lines, varying in intensity throughout the drawing. Here and there the faces of a few of the bricks can be rendered (Fig. 10.6, Sketch 2).

Bricks at larger scale—say ¼ in. = 1 ft—can best be rendered by the use of a broad stroke, the width of a single brick course, leaving the joints white. Monotony can be avoided by the occasional omission of bricks and the inclusion of diagonal strokes made in the direction of light rays (Fig. 10.6, Sketch 3).

Bricks in shade are merely rendered darker by the use of a softer pencil. In shadow, bricks are rendered individually with clean, sharp strokes, leaving the joints white and giving an occasional shadow next to or on top of some of the bricks (Fig. 10.6, Sketch 4).

Rendering Windows
As mentioned in Chapter 6, one of the most important things to remember in rendering windows is that sash and glass usually occupy a position slightly back from the face of the wall. In addition to the outside reveal thus formed, an inner reveal, which may or may not be covered by curtains, also exists. In small window openings (particularly if venetian blinds, shades, or curtains are used) the amount of the inside of the building that can be seen is so limited that dark shading of varying intensity can be used to indicate the interior.

A small window such as the one shown in Fig. 10.7A is best rendered as follows:

1. Draw the window complete with shade, blinds, curtains, etc.

2. Darken that portion of the window not obscured by the items in No. 1.

Fig. 10.7   Rendering Windows

A

B

Fig. 10.8   The Perspective of Trees

3. Put in shade at head and jamb.

4. Put in shadows cast by muntins and meeting rail on curtains and blinds.

5. Put in shadows cast on glass by muntins and meeting rail.

In order to avoid monotony, use a varying line pressure when doing the above five steps.

If the glass opening is large, and the glass is not in glare, the glass itself can be treated as nonexistent. Furniture and furnishings inside the building must be meticulously drawn and shaded in values that will not conflict with those on the exterior of the building. Plants and patterned materials inside the glass opening should be rendered in a subdued manner or they will attract undue attention in relation to the whole picture.

After the interior work has been completed, shadows can be cast on the glass and curtains by mullions and muntins (which have been left white). Finally shade and shadow at head and jamb can be put in (Fig. 10.7B).

Rendering Entourage

Foliage: Foliage should be practiced before it is drawn on the final rendering. Its location and size can be determined in the charcoal value study. Remember that while there may be large trees and certain bushes on the site that cannot be moved, those that you add can be placed wherever you wish. Before practicing the drawing of foliage, the following rules should be kept in mind:

1. Limit the amount of foliage to the necessary minimum. Too much will draw attention from the building itself.

2. Remember that foliage should complement the architecture and not detract from it; therefore, do not make it more conspicuous than the building itself.

3. Show only live-looking specimens. This is no time to indicate trees that have been struck by lightning or otherwise partially destroyed.

4. Rarely, if ever, should only one tree or bush be indicated in any location; a grouping is always much more pleasant to look at.

Realism in the indication of trees comes with the realization that a tree is never an isolated thing. The greatest realism in shrubbery is obtained by drawing generalized, light-valued trees in the distance, slightly detailed; larger, darker trees in the mid-distance, and still larger, darker, and more detailed trees in the foreground (Fig. 10.8). The latter are near the spectator's eye, and therefore the bark, tree structure, and leaves must be exceedingly well drawn. A general description of tree structure is given in Chapter 9, so we will confine our discusson here to the various ways of rendering trees in pencil.

Note: Always draw tree structure from the ground up, as the tree grows, and in short, straight strokes, each deviating in direction from the one below.

Fig. 10.9 Drawing the Tree Structure with Growth Motion Strokes

To draw trees in pencil, first block out the rough shape of the tree with a 2-B pencil, then draw the trunk, branches, and twigs lightly, but as completely as possible. Remember that the branches and twigs radiate from the trunk in all directions, not only to the left and right. Remember also that the total cross-sectional area of any particular group of branches, twigs, etc. must be slightly less than the part of the tree from which this group springs. Draw all parts of the tree from the ground up, using "growth motion strokes" as shown in Fig. 10.9. Most of all, remember that even though it will take some time to do it, the *entire* structure of the tree, including a number of twigs, should be drawn or it will not look real.

Strokes: In drawing the structure of the tree, some of the shading strokes may follow the length of the members that they fall on, and some strokes, particularly shadows, can be drawn around the members. As in all pencil work, leave some of the areas of the tree structure white.

Foliage in the mid-distance: As foliage is made up of a series of masses, it is first necessary to block these in lightly. Leave holes in the foliage masses and draw branches in these spaces. Using the side of the pencil (remembering that there should be no hard edges to the foliage masses), practice making light strokes. Use an F pencil for the foliage in sunlight, and a B or 2-B for foliage in shade and shadow (Fig. 10.10 Sketch A). Touch the paper with the flat of a broad stroke pencil and go back and forth in as many different directions as you can without taking the pencil off the paper, turning the pencil as you go. This method can also be used for bushes (Fig. 10.11).

Trees and bushes in the foreground: For detailed trees or bushes in the foreground, groups of individual leaves must be shown (Figs. 10.10A and 10.11A and C). The shape of the leaves will vary with the species shown.

Trunk textures: The trunk texture, of course, depends upon the kind of tree. It need not be detailed, but can be shown in a generalized way. Texture on tree trunks in the foreground should be detailed as carefully as

Fig. 10.10　Drawing Foliage Masses for Trees

A. Branches of a foreground tree
B. Radial broadstrokes used for foliage of a mid-distance tree
C. Locating shade areas
D. Leaving the pencil on the paper and radiating strokes in all directions.

A

possible. Some suggestions are shown in Fig. 10.11. Generally, if one remembers that a tree is made up of a series of cylindrical (not flat) members, more realistic tree drawings will result.

Grass can be rendered in several ways:

1. By the use of parallel vertical strokes for the entire grass area.
2. By the use of some vertical strokes for only those areas of grass which are in shadow, leaving the remainder of the lawn white.
3. By the use of horizontal strokes.

No matter what technique is used, the grass will become lighter as it recedes into the distance.

Tree shadows on grass:　Shadows on grass areas should first be constructed on tracing paper so that they look realistic. First draw the shadow of the tree trunk and its branches upon the ground, remembering to foreshorten

Rendering Grass

B　　　C　　　D

A

B

C

D

Fig. 10.11   Bushes and Tree Trunks

A.–D. Four methods of rendering shrubbery
E.–H. Tree trunk textures
E. Paper birch; F. Sycamore; G. Shagbark hickory; H. Black locust.

E   F

G   H

the total shadow sufficiently so that it appears to lie flat on the ground. Each portion of the foliage mass, which is approximately spherical in shape, will cast its own small elliptical shadow upon the grass. These will overlap to form a shadow which will have a number of light areas in it (Fig. 9.5). Grass in the shadow areas will, of course, be darker than the grass in the sun. Effort should be made to minimize detail in the shadow; otherwise it will detract from the building.

Walkways and roadways are generally kept light (see Fig. 14.25). It is usual to show roadways without texture, but some delineators prefer to indicate the motion of traffic by the use of an overlapping series of tire marks. Walkways, on the other hand, may be built of any of several materials of distinctive texture, such as brick, flagstone, cobblestone, etc., and for these the foreground at least may be detailed by shading the individual components of the walk, joining the values together here and there by the use of an H or 2-H pencil. Whatever joints are indicated, either in roadways or walkways, must be drawn with a fine light stroke, since they are invariably seen in quite a foreshortened manner.

Outdoor steps: Vertical strokes are usually used to express the verticality of outdoor risers and to draw attention to them.

It should be remembered that the value of a shadow, wherever it falls, is determined by the material it falls upon. On grass, it is quite dark. On a roadway or walkway made of light material, it is correspondingly light. As with shadows on lawns, tree shadows on roadways and walkways should be constructed so that their appearance is believable.

For additional interest, the streets and walks may be assumed to be wet, as from rain, and reflections of the building, passers-by, automobiles, etc. may be made upon them. This is particularly successful if the scene is taken at dusk or at night (see Plate IV).

Some delineators prefer to leave all skies in pencil renderings white. A number of others, however, prefer to shade skies or to render clouds in them. If a sky is rendered, it should complement the building; that is, it should be dark if the building is light, and light if the building is dark. A good rule of thumb is this: If the building has a static quality so quiet that the picture appears to require more life, then a cloudy, busy sky will help. If, on the other hand, the building is dynamic, with many exciting elements, the sky should be quiet, without clouds and with a minimum of texture.

If the perspective of a building is so sharp that the drawing seems to slip out at the side, the motion can be stopped by using a sky made of strokes which counter the movement (Fig. 10.12). This can be a plain sky or a cloudy one, depending upon the type of building.

Since the pencil strokes themselves are so definite that they do not lend themselves to clouds, the clouds are sometimes rubbed down and softened in the surrounding areas by the use of a cardboard stomp. Some delineators find that the side of the pencil technique is better for skies than the broad stroke technique, because it minimizes texture.

See the notes on these embellishments given in Chapter 9.

Skies

Scale Figures

Scale Figures

Fig. 10.12
The House on the Hill
rendered by
Edward G. Schildbach
Student project

MATERIALS: *Kid finish Bristol board; F, HB, B, 2-B, 3-B, and 4-B pencils; pink pearl and ruby erasers.*

Making a Pencil Rendering

A line perspective (Fig. 10.12) was drawn on white bond tracing paper. Another piece of tracing paper was placed over the perspective and the lines of the building and the surrounding areas were traced upon it. This paper was then placed upside down and each line was drawn on the back. Then this drawing was placed right side up, with the perspective in the proper position, and each line was traced through to the kid finish Bristol board below with an HB pencil. Care was taken not to groove the Bristol board, since grooves show up as white lines in a finished rendering.

Charcoal Study

A new piece of tracing paper was placed over the tracing paper perspective and a charcoal study was made as described in Chapter 8. In this study in charcoal it quickly became apparent that the perspective of the building at the left side of the sheet would have to be stopped in some way, so several trees and a tree branch in the sky were introduced. The horizontal sky accomplishes a similar task. A light source from the front and upper right was chosen because it gave the opportunity to express the forms of the building most clearly. It was decided at this time that the roof fascias of the building should be left light and that a dark sky and trees behind it should be used to make the building stand out.

Shading

The actual shading was done as follows:

1. Shades on the vertical wood members at the front of the building were put in, using an HB pencil with vertical strokes and counter strokes in perspective.

2. The shade areas under overhangs, mullions of windows, undersides of mullions, railings, and copings were put in with an F pencil.

3. The dark areas of windows were put in with pencils from F to 3-B; the darkness was varied for interest.

4. The convolutions of the curtains at the rear windows were indicated by the sharp edge of a broad stroke F pencil.

5. Each stone was rendered separately with strokes in perspective, using an F pencil. Monotony was broken by the use of an HB pencil in certain areas. The vertical joints were permitted to remain white. Sharp joint shadows were put next to and under each stone with an HB pencil.

6. The shadow of the building on the stonework below was put in as follows: Each individual stone was rendered separately with a B pencil. Then all the stones were drawn together and the shadow deepened into a general shade area by the use of 2-B strokes over the entire group.

7. The illusion of depth was obtained by introducing trees in the distance and mid-distance. Distant trees in the center and right side of the drawing were blocked in with horizontal broad strokes. Then the mid-distance trees were drawn over these in quite a detailed manner, using B and HB pencils. The spruce trees at the left and right were drawn by first indicating the structure with the sharp edge of a B pencil, then drawing the foliage with a series of individual strokes of HB and 2-B pencils. The large tree at the right of the drawing, with out-stretching branches, helped to fill an otherwise empty sky and provided an interesting pattern. This was blocked out with a B pencil and detailed with a B and a 2-B.

8. Earlier value studies revealed that too much foreground would detract from the building itself. It was decided, therefore, to show only

tree shadows and steps. The risers of the steps were shaded in with vertical strokes with an F pencil. The tree shadows were drawn with a B pencil; making them relatively indistinct gave them a nebulous quality. When these shadows and the stairs were completed, the drawing was "fixed" with clear pastel fixative. After it had dried, the entire foreground was erased with a ruby eraser, to make the shadows and steps appear softer than the building.

9. The tones of the building were made sufficiently strong so that no other area or element of the drawing would compete with it.

10. Pastel fixative was used on the finished drawing.

MATERIALS: *Kid finish Bristol board; HB, B, 2-B, 4-B, and 2-H; pink pearl, ruby; clear pastel.*

Fig. 10.13

Office Building rendered by William Spence Black Student project

The preparation for Fig. 10.13 was similar to that for Fig. 10.12. After making several value studies in charcoal, it was decided to use a light source from above and from the left, since this permitted the clearest expression of the building masses. This light source determined that the face of the grid at the front of the building, and the faces of mullions and muntins at first floor level, would be left white.

Shading

1. The first values to be rendered were those on the sides and soffits of the grid. All these, excepting those on the second floor, were put in with a broad stroke point of an HB pencil, in perspective, in order to help express the shape of these members. The shading on the first floor was purposely made vertical to relieve the monotony.

2. The light values on the glass of the upper floor were next washed in with an H pencil and the shadows upon the glass were rendered in with long, clean strokes with a 2-B pencil.

3. On the shade side of the building, the smooth cut stone was shaded with an F pencil, the strokes being made in perspective. The cut stone was shaded by rendering each stone separately, some light, some dark, for interest and local color. The joints were permitted to remain white, and the monotony of the stonework was eventually relieved by the erasure of white streaks with a ruby eraser.

4. The shadow on the adjoining portion of the building was rendered with HB and B pencils, and reflections on the lighter part of the building were introduced with the ruby eraser.

5. The lower portion of the building was rendered with an F pencil for the light areas and a B pencil for the dark areas. The street and the building in the distance to the left were put in with an HB pencil, as was the sky.

6. The stone of the plant pocket at street level was rendered with H and HB pencils, while the shrubbery and the palm trees were indicated with F, B, and 2-B pencils.

7. The perspective was fixed with clear pastel fixative.

The light source was assumed to be from above and from the right. This produced sharp contrasts between light and shade areas. The chief job for the renderer lay in the study of reflected light within the shadows themselves; dark shadows were required, yet they had to be luminous. Light rays would strike the deck areas, bounce up, hit the ceilings, and ricochet back into the shadows on the walls (see Chapter 6—A Study of Light). Further luminosity within the shadows was obtained by leaving white spaces between the strokes, and by leaving light joints between the stones at first floor level.

The windows were given the deepest values in the rendering, but they were graded so as to give the illusion of glare. The background was rendered quite simply; 45-degree strokes were applied in a loose manner. Foreground

MATERIALS: *Pencils: HB, B, 2B, 3B; pink pearl.*

Fig. 10.14

House on a Stream
rendered by Paul Gene Zafren
Student project

bushes were detailed in character, that is, the leaves were delineated. The background trees were carefully placed in relation to the building and to each other, the intertwining twigs creating a pleasant pattern against the pale sky which was made with horizontal HB strokes. After the water and deep shadows were applied, the white areas were erased clean by the use of a pink pearl eraser, using a T-square as a guide.

Pencil Drawings on Tracing Paper

Schell Lewis makes his pencil renderings on tracing paper, using a rag bond with a good "tooth"—not slick or smooth. After perspective line drawing and preliminary study (Fig. 10.15A) are made, another sheet of tracing paper is placed over the line drawing, and the finished rendering is made, beginning at the left and finishing at the right, as shown in Fig. 10.15B, being guided by the line perspective which can be seen through the top sheet of tracing paper.

Fig. 10.15A
Preliminary Study
for a church
O'Connor and Kilham,
Architects
rendered by Schell Lewis

Fig. 10.15B

Partially finished
rendering:
Preliminary study
for a church
O'Connor and Kilham,
Architects
rendered by Schell Lewis

Fig. 10.16

Study for Cadet Barracks
United States Military
Academy
O'Connor and Kilham,
Architects
rendered by Schell Lewis
Size: 21 x 30 in.

Fig. 10.17

These two masterly renderings were made on tracing paper and were then mounted on illustration board. Preliminary pencil studies were first drawn and presented to the architects for their selection of view (Figs. 10.17 and 10.18). Although these were rough, they were complete enough to show the disposition of the major elements.

The final renderings contain numerous "tricks" that the novice should analyze and practice. Above all, notice the sharp value comparisons that make the buildings seem to stand out. Dark is always used against light, light against dark.

Note also the wide tonal variations in the buildings themselves; stark white, jet black, and hundreds of grays between! Every line is freehand. Line widths vary from $\frac{1}{16}$ to $\frac{1}{4}$ in., according to location, those in foliage masses being widest.

Whereas Charles Spiess's approach is relatively simple (Figs. 10.20 and 10.21) Lewis's is more complex. Look at the tree groupings in any of these renderings and you will see a three-dimensional approach. Spiess renders his foliage masses flat, Lewis in the round. Both men are correct: each has his own approach.

Fig. 10.18

Study for a Church
O'Connor and Kilham,
Architects
rendered by Schell Lewis
Size: 21 x 30 in.

Fig. 10.19

An analysis of Schell Lewis's technique of indicating building materials reveals some interesting things. Brick is made in single strokes, with a pencil point the exact width of one course. Its pattern is purposely made imperfect so it will not appear stiff. Stone is treated with great tonal variation. Sometimes the stones are plainly shown; elsewhere they are so light that they are the color of the paper. Occasionally stones are omitted altogether and angular smudges as well as white spaces are used to relieve the monotony. Where stones are in shadow, they are rendered dark, and the joints are left white. But aside from the variation of the stones themselves, notice that there is a definite gradation from dark at the bottom of the building to light at the top. In Fig. 10.19, however, the brick is graded from dark at the top to light at the bottom. Each is interesting in its own way.

Foliage is rendered with rather wide strokes about ¾ in. long, most of which are diagonal. Shadows cast on trunks and branches by foliage masses are soft in quality and have wavy, indistinct edges. Finally, some trunks and branches are outlined for emphasis.

The skies in Schell Lewis's renderings were made with broad strokes of the pencil, the washes then being muted by rubbing with a paper stomp.

Scale figures and automobiles complete the renderings.

STANLEY J. SHAFTEL, A.I.A
ARCHITECT

These two renderings were produced by Mr. Spiess on a Strathmore plate finish Bristol board. He prefers this to kid finish because it permits indication of small details most accurately. Before beginning, he removes the high gloss by scrubbing the entire sheet with a pink pearl eraser, using vertical overlapping strokes. Pencils used vary from H to 2-B. One set of pencils is sharpened as if for writing, another set is "chisel sharpened." When using a newly sharpened chisel point, Mr. Spiess holds it vertically at first, then at an increasingly acute angle until it is worn down to the natural position of the hand.

Mr. Spiess draws the perspective directly on the board, using an HB pencil. Only the main elements of the building, such as windows, doors, and mullions, are drawn; smaller elements such as muntins are added as the rendering is being made. A sheet of tracing paper is then laid over the perspective drawing, and a charcoal study, setting the values, light source, bushes, trees, etc. is made. This is fastened to the wall in front of the delineator and he begins the final rendering. If there are trees or bushes that "cut through" the building, their outlines are sketched in lightly.

Fig. 10.20
Kaltman Residence,
Westbury, L.I.
Stanley Shaftel, A.I.A.
Architect
rendered by Charles Spiess

Moore and Hutchins, Architects

Fig. 10.21

Glen Rock Community Church

Glen Rock, N.J.

The Moore & Hutchins Partnership, Architects rendered by Charles Spiess

The entire building is then rendered completely, and this is followed by the rendering of the base planting. The surroundings are rendered by beginning as far away from the building as possible, and working toward it. Every element is completed as Mr. Spiess works from top to bottom using the values set up in the charcoal study. Large trees are rendered before the sky, which is the last part of the rendering to be completed. If there are clouds, these are first blocked out, then filled in.

For the sake of clarity, Mr. Spiess prefers to limit the number of values in a rendering to a few that are clearly defined. His trees, for example, are first drawn so that shape and structure are correct and believable. Then each portion of foliage is shaded with a simple flat wash, with no complicated attempt to obtain a three-dimensional quality. A few foliage shadows added on the trunk and branches contribute to the illusion of reality.

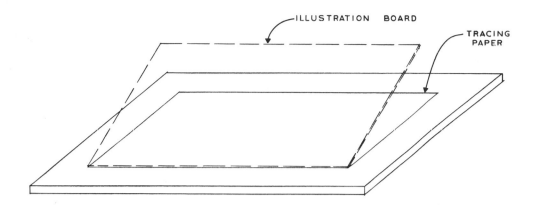

Fig. 10.22 Dropping the Illustration Board onto Tracing Paper

Short Cuts in Pencil Rendering

Many renderers save time in pencil work by the use of a good grade of rag tracing paper. Instead of laboriously transferring the perspective from one sheet to another, they merely place a clean sheet of tracing paper over the line perspective, and, after making a value study, render.

Tracing paper requires the use of slightly harder pencils than kid finish Bristol board, but provides an excellent surface. When the rendering has been finished it may be fixed with pastel fixative and either the original may be shown to the client, or any number of black and white prints may be made from the tracing. If the tracing is to be mounted, it can be fastened to an illustration board with Scotch tape, or it can be "floated" on the illustration board by the following method:

1. Mix a batch of Sanford library paste to a creamy consistency (free of lumps) in a cup or other container.

2. Turn the tracing upside-down on a smooth surface and thoroughly saturate it with the paste, using a sponge. Remove the excess.

3. Sponge an illustration board larger than the drawing with the same paste.

4. Hold the illustration board on one edge next to the tracing, then let it fall onto it (Fig. 10.22). When you turn the illustration board upside down, the tracing will be fastened to it, but will be wrinkled. To remove wrinkles, and any excess paste, cover the drawing with a clean piece of tracing paper, and, using the edge of a large triangle, gently stroke outward in all directions, radiating away from the center.

An illustration board that is wet by such a mounting process will usually curl. To counteract this, a sheet of tracing paper should be paste-mounted as described above, on the back of the illustration board, or, if the board is quite thick, merely wetting the back will do. Finally, the mounted drawing should be placed on a flat, even surface, covered with clean paper, and weighted with heavy books until it is thoroughly dry.

The Carbon Pencil

The carbon pencil is a much more versatile instrument than the graphite pencil. Basically the drawing part is made of a combination of carbon and a sort of gum paste pressed into a stick, and then encased in a wooden container in much the same way as a graphite pencil. Beyond this basic similarity of general appearance, the two have little in common. Whereas the graphite pencil glides across the paper, the carbon pencil grips it. When it is drawn across the paper it produces a clean, dry line, jet black in tone, velvety in quality.

The carbon pencil, of which the Wolff pencil (made in England) is most widely known, is made in six degrees:

HH — very hard
H — moderately hard
HB — middle degree
B — black
BB — very black
BBB — extra black (this is also made in Extra Heavy)

It can be used in various ways, such as:

1. Strokes
2. Hatched strokes
3. Hatched strokes smudged with chamois
4. Strokes combined with chalk
5. Strokes combined with white pencil
6. Strokes combined with tempera

The carbon pencil is one of the fastest and easiest media to use, and is capable of producing a wide range of effects. It erases fairly easily with a kneaded eraser, and produces dramatic effects when used on the proper paper or board. It has a fabulous quality for the "indication" of detail with a minimum of effort. It may be used on a variety of papers or boards, but is most effective when used on a soft-textured paper such as kid finish Bristol board, tracing paper, vellum, charcoal paper, pastel paper, or any of the colored illustration and poster boards. Its sole disadvantage is that the point breaks easily, and for this reason it is advisable to hand-sharpen the pencil very carefully with a sharp knife, exposing only about ¼ in. of the carbon. Care must be taken not to nick the carbon during the removal of the wood. As with the graphite pencil, the final shaping of the point is done on a sandpaper block or a fine file.

The carbon pencil is effective on colored as well as white paper, particularly when it is combined with white pencil, chalk, or tempera. American-made charcoal paper, which is available in a standard size of 19 x 25 in., comes in about thirteen colors. Colors which are relatively "grayed" are most suitable for use in architectural rendering, and these have been marked with an asterisk in the following list:[1]

*Fog blue
Powder pink
*Pottery green
*Peach glow
*Cadet blue

[1] Strathmore Paper Co., courtesy Robert Rosenthal, Inc.

Golden brown
Minton yellow
*Velvet gray
*Storm gray
*White
Black
*Bright white
Maize yellow
Autumn brown
Harvest gold

Poster boards are available in more colors than colored papers. One company makes 41 colors, which includes colors representative of the entire spectrum. As with colored papers, only the relatively "grayed" colors should be used for architectural renderings, because bright colors detract from the rendering itself. Some of the colors that are useful for rendering are:

Brown
Dark green
Silver gray
Charcoal
Ecru
French blue
Dull white

Some colored poster boards are coated on one side, others on both sides. The standard size for these boards is 28 x 44 in., 14 ply, and they can be cut to the size desired.[2]

Herga (English-made) pastel papers are also excellent for working with the carbon pencil, and these are available in many colors. The author recommends the colors marked with an asterisk for architectural renderings.

*Light gray
*Dark gray
*Green
*Light brown
Brown
*Buff
*Light green
Blue
Black

These papers are sold in size 22 x 30 in.[3]

---

[2] Charles T. Bainbridge's Sons, courtesy Robert Rosenthal, Inc.
[3] Winsor & Newton, Inc., courtesy Robert Rosenthal, Inc.

Equipment Required   The equipment required will be determined by the color of the paper used. The following list is for complete experimentation in the various techniques described in the following pages:

1. A sheet of soft paper
2. Black carbon paper
3. White carbon paper
4. B, BB, and BBB pencils
5. Kneaded eraser
6. Chamois
7. Jar or tube of Chinese white or poster color
8. Jar of black
9. Several sticks of white chalk
10. White pencil
11. Jars of warm gray tempera in grades 0, 1, 2, and 3
12. Pastel fixative

The entire perspective for this rendering was constructed on a tracing paper and then reproduced on the charcoal paper by placing a large sheet of white carbon paper between the tracing paper and the charcoal paper (carbon side down). Each line of the perspective was traced with a 3-H pencil, lightly but firmly, to reproduce it on the rendering paper below. It is necessary to use carbon paper because the carbon pencil will not "take" on lines which have been drawn by a graphite pencil, but will slide off.

Fig. 10.23

First Unitarian Meeting House
Madison, Wis.
Frank Lloyd Wright, Architect
rendered by
Jaroslav Sichynsky
Student project

Charcoal study: While the value study was being made in charcoal on tracing paper, the following decisions were made:

1. The light should come from above and to the left in order to express the architectural forms most strongly.

2. The trees should occupy the position shown in the final rendering in order to stop the violent perspective motion of the roof lines.

3. The grass, trees, and flowers in the foreground should be made dark in order to "push the building back" into the mid-distance, while the trees in the background at the right side of the drawing were placed there to keep the building from "falling out of the back of the sheet."

4. It was felt that no clouds were necessary, and that the tone of the paper alone would provide a sufficiently luminous sky.

Shading: The strokes used for textures and shading were differentiated according to location, the texture to be indicated, the direction of the plane, etc., as follows:

1. The shade side of the building at the left, as well as the eaves, was rendered individually in strokes with a pointed B pencil (Fig. 10.24 Sketch 1).

2. The windows in this area were darkened by hatching with the flat side of a BB pencil. Edges were kept straight by the use of a triangle which

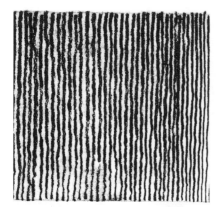

Sketch 1

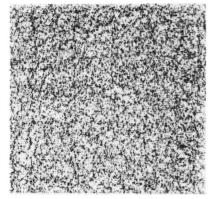

Sketch 2

Sketch 3

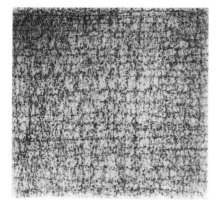

Sketch 4

Fig. 10.24   Shading Made with a B Carbon Pencil

Sketch 1. Pointed
Sketch 2. Side of Pencil (Cross-hatched)
Sketch 3. Hatched, Rubbed with Chamois
Sketch 4. Hatched, Rubbed and Textured

was held in place as the pencil was moved back and forth (Fig. 10.24 Sketch 2).

3. The shade area under the roof was rendered in the same way, with the outer edge of this wash being made darker than the inner edge because of reflected light.

4. The shadow on the glass area was put in by hatching with a BBB pencil and was finally darkened by the use of strokes with the dulled point of the BBB pencil.

5. Shadows on the mullions were put in with a B pencil in short strokes, care being taken to permit the color of the paper to "shine" through for the effect of reflected light.

6. Stonework: The stonework of the side wall in sunlight was indicated by a series of rather isolated stones set in a gray tone (Fig. 10.24 Sketch 3), since an attempt to show more than this in the charcoal study took away the sunny effect it was felt that this wall should have. The stones in the shade area cast by the roof at the left were indicated completely before they were hatched vertically with a BB pencil.

7. The shadows under the mullions were put in freehand in continuous strokes.

8. The complicated texture of the roof was simplified by the use of large freehand strokes simulating the shadows under the shingle butts. If these had been put in solidly, the roof would have been monotonous in appearance; therefore they were made in a series of short, slightly wavy strokes with a B pencil. The small roof at the right and the low roof at the left were made by a series of strokes parallel with the roof in both directions, with some of the paper allowed to shine through.

9. The shingles of the roof in the lower portion of the building at the right were indicated in the same way with a B pencil.

10. The dark windows were indicated by hatching with the point of a BBB pencil, leaving the mullions the color of the paper.

11. The shadow on the ground was indicated by the use of short vertical strokes using a sharp BB pencil.

12. The stonework in this area was indicated by drawing an occasional stone and then placing a smooth wash of white pencil over the stone area.

13. White pencil was also used at various places such as the edges of the roof at the right, on parts of the shingle roof at the left, and on the stones of the wall in sunlight in the foreground.

14. The grass in the foreground was indicated by the use of a B pencil held as flat as possible. Strokes about 1½ in. long were made, care being taken to vary the intensity here and there and to allow the color of the paper to shine through in order to prevent monotony. The grass in the immediate foreground toward the bottom edge of the picture was darkened considerably with the same horizontal strokes in order to help provide a dark frame for the picture.

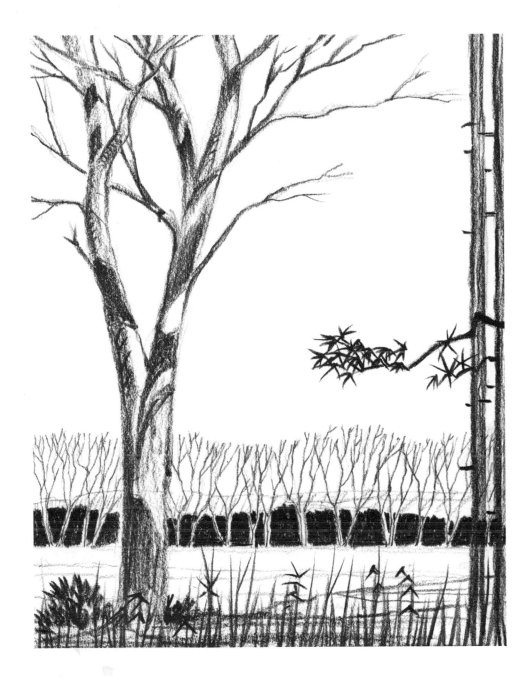

Fig. 10.25 Details of Flowers and Grass in Carbon Pencil

15. The flowers and grass in the immediate foreground were put in with pencils varying from B to BBB, using a pointed pencil. The strokes were made from the ground up with a wiping motion in order to achieve a natural-looking growth pattern. The details were made individually with a pointed BB pencil, beginning with strong pressure and ending with no pressure (Fig. 10.25). Some of the flowers were whitened with the white pencil.

16. The trees were put in last, the bark being indicated with B and BB pencils by a combination of strokes around the trunks as well as vertical strokes. The branches were shaded on the underside with a BBB pencil, and the pine needles were put on last with the same wiping motion described in Fig. 10.25.

17. Pastel fixative was used to "fix" the finished drawing.

MATERIALS: *Sheet of black carbon paper; American-made charcoal paper, 19 x 25 in.; B—BB and BBB pencils; kneaded eraser; chamois.*

Preparation for Fig. 10.26 was similar to that for Fig. 10.23, but a black carbon paper was used to transfer the perspective drawing.

The value study in charcoal disclosed that the most dramatic effect could be obtained by the selection of a light source from above and to the left, giving a definitely light side and a dark side to the building, and providing a dark frame of low adjoining buildings as a base. It was decided to make the tower darkest at the top and at the edges next to the sky.

Fig. 10.26

An Office Building
New York City
rendered by
Edward Devine White, Jr.
Student project

Detail in this project was almost eliminated because of the smallness of scale. A general impression was sought rather than a detailed rendering. The dark shadow in the foreground (from a building assumed to be behind and to the left of the spectator) and the two scale figures were included in the composition in order to "push" the building into the mid-distance.

Shading: This rendering was made by the smudge process; that is, strokes were applied and then smudged with a chamois as follows:

1. A general gray value was given to the shade side of the office building by hatching with the side of a BB pencil in several directions, then each portion of this side was in turn masked with 8½- x 11-in. pad paper and rubbed with a clean chamois (see Fig. 10.24, Sketch 4). The spandrels were then given the same treatment in order to make them darker than the glass areas. They were shaded with a BB pencil.

2. The general light grayed tone on the light side of the building was applied by hatching, care being taken to darken the left upper edge.

3. After this had been done, the spandrel areas were lightened by masking each spandrel with 8½- x 11-in. white pad paper and erasing with a kneaded piece of kneaded eraser. The strokes in the erasing process were made from the left- and right-hand edges of the spandrels.

4. The small dark openings in the center of the light side of the building were applied with a BB pencil, and each opening was made separately in order to obtain gradation.

5. The upper left-hand section of the light side of the building tower was then darkened by hatching softly with the side of a B grade pencil.

6. Shadows cast by spandrels were introduced by the use of a T-square and a loosely held B grade pencil. Reverse shadows on the shade side were cast by the same method.

7. The dark areas at the top of the tower were next indicated by hatching, using clean, short strokes with a B pencil. Shadows were put in in the same manner.

8. After the entire office building had been rendered, rough edges (places where hatching had gotten into the sky area) were cleaned with a kneaded eraser by masking the building with pad paper and then erasing in a wiping motion away from the building.

9. The low surrounding buildings were next rendered by hatching in several directions with the side of a BB pencil, masking with pad paper, and then rubbing with a chamois. After the general tones had been put in, cornices, window, canopy, and other details were drawn by hatching with the point of a BB pencil. The low building at the right of the picture was indicated in the same way.

10. The values on the street were put in unevenly to avoid monotony, and a dark shadow cast by a building to the left and behind the spectator was put in in the immediate foreground.

11. Scale figures were distributed throughout the picture to draw the eye to the entrance of the building. Like all values, these were dark in the foreground and lighter in the background, and were drawn with B, BB, and BBB pencils.

12. Reflections in the street were made with a wiping motion by the use of a kneaded eraser held against a T-square tilted at an angle.

Fig. 10.27

Bridge
rendered by
Valerius Leo Michelson
on dark green charcoal
paper
Student project

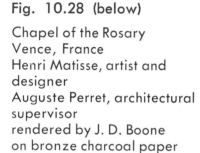

Fig. 10.28 (below)

Chapel of the Rosary
Vence, France
Henri Matisse, artist and
designer
Auguste Perret, architectural
supervisor
rendered by J. D. Boone
on bronze charcoal paper
Student project

Figures 10.27 and 10.28 were made by using carbon pencil strokes and chalk, and were rendered in a manner similar to that described for the preceding figures. White pencil may be used instead of chalk in this type of rendering, the difference being that the white pencil has a waxy quality which does not permit any overlaying of carbon pencil lines.

The transfer for Fig. 10.29 was made by covering the reverse of the perspective drawing with *Conté crayon*—a very black waxy crayon—placing it on the gray illustration board, and pressing each line through with a 2-H pencil.

The value study was made in charcoal on tracing paper. It was decided that a light source from above and to the right should be used because it permitted the best expression of architectural forms. The parking areas and roadways were considered to be part of the architectural problem, so these were shown. When the perspective was constructed, it became obvious that they would compete with the building in area, so a shadow was cast over the foreground to diminish the roadway's importance. The ground value

Fig. 10.29

Tokeneke Elementary School, Darien, Conn., rendered by Vincent Furno
O'Connor & Kilham, Architects
Size: 16 x 38 in.

MATERIALS: *1 sheet gray illustration board; B, BB, BBB carbon pencils; 1 sheet white carbon paper; 1 jar Chinese white; 1 jar black tempera; 1 No. 4 pointed brush; Conté crayon.*

was made gray in order to make the building stand out. The trees around the building were vignetted so they would not compete with the school itself in importance. An analysis of the tree groupings shows that the eye is drawn from group to group in a circular path, beginning with the circle in the driveway and ending at the entrance to the school. In other words, the trees exist for the purpose of locating the building and also for leading the spectator's eye to its important parts.

Shading: This rendering, made on gray illustration board, was executed by using a combination of strokes and Chinese white. In this combination, of carbon pencil with chalk, or white pencil, it is advisable to leave the white until last (as Mr. Furno did in this presentation), since powdered carbon shifts from one part of the drawing to another and would soil the white if it were put in first.

Like most professional delineators, Mr. Furno prefers to render by beginning at the top of the drawing and proceeding on a rather even line,

Fig. 10.30

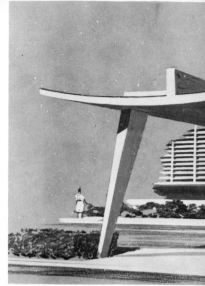

Fig. 10.31

working horizontally from left to right, and from top to bottom. In this rendering the tempera was added later, of course, but all the carbon pencil was finished in one "pass" across the illustration board.

1. The grass areas were put in with long strokes made with the side of a B pencil. Variations in value were purposely introduced in order to obtain the feeling of perspective. The grass areas are darker in the foreground and progressively lighter in the distance in order to introduce natural variations and relieve monotony. Their direction was governed by the rise and fall of the land, but sometimes they are horizontal. It should be noticed that cloud shadows were also occasionally used to relieve the monotony.

2. The trees were first blocked in by the use of the edge of a BB pencil, care being taken to locate them exactly as they had been indicated on the charcoal study. While the structure of some individual trees, particularly in the foreground and mid-distance, was shown, large groupings in the distance were indicated almost without structure. The foliage of the trees and bushes was rendered by using pencils varying from B to BBB, by holding the pencil at an angle of about 20 degrees with the horizontal and making short strokes in different directions. Care was taken to avoid hard edges in the tree foliage. The shadows of the trees on the ground were made next and these were indicated indistinctly to prevent a hard appearance.

3. The shadows on the masonry of the building were sharply delineated by the use of a BB pencil. Strokes in perspective were used for the brick at the left corner and for other shadows.

4. The windows were rendered with BB and BBB pencils, care being taken to show some of the floor within the building in order to add interest.

5. For some areas, such as the edges of fascias and rafters, the Chinese white was applied as thickly as possible with a No. 4 pointed brush. Other areas, such as the roof, were painted with diluted Chinese white so that some of the color of the board actually showed through. Shadows on the roof, which had been previously located, were made by painting these areas with light gray tempera. Mullions and muntins were applied with a fine brush used with a T-square as a guide. Shadows on the mullions were left the color of the paper itself.

6. In general, the walkways received a coat of diluted Chinese white and the joints were drawn with a fine brush and gray tempera when the

Fig. 10.32

base coat was dry. The shadow on the walk of the entrance at the left was made by leaving the paper color itself as the base and drawing in the tones with a T-square, brush, and gray tempera.

7. In order to add reality, a bus was rendered at the entrance, and tire streaks from previous traffic were shown on the road, both in sunlight and in shade, by the use of gray tempera and a rather dry No. 4 brush. The streaks were drawn freehand.

8. The large shadow in the foreground, which was assumed to have been cast by something behind the spectator, was drawn on the grass with a BBB pencil, using the side of the pencil. In order to suggest the smooth quality of asphalt, the shadow on the roadway was brushed in with gray tempera and traffic streaks imposed upon it in light and dark gray tempera.

9. Automobiles and scale figures were rendered last by the use of a brush, gray tempera, and Chinese white.

The same method of approach was used by Mr. Furno in rendering Figures 10.30, 10.31, and 10.32. Charcoal studies were first made on gray illustration board; the carbon pencil work was done from the top down in one operation, and the tempera was added last. It is worth noting in all three presentations that while the surroundings are made realistic and interesting, they play a minor role. In addition, in Fig. 10.30 in particular, the inside of the building is shown as clearly as possible. The interior is always rendered before the outside is begun because this order is not only easier, but more practical. If the outside work (such as mullions) were put in before the interior, it might easily be damaged when the interior work was drawn in.

In all of these examples, the surfaces receiving direct sunlight are painted with a strong white, while those receiving indirect or reflected light are painted in various shades of grayish-white. Smooth surfaces, such as the sign in Fig. 10.30 (511 Fifth Ave.), the shade area under the canopy, and in shadow areas in Fig. 10.31 (Entrance, Standard Vacuum Oil Company), and shadows cast on the building in Fig. 10.32 (A Country House), are all painted in shades of tempera which produces a smooth and precise appearance impossible with the carbon pencil. The combination of gray board, jet black carbon pencil, Chinese white, and gray tempera produces a smart, tailored effect that is difficult to match, and photographs exceedingly well.

Fig. 10.30

Alteration and Renovation to 511 Fifth Avenue
Emery Roth & Sons, Architects
rendered by Vincent Furno

Fig. 10.31

Entrance, Standard Vacuum Oil Company
Saigon, Vietnam
Chauncey W. Riley, Architect
rendered by Vincent Furno

Fig. 10.32

A Country House
Vincent Furno, Architect
rendered by Vincent Furno

Fig. 10.33

Porch Detail
rendered by Emil Kempa
Student project

After the perspective was transferred to the pastel paper by the use of a white carbon paper, a value study was made over the tracing paper perspective. It is impossible to make a value study over a dark sheet, as the values become confused.

The light source was assumed to be directly in back of the spectator, since this would create shades and shadows which would best express the architectural forms.

Shading: This rendering was executed with carbon pencil combined with chalk on Herga green pastel paper.

1. The shade under the canopy was made by hatching in the direction of the perspective by the use of B and BB pencils. Care was taken to permit the inner edge of this shade area to be lighter—almost the color of the paper itself—to create the illusion of reflected light. The shade under the other members of the canopy was put in by the use of a T-square and a BB pencil.

2. The interior was drawn and shaded with B and BB pencils, care being taken to show the chair and to indicate some other pieces of furniture inside the glass. Variations in value with the dark portions next to mullions and wall area were introduced into this area as well as the partly drawn curtains.

3. The beams above the glass were drawn with a T-square and a sharp B pencil.

4. The shadows were rendered on beams, glass, mullions, and stone by the use of strokes made with the side of a BB pencil. The outer edges of the mullions were then darkened in order to make them stand out.

5. The top of the shadow on the building cast by the canopy was kept lighter than the bottom edge in order to give the feeling of reflected light.

6. The front fascia of the canopy, the front edge of the mullions in sunlight, as well as other portions of the front face of the building, and the sky, were permitted to remain the color of the paper itself, as well as portions of the porch floor.

7. The shadows in the vertical joints of the boarding at the front of the building were introduced by the use of a loosely held, sharp B pencil and a T-square. Care was taken to draw them with varying intensity in order to avoid monotony.

8. Stonework in sunlight was drawn with joints the color of the paper, with only an occasional joint darkened here and there with a B pencil. Because of the angle, and in order to obtain a definite break, the narrow edge of the masonry mass was rendered darker than the longer side of the masonry mass, and the stone was hatched with a B pencil here and there, the joints remaining the color of the paper.

9. In the use of chalk (as well as in other kinds of white used in combination with carbon pencil) care must be taken to limit the amount of white, because too large an area will reduce the importance of the carbon pencil itself. A careful analysis in the value study indicated the use of white in the places shown on the finished rendering.

The chalk was first sharpened so that it made a conical point similar to that of a pencil used for writing. The graining on the board at the left of the rendering was put in freehand. The highlights on the sides of the vertical boards at the front are indicated with a wavering line of chalk, put in with a T-square. Some highlights on the curtains to the left and right were put in freehand with a curved motion to simulate the folds of the curtains. The highlights on the lower portions of the window mullions were put in by masking those areas with pieces of pad paper as previously described, and then hatching over and over with the chalk. The light portions of the roof overhang were done in a similar manner, except that some strokes were introduced at the left.

10. The flagging in the porch floor was whitened by the use of strokes and counterstrokes in perspective. It was graded from solid at the left, to paper color at the right. The grass in the joints was then drawn with a B pencil held flat. The steps were rendered in strokes. The ground was rendered by holding a B pencil at an angle of 20 degrees with the paper and making strokes in perspective. The hill in the back was rendered in the same way, except that the strokes were pitched in order to indicate the slope. The trees were first constructed with a loosely held, sharp BB pencil. Portions of the tree trunks were permitted to remain the color of the paper, and shading was made with short strokes around the trunks themselves (Fig. 10.25).

11. The tree mass at the right was indicated by first softly delineating the mass with a BB pencil held flat, and then shading the foliage with a series of short converging strokes. The flowers in the foreground were put in freehand with a sharp BB pencil and chalk.

As this rendering was being made, errors in carbon pencil were corrected by masking the area to be changed with pad paper and erasing the unwanted portions of the wash with a small piece of kneaded eraser, wiping it away from the edge of the pad paper.

12. At the very end of the job, small tree shadows were introduced with short vertical strokes made with a B pencil, held lightly.

13. A small amount of charcoal fixative was applied from a distance of about 5 ft. *Note:* Too much fixative will diminish the white value of chalk areas and make them disappear.

The Lithographic Crayon Pencil

While the carbon pencil has a slightly gritty "feel" when used on paper, the lithographic crayon pencil is smooth and somewhat waxy. It is used in the same manner and on the same kinds of paper as the carbon pencil (when it is used alone) and is capable of producing the same jet blacks, atmospheric

Fig. 10.34

A visualization based on the architect's plans,
United Nations Headquarters, New York
Architects: United Nations Headquarters Planning Staff,
Wallace K. Harrison, Director
Drawn by Hugh Ferriss

effects, and tonal variations. The best known are Korns Lithographic Crayon Pencils, which are made in the following grades:

No. 1—Soft	No. 4—Extra hard
No. 2—Medium	No. 5—Extremely hard
No. 3—Hard	

Like the carbon pencil, the lithograph pencil is excellent for indicating large expansive projects without actually showing detail (Fig. 10.34 and Fig. 10.35, both drawn by Hugh Ferriss). In these two powerful renderings, the eye is drawn to the center of interest by leaving the tones in that area light, and by surrounding the focal points with rather deep (sometimes almost black) values.

Direction is given the various planes in each rendering by the simple expedient of building tones with final strokes in perspective. By placing wash upon wash, and by leaving small spaces between strokes, lightness and transparency are obtained. The appearance of natural or artificial light is skillfully reproduced in both these renderings by the use of sharp value comparisons: light areas are permitted to remain *very* light, and are always adjoined by dark building surfaces. Gradually diminishing the intensity of light on the wall and street surfaces also contributes to the extraordinary illusion of reality: the farther an area is from the light source, the dimmer its light becomes.

Fig. 10.35

Impression of the RCA, French and British Buildings
Rockefeller Center, New York
Reinhard & Hofmeister, Corbett, Harrison & MacMurray, Hood & Fouilhoux, Architects
Drawn by Hugh Ferriss

Pen and ink rendering

THE PEN EXISTED as a writing instrument long before it was used by artists and architects. It was first made of the bamboo root, or other hollow woody plant forms, with the end prepared by fraying. The Greeks and Romans later cut reeds to a point and slit them like modern pens. Later pens were made of such metals as copper and bronze; these imitated in form the earlier pointed reeds. Use of goose quills, which were easily prepared, came later.

The modern pen dates from the latter part of the nineteenth century, when it was mechanically (and therefore cheaply) produced in England by Joseph Gillott. The form and style of pens have been improved, and they have been standardized according to number, and produced in many sizes. The smallest of the modern pen points is called the crow-quill, and the earliest of these was actually copied from the quill form. The better drawing pens are produced by Gillott in England and the Hunt Manufacturing Company in the United States. For the purpose of simplification, the numbers of pen nibs specified in this chapter will be those of the Hunt Manufacturing Company, but Table 11.1 gives the corresponding sizes of Hunt and Gillott pen nibs.

Although there are more than 35 different styles and sizes of pen nibs available, only about ten of these are generally used for drawing. The finest of this group is the crow-quill, Hunt No. 102, which is very flexible and can produce a moderately wide line if pressure is exerted upon it. Another small nib is the flexible quill, Hunt No. 108, which is a bronze finish quill pen for crosshatching. The hawk quill, Hunt No. 107, has a superfine point but is stiffer than the crow-quill and very durable. It is also used for crosshatching.

For larger drawings, Hunt's No. 99 round-pointed drawing nib is popular, and this, used in conjunction with Hunt's No. 22-B, extra fine (medium stiff) nib, and Hunt's No. 56 school drawing pen, provides an assortment adequate for nearly all work. There will be occasions mentioned later in the chapter when broader lines are desired, and these can be made by using Hunt's No. 512 bowl-pointed nib, Globe 513-EF, and the Speedball pens, such as B-6 and C-6.

The Pen

Table 11.1   Gillott and Hunt Pen Sizes[1]

Gillott	Hunt		
1		101	
13EF		514	
14EF		513	
41		67	
51		67	(nearest)
61		59	
81		67	
91		69	
102		35	(nearest)
105		X98	
170		99	
290		100	
291		103	
292		35	(nearest)
295		35	
303		22B	
351		22B	
390		67	
404		56	
425		69	
427		67	
601		59	
603		5	
604		35	
659		102	
837		107	
849	38 or	65	
850		108	
878		97B	
908		98	
909		5	(nearest)
1000		104	
1008	38 or	65	
1009	38 or	65	
1010	38 or	65	
1043	38 or	65	
1044		59	(nearest)
1045		69	
1046	59 or	69	
1047		67	
1060		97B	
1065		35	
1066		35	

[1] Courtesy of Hunt Manufacturing Co., Philadelphia, Pennsylvania, and Heidl Slocum Co., Inc., New York, U.S. sales representative for Joseph Gillott & Sons Ltd., England.

Table 11.1 (Continued)

1067		67
1068	59 or	69
1071	38 or	65
1083		65
1087		6
1089		69
1095		98
1096	59 or	69
1100		38
1102	38 or	65
5005-1		400-1
5005-1-½		400-1-½
5005-2		400-2
5005-2-½		400-2-½
5005-3		400-3
5005-3-½		400-3-½
5005-4		400-4
5005-4-½		400-4-½
5005-5		400-5
5005-5-½		400-5-½
5005-6		400-6

Pen Holders

Since pen holders are inexpensive, it is usual for the delineator to keep about a half dozen on hand. The crow-quill nib requires a special holder, available with or without a cork cushion. All other nibs fit the average writing holder, which must, however, be small enough to fit into the neck of an ink bottle. One who does a great deal of pen and ink work may wish to have pen holders of different colors, or identified by notching, for the quick identification of pen sizes.

Pen wiper: A soft, pliable chamois will be found ideal for cleaning the pen nib, as it absorbs ink and will not injure delicate points.

Inks

The earliest inks, like the early pens, were employed for writing rather than drawing. They were made of vegetable stains, berry juices, and mixtures of soot, charcoal, resin, and sometimes schist, a crystalline rock. Ink was used in China as early as 2500 B.C. and at approximately the same time in ancient Egypt by the ruler Ptah-Hotep, who used both red and black ink.

Modern inks used by delineators are, for the most part, black. If they are to be used in conjunction with water color or other washes, waterproof ink is used. For those who wish to use them, the following colored inks are available:

Yellow
Orange

Red orange (Vermilion)
Red (Scarlet)
Carmine red
Red violet (Purple)
Violet
Blue
Turquoise
Green
Leafgreen
Neutral tint (Gray)
White
Brick red
Russet
Brown
Indigo

Some manufacturers of American inks are Higgins Ink Co., Inc., Artone Color Company, and F. Weber. A superior drawing ink is Pelikan, manufactured by Gunther-Wagner, Germany.

Ink bottle holders: A simple and inexpensive bottle holder which will reduce the possibility of tipping the ink bottle is commercially available.

Fountain-type Pens Some renderers prefer a fountain-type mechanical pen such as Koh-I-Noor Rapidograph or Pelikan Technos.

The Rapidograph pen uses regular or India ink and is available in 13 point sizes, which are interchangeable as indicated below:[1]

Point	Approx. Line Width	Pen
4X0	0.008 in.	025627
3X0	0.010 in.	104159
00	0.012 in.	113078
0	0.014 in.	113069
1	0.019 in.	113022
2	0.023 in.	113031
2½	0.0275 in.	113087
3	0.0355 in.	113041
4	0.052 in.	113096
6	0.067 in.	025636
7	0.080 in.	025645
8	0.098 in.	025654
9	0.118 in.	025663

[1] Courtesy Rosenthal's, New York, N.Y.

The Pelikan Technos pen is a precision drawing ink fountain pen with interchangeable points for ruling, lettering, and drawing. It has an ink cartridge fill system with an ink regulator to maintain a uniform flow of ink for all point sizes. A typical draftsman's set contains a pen, bellows, cleaner, compensation clip, six blank ink cartridges, one each of the following B points: 0.1, 0.2, 0.3, and 0.4, and one each of the following D points (for lettering and drawing) 0.3, 0.4, 0.5, 0.6, 0.7, 0.8, 1.0, and 1.2.

Paper

As we have seen, early paper was made from the bark of trees and papyrus. In addition, vellum and parchment were produced from the skins of calves and sheep. Parchment, although it was very expensive, replaced papyrus because changes could be made upon it, because it had two sides that could be used, and also because it was thin. The combination of parchment and the pen resulted in greater facility, and hand-lettered illuminated books came into existence as early as the fourth century, developing to their highest point during the next two or three centuries.

There are a number of types of modern paper which lend themselves to pen and ink work. Such papers should be fairly smooth and firm and should accept erasures without any obvious change in the surface. Among those that fit this description are the following:

1. Ledger bond paper
2. Tracing cloth
3. The better grades of firm tracing paper
4. Hot-pressed paper
   This paper can also be purchased mounted.
5. Cold-pressed paper
   While rough, this paper will accept pen and ink work, as well as water color washes, which can be made over waterproof ink.
6. Plate finish Bristol board
   This is the most desirable surface for pen and ink work since it has a smooth surface across which the pen may glide. It will accept gently rubbed erasures without damage and is made in two- or three-ply thickness, either of which is thick enough to form a good cushion.
7. Kid finish Bristol board
   Although the surface is fairly rough, this board is preferred by some delineators to the smoother plate finish Bristol board.
8. Colored illustration boards
9. Prepared acetate

Advantages and Limitations

It should be recognized at the outset that pen and ink should be reserved for small-scale drawings. The very fineness of the pen point is at once an advantage and a disadvantage. Small details may be easily rendered, but the illusion of reality in larger areas is obtained by building values of appropriate combinations of lines or dots of various kinds. Thus, by a careful selection of line groupings, one can easily and magnificently indicate wood grain, stone, trees, foliage, etc.

Something as exciting as reality can be achieved in pen and ink, however: the logical expression of architectural form by the use of abstract conventions. By this method all but the most important elements in a picture are eliminated, and those that are included are rendered in lines and combinations of lines and dots arranged in a striking manner. The success of such a presentation will depend upon the "readability" of each portion of the picture, as well as the manner in which the various parts fit into a meaningful whole.

Getting to Know Your Pen   Before attempting the more complicated means of producing tones, textures, and values, it is well to familiarize yourself with your pens. Using a piece of the same paper or board on which you intend to draw your final rendering, take a medium nib pen, dip it into the ink, shake off the excess, and hold it in a manner similar to that used for writing. Following is a series of practice strokes (see Fig. 11.1):

1. Sets of straight strokes from left to right, about $\frac{1}{32}$ in., $\frac{1}{16}$ in., and $\frac{1}{8}$ in. apart, with even pressure. As you draw the pen across the paper, notice that by holding it lightly, the pen nib works in a natural way and the average line for that pen nib will result. Certainly every pen nib can be made to make a wider line than its average, and in some cases this is desirable, but such treatment will quickly wear out the pen nib.

2. Similar sets of vertical straight strokes.

3. A set of horizontal wavy strokes.

4. A set of vertical wavy strokes.

When you have filled a space about 10 x 12 in. with such experimental strokes, you are ready to practice the various kinds of strokes and combinations thereof normally used in the rendering of a building. Among these are the following (Fig. 11.2):

Fig. 11.1   Pen Strokes

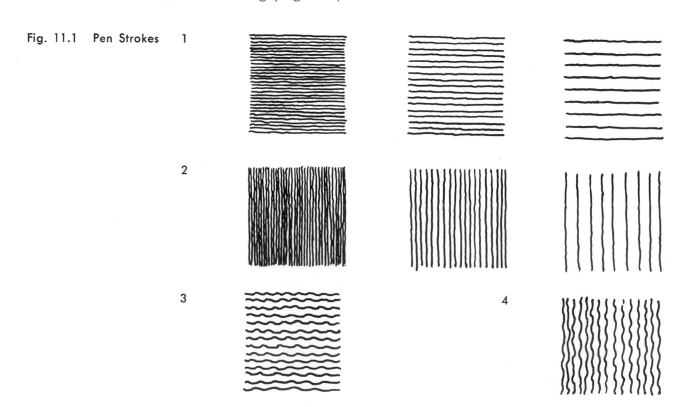

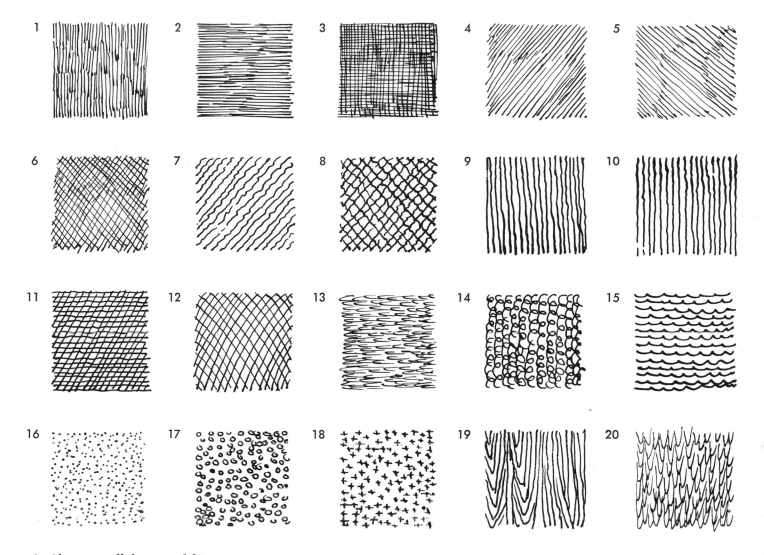

1. Short parallel vertical lines.
2. Short parallel horizontal lines.
3. A combination (hatching) of Numbers 1 and 2.
4. Straight lines at an angle of 45 degrees from right to left.
5. Straight lines at an angle of 45 degrees from left to right.
6. A combination of Numbers 4 and 5.
7. Wavy lines at 45 degrees.
8. Wavy lines with steady pressure, in two directions at 45 degrees.
9. Vertical strokes beginning light and ending dark.
10. Vertical strokes beginning dark and ending light.
11. Horizontal straight strokes with 45-degree hatching.
12. Cross-hatched parallel curved lines.
13. Flat "C's."
14. "E's."
15. Water wave strokes.
16. Dots.
17. Circles.
18. Plus marks.
19. Graining.
20. "V's."

Fig. 11.2   Devices for Forming Tones

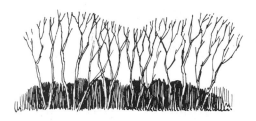
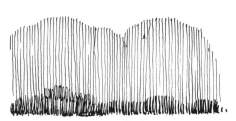

1   2   3

Fig. 11.3   Background Trees

1. Generally speaking, trees in the background are shown by a simple combination of vertical straight or wavy strokes (Fig. 11.3, Sketches 2 and 3). Trunks may or may not be shown in these areas as white spaces (Sketch 1).

2. Trees in the mid-distance are usually shown in quite a developed manner, with the complete tree structure indicated, but with small circles or ovals, or perhaps dots, for leaves (Fig. 11.4, Sketch 4). Sometimes foliage masses are shaded with lines forming continuous convolutions over the foliage areas (Fig. 11.3, Sketch 6).

For best results, block the trees lightly in pencil, and then use a lightly held crow-quill pen. Thin lines will produce the illusion of reality and distance.

3. Trees in the foreground are usually quite detailed, both trunk texture and leaves. Leaves should be characteristic of the type of tree indicated. Pine trees may be shown by combinations of needle groupings (Fig. 11.7). Sometimes these groups are hatched with vertical lines. Individual leaves in the foreground may be abstracted; that is, only a few may be shown, and these may be shaped with simple vertical parallel lines. As in all types of rendering, only a relatively few leaves should be included to express the idea, and these should complement the architecture rather than draw attention away from it. If realistic leaves are desired, each leaf must be carefully drawn around previously constructed tree or bush structure.

Fig. 11.4   Simple Tree Indications

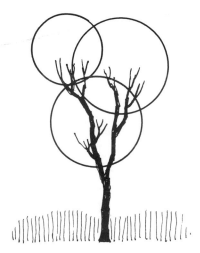

1   2   3

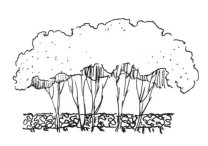

4

5

6

The shading and texture of trees is accomplished in several ways, but usually by a combination of lines that parallel the shape of the tree structure, and short, curved strokes around the tree structure. Figure 11.4 suggests a number of simple tree indications.

Grass can be shown in many ways, by the use of a combination of short, vertical strokes; by individual clumps of grass made with fine strokes of varying heights covered by light crosshatching; by convolutions, or by a combination of short, parallel, horizontal, wavy lines. As in pencil drawing, only a small portion of the actual grass area should be indicated, and only in areas receiving shadow.

Water may be represented by a series of short arcs facing upward, or by wave forms. It may also be indicated by combinations of thin, relatively horizontal lines, with a wavy reflection here and there, or by a series of "moving" wave forms. See Fig. 11.5.

As in pencil rendering, the perspective drawing should be transferred to the rendering paper with a graphite pencil (see Chapter 4). Extreme care should be taken not to dent or gouge the paper, since the pen is easily caught by such irregularities.

Procedure for Rendering

Water

Grass

4

5

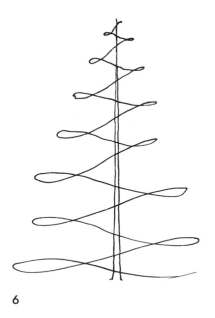

6

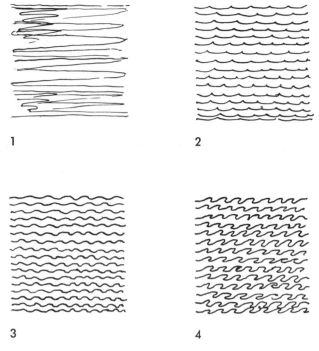

1 2

3 4

Fig. 11.5 Ways of Drawing Water

Value Study A charcoal study is particularly important in making a pen and ink rendering, since it determines not only the light source, location of trees and bushes, the size of the picture, shades and shadows, etc., but also the exact proportion of white, gray, and black. While this is important in any black and white medium, it is doubly important in pen and ink, as the white, gray, and black areas must be delicately balanced in order to produce a successful picture. A picture with no black in it has no punch, but with too much black the gray areas—important as they may be—are lost. If a sufficient amount of white is not left in a rendering, neither the gray nor the black areas have any meaning at all. In addition, the black areas must be strategically located so that they do not form an unpleasant pattern which camouflages rather than expresses the form of the architecture. The same can be said of local color, which, while it may be important in the finished building, sometimes must be modified in order to fit into the total picture.

Before proceeding with the final rendering, a preliminary pen sketch should be made on a sheet of tracing paper placed over the perspective drawing. This, of course, should not be a complete rendering, but rather an experimental drawing in which various parts of the building and textures can be studied. In particular, this study should determine what kind of lines will be used, and where they are to be located. The exact pens to be employed can be selected at this time, and generally it will be found that the broadest pens will be used for lines in the foreground, pens of medium width for lines in the mid-distance, and fine pens, such as the crow-quill, for lines in the distance. This is an important secondary means of expressing perspective in pen and ink.

MATERIALS: *Hunt crow-quill pen, Hunt No. 99 pen, Hunt No. 22-B pen, Hunt No. 56 pen; Higgins' waterproof black ink; plate finish Bristol board, three-ply; chamois; ruby eraser, glass eraser and artgum eraser.*

Fig. 11.6

A Residence
St. Petersburg, Fla.
Twitchel & Rudolph, Architects
rendered by
Pressley C. Thompson
Student project

After the perspective drawing was put on the Bristol board, a charcoal study was made to determine the light source, composition, and amount of white, gray, and black. In this drawing, the lines were done entirely freehand. The outline of the building, mullions, and muntins were first lined in by drawing them of workable lengths of about 1¼ in. each, which could be easily made without moving the hand. The interior walls, furniture, and furnishings, as well as the tree in the center of the building, were next put in with a crow-quill pen. All of this work, with the exception of the black area, was done with short vertical strokes varying in length from ⅛ in. to ¾ in. Deeper values, such as the shadows on the floor, were obtained by crosshatching of 45-degree angles. The black areas were next put in with a No. 56 pen, first by hatching and then by filling in the spaces between the hatching lines. Muntins and similar features in front of the shade areas were left white.

The foliage on the tree in the building was suggested by convolutions (Fig. 11.3). The curtains were next rendered with very short crosshatched strokes of a crow-quill pen. Shadows on the posts beneath the building were blackened in the same manner as the shade areas above. The stone textures were next indicated, with an occasional stone hatched to give interest. The shadows on stone and the woodwork beneath the building were indicated by vertical and horizontal hatching combined with dots, all made with a crow-quill pen.

The wood pylon, roughly in the center and underneath the building, was identified by graining with a crow-quill pen; the shadow on it was crosshatched both vertically and horizontally. The grass area was put in sparingly with a No. 99 nib, with most of it drawn near the stone wall by a combination of continuous vertical strokes of varying heights. These groupings were then held together by horizontal and diagonal hatching.

The palm trees were indicated last by using strokes around the tree to give form to the trunk. The fronds were made with a No. 56 nib used in a wiping motion, starting with pressure at a point on the stem and ending with no pressure at the end of the frond.

The horizon line and island in the distance were lightly indicated by the use of a crow-quill pen, the island being crosshatched at 45-degree angles.

Care was taken in the making of this presentation (as should be done in all pen and ink work) to keep the appearance soft by using freehand strokes rather than hard ruled lines. When all the pen and ink work had been done and was completely dry, the pencil construction lines were completely removed by gently rubbing each line with a corner of an artgum eraser.

Fig. 11.7

A residence rendered by Alfred J. Szcpanski Student project

This presentation illustrates the brilliance that can be obtained with pen and ink by the use of carefully determined light source and by a fine balance of white, gray, and black. It is particularly successful because of the combination of numerous textures, local color, and built-up values.

Several methods were used to outline the building itself. The edge of the roof at the front, for instance, was shown by the use of a series of short, vertical strokes using a crow-quill pen. The edge of the roof at the left side was drawn with a series of short strokes with spaces between, also made with the crow-quill point. The right side of the building was made by a series of dots. The outline as well as the end of the building at the left was made by graining with a crow-quill pen. No attempt was made to draw in hard edges at this end, the open edge of the graining forming the corner of the building.

The roof fascia at the front of the building was textured by the use of dots made with a crow-quill pen, more dots being made at the left end than in any other portion.

The interior ceiling, walls, furniture, and furnishings were next rendered, leaving the mullions white. The local color of the walls was put in with ¾-in. strokes of a crow-quill pen. The pictures were drawn in the same manner, while the picture frames, as well as the wall hanging, were shaded with dots made with a crow-quill pen. Furniture was shaded by the use of short strokes, in perspective. The shadows were put in in the same manner, but by placing the strokes more closely together.

Each individual leaf of the flowers was carefully drawn and rendered with a No. 56 pen. The main shadow cast by the roof was rendered in a combination of short, vertical and off-the-vertical strokes for the wooden surround and 45-degree strokes from right to left for the sides of the mullions, while vertical and horizontal hatching produced the blacks in the fronts of the mullions. Curved and vertical hatching formed the shadows on the curtains. The folds of the hangings were shown by the use of short 45-degree strokes from right to left.

MATERIALS USED: *The same as for Figure 11.6, except that kid finish Bristol board was selected. The value study and preliminary pen and ink study prepared the way for the final rendering.*

The wood graining in the upper portion of the building was done with a crow-quill pen. The shadows on the graining were made with strokes which followed the graining, but were closer together. Where it was necessary to darken the shadow at the left for emphasis, vertical hatching was introduced over the previous graining strokes. The underside of the building was darkened with dots, some made with a crow-quill pen, and some—particularly those toward the front edge—with a No. 22-B pen.

The stonework underneath the building was first drawn in pencil. The sunny sides of the pylons were left quite plain, with an occasional stone indicated by the use of dots with short lines. Stones in shadow were rendered individually in a combination of vertical, angular, and crosshatched lines, with the joints left white. A crow-quill pen was used for this work. The shape of a number of protruding stones was accentuated by darkening some areas of a number of stones. The flagstones around the building were indicated with a crow-quill pen, and those in shadow were hatched and crosshatched until they were almost black, leaving the joints white.

The trees in the distance were made by a series of vertical strokes varying in height, and the water was indicated with a series of long, slightly wavy strokes, using a crow-quill pen. The plants were drawn and shaded with a No. 99 pen, the leaves being crosshatched until they were almost entirely black. The plant at the left was made dark in order to "push" the building into the mid-distance. The tree at the right was drawn with a No. 99 pen, the trunk lines being indicated first. The bark texture was introduced by a combination of long, light vertical crow-quill strokes and short, dark lines made with a No. 99 pen. As in the rest of the drawing, care was taken to make the sides of the tree trunk look soft. The needles on the branches were put in in individual groups with short radiating strokes, heavy in pressure at the center and without pressure at the ends of the strokes, as described in Fig. 10.25. In order to give a three-dimensional appearance to the boughs, some of the groups of needles were darkened by the use of a No. 99 pen. When all the pen and ink work was done, an artgum eraser was used to remove the pencil construction lines.

Fig. 11.8

A residence
rendered by
Philip Gordon McIntosh
Student project

This rendering is an outstanding example of stylization in pen and ink rendering. Although it is usual to vary the direction of strokes in tone building, this entire rendering was made by the use of vertical lines. The charcoal study for this presentation showed that the rectilinear quality of the building should be softened by the inclusion of a bending, curved tree on the left. The clouds in the sky were stylized to complement the shape of the roof itself and to help express its form. The tone differentiations in the building were obtained by varying the distance between the vertical strokes; the shadows on the glass, for instance, which are normally lighter, were drawn by the use of crow-quill lines about $\frac{1}{16}$ in. apart. The shade areas under the curved roof and the shadow on the ground were rendered with lines about $\frac{1}{16}$ in. apart. Each stone of the pylon beneath the building was rendered separately by the use of vertical strokes. The stones at the front of the pylon were then tied together with long vertical strokes of a crow-quill pen. The reflections in the glass were rendered in vertical strokes with a crow-quill pen, and when these were dry, the reflections were lightened by scrubbing them with a ruby eraser until they were much lighter and less distinct.

The foreground was formed by the use of a series of individual parallel grass patches made with short vertical strokes. Trees in the distance were shaded vertically with a crow-quill pen in strokes about $\frac{1}{64}$ in. apart, and those in the mid-distance were shaded vertically with a No. 99 pen. The tree in the foreground was rendered as follows: The shade and shadow areas on the trunk were drawn with a series of vertical strokes, the darker shadow areas being darkened by crosshatching until they were quite black. Individual leaves were shaped with a No. 56 pen with strokes approximately $\frac{1}{16}$ in. apart. The lack of outlining in these leaves, as well as in the rest of the rendering, gives a soft appearance.

MATERIALS USED: *The same as specified for Fig. 11.6 and 11.7.*

MATERIALS USED: *No. 512 Bowl-pointed and No. 513-EF Globe bowl-pointed pens; No. 22-B pen, ruling pen; plate finish Bristol board.*

Fig. 11.9

A residence rendered by Sviatoslav I. Jacuszko Student project

This presentation is notable for the fact that wider pens were employed. What it lacks in delicacy, it makes up in the excitement created by its abstract quality.

Unlike the foregoing renderings, some of the drawing, such as the outline work, was done with a ruling pen. As usual, the interior work was drawn as soon as the outline of the building had been indicated. The shading was done with a combination of horizontal and 45-degree strokes. Black areas were made by hatching lines closely together. The curtains were formed by a series of vertical and continuous "E's." Graining was put in with a No. 512 Bowl-pointed pen and a No. 513-EF Globe bowl-pointed pen. The stone foundation and wall were indicated by outlining each stone with a 22-B pen. The stones in shadow were blackened with the No. 513-EF Bowl-pointed pen, leaving the joints white. The grass in the foreground was totally omitted, except for shadows cast by trees and flowers. The shadows were made by a series of crimped horizontal lines and short vertical strokes.

The shape of the tree, as well as its foliage, was highly stylized, the tree being actually outlined and the foliage being indicated by a series of adjoining amoeba patterns.

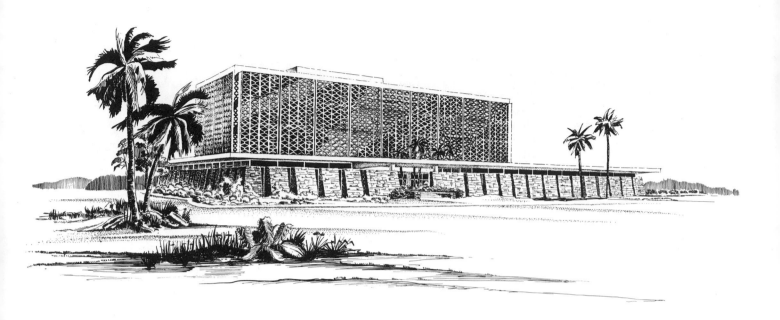

Fig. 11.10

Embassy building
rendered by V. Svalbe
Student project

The small scale of the details of this building, particularly the grille work, made it an ideal subject for pen and ink. The pen and ink study quickly disclosed that if the entire area behind the grille work were blackened, it would become deadly and monotonous; therefore it was decided to leave several light areas at various angles behind the grille work. The spaces between the members of the grille were blackened with a 22-B extra fine pen. The shadows on the glass, cast by members of the grille, and the white streaks, were made with a crow-quill pen. The rendering was made on plate finish Bristol board, and the same pens as specified for Fig. 11.8 were employed.

The building was outlined with a combination of short lines and dots. Dots were also used for the underside of the lower roof. The stonework in sunlight was indicated sparingly with a crow-quill pen and that in shade was made by hatching in various directions, leaving the joints white.

The trees in the distance were drawn with a crow-quill, in slightly wavy lines. The mid-area and foreground were shaded with dots, used sparingly. The picture was completed by drawing the trees and other planting. In this case, some of the palm fronds were darkened and others left white. The form of the palm tree trunk was obtained by shading around the trunks themselves. The grass in the foreground was made with short upward wiping strokes of a No. 56 nib, starting with a strong pressure and ending with no pressure (Fig. 11.4).

In making the value study for this building, it was decided that because of its rather plain exterior quality, additional interest could be given the rendering by a carefully studied tree disposition in the foreground. The simplification of the architecture was enriched by the delicacy of the network of trees in this splendid setting. Liberty was taken in the relocation of the actual trees on the site in order to accomplish this. In addition, a feeling of sunlight on the ground was introduced by the use of long shadows and a pattern of fallen leaves. It should be noted that the foreground is smaller than the building in both area and total intensity, and therefore complements rather than competes with it.

The building itself was rendered in hatching and dots, and a wash made by adding water to a small amount of ink was applied with a No. 4 brush to the sunlit portions.

Fig. 11.11

Sol Friedman House
Pleasantville, N. Y.
Frank Lloyd Wright, Architect
rendered by Homer King
Student project

MATERIALS USED: *Pens as for 11.8; plate finish Bristol board.*

MATERIALS USED: *In addition to pens formerly specified, No. 513-EF Globe bowl-pointed; plate finish Bristol board.*

An otherwise small and open building was made to "read" (made easily understood) by the use of a dark ceiling, the structure supporting it being left gray. As in all pen and ink work, the amount of black in the picture had to be carefully determined in the charcoal study, and it was found that leaving the foreground values quite light would permit the use of the dark ceiling, which was rendered with use of the No. 513-EF Globe bowl-pointed pen.

Generally the building was rendered by the methods described above for other pen and ink work. The pool was indicated by the simplest means possible: showing reflections of the various values above in a series of horizontal and wavy strokes. The foliage on the trees was indicated by a series of irregular scribbled leaves.

Fig. 11.12

A residence rendered by George Eugene Via, Jr. Student project

MATERIALS USED: *As for Fig. 11.6; kid finish Bristol board.*

The technique used in this rendering is quite similar to that employed for Fig. 11.6. It was discovered in the charcoal study that an indication of the interior could be obtained by leaving some white areas instead of blackening each of the openings. The outline of the building, including the stairs, was delicately obtained by the use of a series of dots made with a crow-quill pen. Form in the various parts of the building was indicated by shading in perspective. The shade on vertical surfaces, for example, was made with vertical lines, and on the tilted underside of the roof the shade lines were tilted at the same angle.

Perspective in the entire picture was obtained by using the broad point pens in the foreground, the medium pens in the mid-distance, and the crow-quill pen for the distant trees.

Fig. 11.13

A residence rendered by Charles P. Winter Student project

MATERIALS: *Crow-quill pen; Hunt 99 pen, Hunt 22-B pen, ruling pen; Pelikan black ink; kid finish Bristol board.*

Fig. 11.14

A house by the sea rendered by Julio Cesar Volante Student project

Although pen and ink work is usually carried out without the use of a straightedge and ruling pen, there are times when they can be used to advantage. In this project, ruled and freehand lines are combined. Eaves, columns, window frames, walk, and part of the sky are ruled with fine lines; all else is freehand. Notice the convention used for clouds: a few horizontal lines are drawn; these are softened with dots above and below the lines in the shape of clouds. Another interesting convention is used in this rendering: The tree is light where dark water is behind it, but black where it is in front of the white sky area. Also, stones are white with dark joints in sunlight, and black with white joints where they are in shadow. In other words, values are reversed at will so long as the reversal helps make the rendering "read."

For occasions when a broader penlike instrument may be required, a number of felt-tipped pens are available.

The Flo-Master felt-tipped pens are made in several sizes, such as "Standard" Flo-Master, "Advanced" Flo-Master, and "King Size" Flo-Master. Essentially this type of instrument has a metal fountain-pen-like body, with felt tips which come in various sizes and shapes, some conical, some rectangular, some round. Flo-Master ink is made in eight colors: black, red, blue, green, purple, orange, yellow, and brown, and is sold in metal cans. It is instant-drying, waterproof, and may be obtained in transparent or opaque type. Solvent and thinner for Flo-Master inks are also available for use in softening and rejuvenating felt tips.

While the Flo-Master is a refillable instrument, a number of similar pens which are not refillable are also available. Among these is the Magic Marker, which comes in red, yellow, orange, black, blue, brown, purple, and green. It is available in standard and king size. Studio sets of Magic Markers are available in twelve basic and twelve complementary colors. Special sets of nine assorted warm grays, plus nine cool grays, two blacks, and one white, are also available, as are studio sets. For those who specialize, colors in various sets are available, such as fundamental colors, wood colors, stone and masonry colors, landscape colors. Fine point Studio Magic Markers are available in 34 colors which have been prematched and color coordinated to the Studio Colors. Their nonpenetrating water colors dry instantly.

The Pentel sign pen marker is nylon-tipped and produces a fine line. It can be used on every kind of paper or board. The water-soluble ink does not show through. It is available in seven colors, including black, red, blue, yellow, green, orange, and brown. It is nonrefillable.

Dri-Mark felt-tipped markers are waterproof and smearproof, and are available in numerous colors as well as grays.

Smudge charcoal rendering

Subject and Medium

THE SUBJECT to be rendered often determines the medium to be used. Pencil and pen and ink are pointed and therefore are ideal for rendering buildings heavily textured and fine in detail. Smudge charcoal, on the other hand, is well suited to rendering structures or interiors which have large plain areas and are fairly large in detail (Figs. 12.1, 12.2, and 12.3). It is a fact that more renderers can obtain a fine finished result with smudge charcoal the first time they try it than with almost any other medium. It is easy to apply and is by nature such a loose, soft medium that it is almost impossible to produce a tight, uninteresting rendering with it. What, specifically, is the smudge charcoal technique? It is a rendering process in which powdered charcoal is applied to a rather rough paper by means of absorbent cotton, stomps, or the hands. The smudge pastel technique is similar, except that colored pastel chalk sticks are used instead of charcoal. Smudge charcoal is used on renderings that are to be reproduced in black and white, smudge pastel on those to be reproduced in color.

Materials

A good grade of white linen finish charcoal paper, such as Fabriano Ingres (Italian), should be used in this type of rendering. Avoid the cheaper brands of paper because no matter how hard you work with these, the results will be poor. Not only does the texture quickly wear or become "tired" when it is worked upon, but the color of the paper is usually off-white and therefore does not permit sharp contrasts.

Powdered charcoal can be purchased, but one can also use a "medium" grade of stick charcoal, such as Weber Vine Charcoal, which will be powdered and applied with absorbent cotton. For masking paper it is best to use 8½- x 11-in. thin but firm pad paper without ring binder or other holes and with straight, clean edges. In addition, you will need several stomps, which are made of thin paper strips wound to a point and can be purchased at any art materials store. A kneaded eraser, a sandpaper block, a ruby eraser, and a bottle of charcoal fixative complete the equipment required.

Fig. 12.1

A dining room
rendered by
Harold Edelstein
Student project

Fig. 12.2

The interior of a chapel
rendered by
Joan Willet de Ris
Student project

144

Since the process that you are about to try involves the use of pressure on the drawing board, it is wise to make sure before you begin that your drawing board is clean, and as free from imperfections as you can make it. It should then be covered with one or more sheets of detail paper to form a cushion. If detail paper is not available, several sheets of charcoal paper may be used. These should be firmly fastened to the board with thumbtacks and the sheet of charcoal paper that is to be used should be fastened upon them. When handmade charcoal paper is held up to the light, the side from which the watermark or name can be read is the right side to use. If no watermark can be found, either side can be used.

Assuming that you have already drawn your finished perspective at a size of about 14 x 21 in. on a sheet of tracing paper, and have it backed up as described for pencil rendering in Chapter 10, you are now ready to reproduce it on the charcoal paper. This must be done with extreme care, as an erasure on the charcoal paper at any stage of the rendering, before the finishing touches, will show up in the finished rendering as a black smudge that cannot be removed. Similarly, any grooves made by the heavy pressure of the pencil will show in the finished rendering as white lines; therefore the drawing must be pressed through to the charcoal paper with a light but firm stroke.

Fig. 12.3

Detail of a house
rendered by
Paul Hilary Pinter
Student project

Freehand Charcoal Study

Before proceeding with the actual rendering of your perspective drawing, you should make a freehand stick or block charcoal study, as described under "The Value Study" in Chapter 8. This will permit quick experiments with various light sources, value comparisons, and sheet composition. Fix this study and hang it on your tack board or on the wall in front of you, so that you may use it as a guide during the progress of your rendering.

You are now ready to prepare the charcoal. Fasten a large sheet of pad paper on a table or board next to your drawing board with drafting tape— on the right side if you are right-handed, and on the left side if you are left-handed. In this way you will avoid crossing your entire drawing with the powdered charcoal while you are using it. Now make a pile of powdered charcoal, about 1½ in. in diameter and ¼ in. deep, by rubbing the stick charcoal across the sandpaper. Do this slowly, so that the charcoal is finely and evenly powdered, with no lumps. If the charcoal scatters, it may be drawn together with a pen knife or palette knife.

The powdered charcoal, at least for most large areas, is applied by dipping a piece of absorbent cotton into the pile of powdered charcoal, tapping it on a piece of waste paper to remove the excess, and rubbing it on a previously masked area. It can be applied in long, overlapping strokes (Fig. 12.6, Sketch 2), or in long strokes in several directions (Fig. 12.6, Sketch 3). Variations in tone and gradations are obtained by taking more or less charcoal on the cotton, by varying hand pressure and by applying more or less coats of charcoal, see Fig. 12.6, Sketch 4—light to dark, Sketch 5—dark to light, and Sketch 6—light at the upper left to dark at the lower right.

It is well to wash your hands often when working in this medium, since oil marks from the fingers will stain the rendering.

Because of the fugitive nature of powdered charcoal, the rendering is best accomplished in three steps:

1. A general attempt is made to obtain the correct relative values in the several parts of the drawing.

2. The values obtained in Step 1 are refined and corrected.

3. Further refinements and corrections are made, darkest tones are deepened, textures are inserted, and erasures are made for highlights.

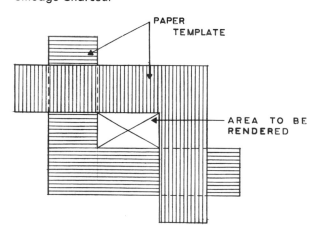

Fig. 12.4 Use of Two Right-Angle Templates to Make a Rectangle in Smudge Charcoal

PAPER TEMPLATE

AREA TO BE RENDERED

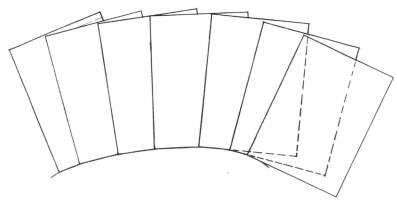

Fig. 12.5 Template for Curves, Made by Overlapping Several Sheets of Paper

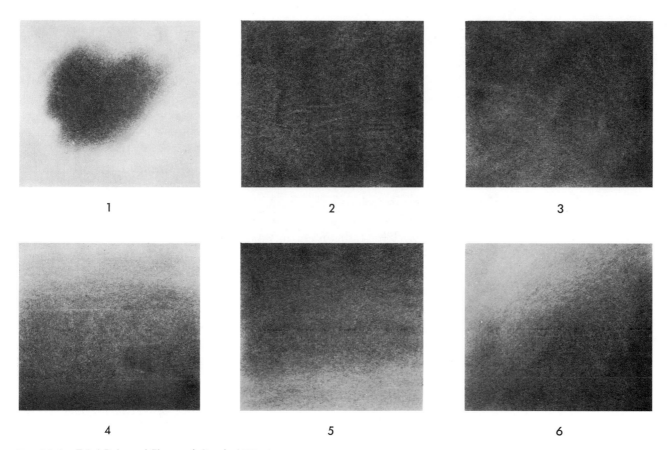

Fig. 12.6   Trial Rub and Flat and Graded Washes

Masking paper is used to surround the edges of the area to be rendered, and as many sheets as the area has sides will be required at one time. Since it is difficult to hold four sheets with one hand while applying charcoal with the other, you may find it helpful to make two right-angle templates, which used together make it easy to lay down a rectangle or square of any size in a short time (Fig. 12.4). If your rendering has large curved areas, these may be masked by forming the curves with a number of sheets of overlapping pad paper, as in Fig. 12.5, or by cutting a piece of pad paper to the exact curve.

An appropriate place to start a rendering of an interior such as that in Fig. 12.1 would be the ceiling. Place a sheet of masking paper on each one of the edges of this area and hold them firmly in place with your fingers. Dip a piece of cotton about the size of a walnut into the charcoal and tap it lightly on a spare piece of paper to remove any excess charcoal. Take a trial rub on this same piece of paper to make sure that there are no lumps and it will make a smooth wash (see Fig. 12.6, Sketch 1). The charcoal may then be applied to the masked area of the rendering. Gently brush the cotton into the area in long, clean, overlapping strokes, proceeding away from the edges of the masking paper toward the other end of the area that you are shading (see Fig. 12.6, Sketch 2). Cross the same area with other strokes and try circular strokes (Fig 12.6, Sketch 3). Variations and gradations in tone, previously determined in the charcoal study, should be carefully followed,

Order of Drawing

Step 1

and may be executed as shown in Fig. 12.6, Sketch 4 (Gradations from light to dark), Sketch 5 (Gradations from dark to light), or Sketch 6 (Diagonal gradation).

When this area has been shaded, lift the sheets of masking paper, move them to the other end of the area being shaded, and repeat the process, this time shading toward the opposite end, where you began. If necessary, this process may be repeated on the other sides of the area being shaded. When you lift the masking paper you may find a small ridge of charcoal which has seeped under the paper. To remove this, take a clean piece of cotton, about the same size as the one you have been using, and gently dust the charcoal ridges off your drawing.

Discard masking paper when it has become soiled, or when the edges become fuzzy. The ball of cotton should be discarded when it becomes lumpy or produces streaks.

You may now proceed in a similar manner with shading all other areas of the perspective, such as the back wall and curtains in Fig. 12.1. The lightest background values of the screen, furniture, floor, and pictures may also be put in during this step. Be careful to work around legs of furniture and other similar details, so that you will not lose their location before you are ready to render them.

Step 2   After you have put in the first set of washes, stand your drawing next to the freehand value study and look at it from a distance of 5 ft or more. How do your values compare with those you have determined in your value study to be correct? Are any of the areas too light or too dark? If so, you may correct these mistakes when you repeat the process outlined in Step 1. It is advisable from now on to work from the top toward the bottom of the rendering, so that you will not disturb charcoal that has previously been applied in adjoining areas. This second step is more than a reinforcement and correction of previous values. It is here that you begin to apply general detail such as the squares in the floor pattern and the differentiation of the sides of chairs, the shadows on the legs of the table and chairs, and the shadow side of the various members of the screen in the foreground. Small or narrow washes such as those on members of the screen, the squares of the floor, and place mats are all carried out in the same way as the large washes, with the pieces of masking paper held close together.

When Step 2 has been finished, you may feel that your rendering has reached a hopeless stage and be tempted to blow fixative on the charcoal that you have already applied to keep it from rubbing off your drawing. Resist this temptation, because if you apply fixative before the rendering is entirely finished, no further charcoal may be applied on the paper, nor will you be able to refine the rendering as you will want to do in Step 3.

Step 3   To complete the rendering, re-assess it as in Step 2, with an increasingly critical eye. You will now make your final value correction throughout the drawing. In order to obtain the darkest values, such as those in the chairs in Fig. 12.1, mask these, dip your finger into the powdered charcoal, and gently but firmly rub the areas to be darkened. The oil from your skin will combine with the charcoal to produce the desired effect. Remember, however, that once values have been darkened in this way, they cannot be lightened.

Small details, such as vases, flowers, lighting fixtures, and pictures may best be rendered with a stomp. The stomp is dipped in the powdered charcoal, the excess is removed, and then the stomp is used to draw in the details. You will find that this produces a soft, but definite, result. Fine lines like those in the place mats in Fig. 12.1 may be applied with a sharp stick of charcoal and then softened with the stomp. Definite patterns, such as figures etched in glass panels, may be inserted at this time by rubbing charcoal through the openings of a carefully cut stencil. If the lines of the pattern are to be lighter than the background, they may be erased with a kneaded eraser and the same stencil.

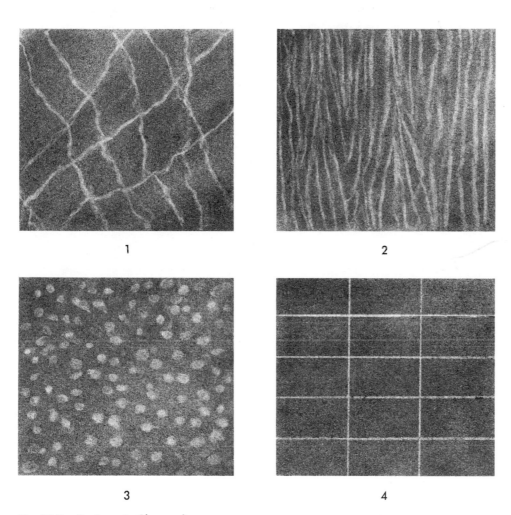

Fig. 12.7   Textures in Charcoal

One can easily obtain various textures by erasing parts of a charcoal wash with a pointed piece of kneaded eraser. The latter, if rolled between the fingers for a short while, becomes pliable and can be rolled to a point. The marble and wood grain textures shown in Fig. 12.7, Sketch 1 and Sketch 2, were drawn freehand with the eraser. The texture in Sketch 3 was made by carefully dabbing with the point of an eraser. Each line in Sketch 4 was made by erasing between two pieces of paper, held tightly and close together.

To erase lights such as those on the back wall, in the curtains, and on the edges of the place mats in Fig. 12.1, use a clean piece of cotton and masking paper. Clean cotton will lighten the area but will not produce a highlight. In similar fashion, clean cotton may be used to lighten whole areas that have become too dark.

Highlights   To produce highlights such as those in the legs of the chairs and tables and on the edges of the picture frame on the rear wall of Fig. 12.1, a kneaded eraser is used. Break off a small piece about the size of the first joint of your little finger and roll it between your fingers until it has become soft. Then, after masking the area to be lightened, gently rub the eraser several times in long strokes until the excess charcoal has been removed. If some of the areas will not lighten with the kneaded eraser, use the ruby eraser in the same way.

If you feel that you have completed your rendering, appraise it again from a distance of several feet. Any changes or corrections that you wish to make should be done at this time.

In order to fix a charcoal rendering, use a nongloss charcoal fixative spray such as Krylon or Spray-Fix from a distance of 4 or 5 ft. If the fixative is sprayed at too close a range, there is danger of large droplets striking the drawing and staining it.

After it is fixed, the drawing may be matted, as described in Chapter 7.

Chapter 13

Rendering with Chinese ink

When you have mastered the basic skills in pencil, pen and ink, and smudge charcoal rendering, you will be ready to try the most basic of all liquid media. Whereas dry media are applied directly to the paper without mixture with any vehicle, and ink is applied with a specially designed instrument, the pen, such liquid media as Chinese ink, water color, and tempera are applied with brushes after they have been mixed with water. The use of water, of course, implies an entirely new set of problems, which we shall take up in this chapter. Liquid media are applied in washes, by dropping and scrubbing pigment into wet surfaces, by the stipple method, by spatter, and by spraying with an airbrush.

Preparation of Ink

Media of the water color type, including Chinese ink, are prepared by suspending particles of the pigments themselves in water. Sometimes water colors that do not suspend evenly in water are used deliberately, as described in Chapter 14. But to make a rendering of clear, unadulterated, transparent washes, Chinese ink is the best choice. Applied correctly, this medium makes possible amazingly real illusions of light, space, and air. It is meant for those who wish to study their designs clearly, concisely, and beautifully.

Materials

Paper: Handmade water color paper is available in three different finishes: *cold-pressed* (medium texture), *hot-pressed* (smooth finish), and *rough* (used for water color paintings).

For our purposes we will use medium texture, since it accepts washes more easily than the other two. There are a number of different brands of paper, such as D'Arches (French), Fabriano (Italian), J. B. Green (English), RWS (English) (each sheet of this paper is inspected separately and individually marked and embossed with the seal of the Royal Watercolor Society), and Strathmore (American). The weight of the paper, based on the weight of a ream of standard size, is as important as its name. Too light a paper will not stand up to the rigors of stretching, nor does it have the body to withstand sponging. Therefore, it is best to use a paper no lighter than 140-lb, based on the Imperial size of 22 x 30 in. Water color papers are available in 44-lb, 72-lb, 140-lb, and 300-lb weights.

An increasing number of delineators are using illustration board, which consists of several thicknesses of cardboard faced with water color paper.

It is wise to look at a sheet of paper carefully before purchasing it. Since it is handmade, it may have imperfections. If you hold it up to the light and see any thin spots, or if you discover any mounds on the surface, return it and ask for another sheet. Do not be concerned if the paper appears to be old and creamy rather than white, since the older the paper, the more seasoned it is likely to be.

Stick Inks   Chinese ink is available in stick form (the way it was originally prepared in China and Japan). It is made of finely ground lamp black baked with a glutinous binder. The better sticks are delicately perfumed, and the older a stick is, the better it is considered to be. Some sticks 300 to 400 years old are still in use.

If stick ink cannot be obtained, tube ink will do.

Brushes   Good brushes require a major expenditure, but they may be used for water color as well as wash rendering and will last virtually a lifetime. The best available are red sable, made by Winsor & Newton, Inc., and are known as their Series No. 7, Albata. Brushes are numbered from the smallest size, No. 000 ($\frac{7}{32}$ in.), to the largest, No. 14 ($1^{17}\!/_{32}$ in.)—seventeen in all. If money is no object, buy a No. 4 and a No. 12. If the budget must be considered, a No. 4 red sable in the less costly Series No. 133 or No. 33 (which offers fourteen sizes) and a large camel's-hair brush, which is much less expensive, will do.

As a brush is a major investment, it should be selected with care. There are several ways of testing brushes. To begin with, do not buy the first brush that you look at; ask the dealer to show you a number of them. Take them in hand and look at them carefully. If you discover a loose ferrule, discard that brush immediately. But even more important, ask your dealer for a small container of water and dip each brush in it. Move the brush around in the water to get all the air out of it, then take it out of the water and hold it vertically. If the brush is conical, comes to a sharp point, and does not have any loose hairs sticking out at the sides, it is a pretty fair brush. Now look more closely. Dip it in the water again. Shake the water out by slatting the brush toward the floor. If it has one point and is smooth and symmetrical, you are ready to try it further. Wet it again and, holding it like a pencil, draw it across a sheet of paper, pressing down upon it as you do so. If the brush springs back into a conical shape after you have done this, it is a good brush, but if it stays in a bent position, it is not good.

In addition to the red sable and camel's-hair brushes, a Chinese bamboo bristle brush is also frequently helpful. These are inexpensive and may be discarded when they become too frayed, but when they are new at least they hold a good point and are extremely helpful in many ways.

Care of the brush: Moth larvae enjoy chewing on red sable brushes; therefore when these brushes are not in use they should be kept in a box with a few camphor balls. Make sure that the brushes are dry before they are put away. After use, rinse them thoroughly, and above all, never leave them standing in water; they may acquire a bend that can never be corrected.

Some other supplies that will be needed for Chinese ink rendering are the following:
1. Grinding slate and glass
2. A bottle of Higgins' waterproof ink
3. A silk or "baby" sponge
4. A small box of alum
5. A small box of cheesecloth
6. Six or more white wash pans (enameled metal or plastic)
7. A water bucket or other container that will hold at least a quart of water
8. A jar of Elmer's Glue-All or Sobo glue
9. Half-dozen white blotters
10. A drawing board about 3 in. larger all around than the rendering you intend to make

White cold pressed, hot pressed, and rough water color paper may be purchased mounted in the form of an illustration board, but a tougher, tighter surface may be made by "stretching" the paper on a drawing board. But why do we make a stretch at all? The answer is that any liquid medium has a tendency to buckle the surface of the paper upon which it is used. Just place a few drops of water on any sheet of paper and you will see what we mean. While a sheet of paper which is made taut and drumlike by a stretching process may temporarily buckle, it will immediately become flat again as the washes dry. Since there will be occasions when the entire sheet is wet by brushing or sponging, the importance of a stretch can easily be seen.

Before proceeding further, look carefully at the drawing board that you intend to use. It should be clean and free from lumps of glue or dirt which would be magnified by the stretch. If you discover such imperfections, try gently scraping them off in a way that does not further mar the surface of the board. If there are any large open cracks in the board, it is well to discard it and get another.

For practice rendering throughout this book, 14 x 21 in. is suggested as a picture size; therefore, the sheet of paper that you intend to use should be cut to a minimum of 20 x 26 in. But before you cut the paper you will want to know which side you are to work upon. Hold the full sheet that you have purchased up to the light and you will see a water mark (usually the name of the manufacturer) in one corner. The side from which you can read this water mark is the side upon which you will render. The other side is the one to be glued. To avoid confusion, mark a small "X" with a graphite pencil in the center of the usable side of the paper.

Now, with T-square and triangle, lay out the size that you want your paper to be and cut it to this size with scissors, sharp knife, or razor, being careful not to cut it upon the drawing board that you intend to use—or on your best table.

After you have cleared away the scraps of paper, cover the drawing board entirely with several thicknesses of newspaper to protect it from moisture. You are now ready to soak the rendering paper so as to relax the fibers, then to stretch it. When the paper dries, the fibers will again draw close together.

Soaking   The paper can best be soaked in a large, flat, clean, tray-type sink, but if the paper is larger than any sink available, a bathtub will do. Fill the sink or tub with 3 or 4 in. of cold water and place the paper in it. It will float at first, so force it under the water. Let it soak for no more than two minutes; over-soaking (or soaking in warm water) will eventually totally disintegrate the fibers of the paper. At the end of two minutes, and if possible with someone else's help, lift the sheet out, let most of the water drain off, and place it upside down upon the newspaper on your drawing board.

Blotting   Using clean white blotters, blot about 1½ in. of the entire edge of the paper on all four sides. Make sure that these edges are entirely dry. Open the squeeze bottle of glue and take a generous amount of the glue upon your forefinger. Spread this generously, but not wastefully, upon the dried area on all four sides of the paper. Make sure that you do not miss any spots. Then wash your hands.

Lift the paper again by holding it by two corners, and have someone else remove the wet newspapers from the drawing board. If your assistant will hold the other two corners, you may now reverse the sheet so that the rendering side is up and the glue side down, and place it in the center of the drawing board and as parallel with its edges as possible. Now you are ready to stretch the paper.

Stretching   While you gently pull the paper, starting at one corner, have your assistant pull in the opposite direction. When this section has been stretched, move your hands about 2 in. and repeat the process. When the paper has been stretched in one direction (Fig. 13.1), change sides and stretch it in the opposite direction. If you pull too hard, you may break the paper, so pull gently.

Now close the bottle of glue and, with your fingers or the bottom of the bottle, press the glued edges of the paper tightly upon the board. Start at one corner and, moving your hand or the bottle, press down and pull the edge of the paper toward your body for a distance of about ¾ in. Repeat this process all around the edge of the paper until you can see no place where the paper has not been adequately fastened to the board. Using paper towels, facial tissues, or clean rags, remove the excess glue that has been squeezed from under the paper. Wash your hands again. Then, using clean water and the silk sponge, dampen the picture side of the paper—not the edges under which the glue is located—being careful to remove any puddles of water which may form.

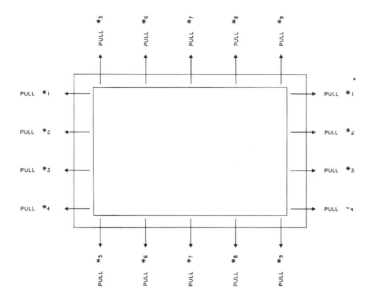

PULL #5　PULL #6　PULL #7　PULL #8　PULL #9

PULL #1

PULL #2

PULL #3

PULL #4

PULL #1

PULL #2

PULL #3

PULL #4

PULL #5　PULL #6　PULL #7　PULL #8　PULL #9

Fig. 13.1　Stretching the Paper

When you have completed making the stretch, lay it aside, being careful not to put it near a heat source (such as a radiator) while it dries. After about 10 or 15 minutes, look at it again and see if any of the edges of the paper have risen from the board. If so, take a small amount of glue on the end of a pen knife and insert it under the paper at these areas, then carefully press the paper into position again. Stubborn spots such as these may be held in place with a thumbtack until they have dried, after which the tack should be removed.

If this procedure is carefully followed, a good stretch will result. If the paper does not remain glued and taut when it dries, do not try to rescue it, but remove it from the board and start all over, being careful to follow the steps described above. The remnants (the glued edges of the paper) may be removed by scraping with a knife after they have been soaked by placing wet newspaper upon them for about half an hour. Do not attempt to lay the second stretch while remnants of the first stretch are in place, or while the board is still wet. If the opposite side of the board is in good condition, and dry, this may be used.

Preparation of Mother Wash

The mother wash, from which all the lighter washes to be used in the rendering are made, can be prepared while the stretch is drying—a process that usually takes about an hour.

If you have purchased a tube of Chinese ink, your process will be enormously simplified, since tube ink merely needs to be mixed with water and strained several times. However, there are those who consider stick Chinese ink so far superior to tube ink that they invariably use it. This is prepared as follows:

Grinding the Ink

Place about 1/4 in. of clean cold water in the bottom of a clean slate dish. Grasping the stick of ink between your fingers, rub it in the water using a rotary motion, gently pressing it against the rough slate surface of the dish. After a few minutes you will notice that the ink that you ground has dissolved in the water. It should be very black, and you may test it by dipping a brush in it and trying it on a piece of white paper. If it is not yet black enough, grind some more.

When this is finished, pour the ink into a small sealed glass container about 3 in. high and 1 in. in diameter, such as those used by pharmacists in dispensing pills. Repeat the process of grinding ink until this container is at least half full. You are now ready to strain the ink.

Straining the Ink

The ink that you have prepared is not yet ready to use; it contains a number of small particles that have not dissolved in the water and must be strained by the following process:

1. Place the ink in a wash pan supported upon a number of books so that it is about 12 or 15 in. from the surface of a table or desk. Place another clean wash pan on the desk below the pan containing the wash. Cut a strip of cheesecloth about 1¼ in. wide and 18 or 20 in. long, and holding the ends, roll it so that it forms a wick. Wet this wick thoroughly in clean, cold water, then place one curled end in the container of Chinese ink and arrange the rest so that it hangs above the dish below. The capillary action of the water will draw the ink from the top pan through the wick and permit it to drip into the pan below. The water which first drips out should be thrown away so that the undiluted ink will not be weakened by water.

2. This process should be repeated at least twice more, each time with a clean piece of cheesecloth and a clean receiving pan. By this time all of the imperfections will have been removed from the mother wash and it should be stored in a clean bottle such as the one previously used, in order to keep it free from dust in the air, eraser crumbs, or other impurities.

(Note: If filter paper is available it may be used as an alternate for straining the mother wash.)

Fig. 13.2 Chinese Ink Washes

1

2

3

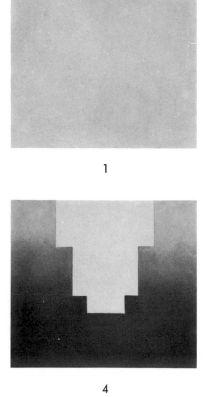

4

5

6

Once prepared, the ink should be used as soon as possible. At most it will last for only a couple of days. Some people find that it will keep a slightly longer time in a refrigerator. Beyond this period, however, it becomes sour, the particles of ink again separate from the water, and the ink acquires a foul, sour odor. When this occurs it is no longer useful. With experience one will learn the approximate amount of ink required for each day's work and will not grind more than is needed.

To prepare tube ink, mix it with a small quantity of water, then strain it several times as described above.

As perfect as it is, pure mother wash cannot be applied undiluted to the paper. Instead, it is mixed with water in a clean pan and used in a series of light washes. Washes such as these, with a small amount of sediment, are easier to handle. They also provide an opportunity for greater uniformity, since it is easier to build a tone of a number of light "layers" than it is to make it of one heavy wash. In addition, such heavy, carbonaceous washes have a dead look.

To begin with, let us practice laying the various kinds of washes used in rendering. The simplest wash is, of course, a flat wash of uniform intensity throughout and it is made as follows (Fig. 13.2, Sketch 1):

Tilt the board about 10 or 20 degrees by placing books or a wood block under the edge farthest from you. Using a small brush, place several drops of the mother wash in 1/4 in. of clean water in a wash pan. Stir this until the ink is thoroughly mixed. For practice, a cold pressed illustration board rather than a stretch may be used. Draw six graphite pencil rectangles upon the board, each about 4 in. wide and 6 in. high. For practice, dilute a few drops of Higgins' waterproof ink in some water, and outline each of these rectangles with a ruling pen. After the diluted ink is dry, remove the graphite lines.

Before making any ink washes it is well to dampen the surface of the paper with clean water, using a No. 12 brush. When this has dried to the point where it no longer feels cool to the back of a finger, it is ready to use.

Take your large brush (not the one which was used for mixing the ink), dip it into the wash that you have prepared, and move it around until all of the air has been removed from the brush. Gently shake off the excess wash, and holding your other hand under it as you cross your illustration board, begin by wetting the entire top of the first rectangle. Draw this down about an inch, using a rotary motion with the brush, being sure to touch only the liquid and not the surface of the paper.

Take another brushful of wash and drop it into the first wash above the puddle created by the tilt of the board. Mix this with the same rotary motion and draw it down another inch. Repeat the process, being careful not to touch the paper, until the wash has reached the bottom of the rectangle. It is important to keep the wash within the inked lines of the rectangle.

The puddle at the bottom can be removed by shaking or squeezing the wash from your large brush and touching it to the puddle, squeezing the brush out, and repeating the process until the puddle is all gone. It will dry evenly if the board remains tilted.

Superimposing Washes

Since just about every section of a rendering will be made up of more than one wash, it is worthwhile to experiment with superimposed, uniform flat washes (see Fig. 13.2, Sketch 2). Each wash is done as in Fig. 13.2, Sketch 1, but care must be taken that the first wash is dry before the second one is applied.

Graded Washes

Graded washes can be run most easily from light to dark (Fig. 13.2, Sketch 3). In laying a graded wash, the simplest method is as follows:

Use two wash dishes, one containing about ⅛ in. of water, the other containing mother wash. Place a pencil dot at 1-in. increments of the height of the rectangle to be washed. Use two brushes as before—the smaller one for handling and mixing the wash, and the larger one for running the wash itself. Begin by introducing two small drops of mother wash into clear water and mix thoroughly with the small brush. Dip the large brush into this mixture and introduce it to the top of the rectangle as in Sketch 1, being careful to keep to your inked lines. Carry it down to the first increment, then introduce two more drops of mother wash into the mixture with the small brush. Mix this thoroughly and again take up a brushful of the new mixture with the large brush. Drop the new wash into the one previously made as before, and mix it in with a rotating motion, carrying it down to the next increment. Repeat this process, introducing the same amount of additional mother wash each time, until the bottom has been reached. Remove the excess wash as before, keeping the board tilted until the wash dries.

Graded washes are built up in the same way as flat washes, but the first wash must be discarded and the entire process repeated, beginning with water and mother wash.

Gradations from dark to light are made as follows:

Make a mixture of medium intensity wash by mixing water and mother wash—about ⅛ in. in the bottom of a pan will do. Divide your rectangle into increments as before, and after introducing the medium wash to the top of the rectangle, carry it down with a rotating motion for about an inch. Introduce a small brushful of clean water into the medium wash and mix it thoroughly with the small brush. Use this new mixture, and dropping it in above the puddle, using a rotating motion and being careful not to touch the paper, carry it down to the next increment. Repeat the process until the bottom of the paper has been reached and remove the excess, as above.

Double graded washes: In making an actual rendering, it is often necessary to reverse the gradation of washes during a single wash (Fig. 13.2, Sketch 5). This can be accomplished as follows:

Begin by grading from dark to light, but prepare two wash pans full of the same medium intensity wash. When the halfway mark has been reached, begin adding a couple of drops of the medium intensity wash into the mixture in order to darken it. Keep adding the same amount for every increment so that the wash will be dark at the bottom.

It is often necessary—as when a sky is being rendered—to run two washes simultaneously, keeping them at an even gradation, (Fig. 13.2,

Sketch 4). This process can be practiced if a rectangle piercing the sky is drawn about two-thirds of the way down from the top. The height of the rectangle should be divided into increments as before, and the wash, which we will assume will run from light at the top to dark at the bottom, is run as in Sketch 5, except that the wash of equal intensity should always be introduced concurrently at the left and right sides and carried down. Care must be taken that the washes are moved along quickly enough to prevent formation of horizontal lines by settling wash.

A sure-fire method of grading washes is described below:

French Method of Gradation

Divide the rectangle into increments as before, but this time actually draw horizontal lines with dilute ink at every increment. Assuming that you wish to make a gradation from dark at the top to light at the bottom, you would proceed as follows (Fig. 13.2, Sketch 6):

Use a light mixture of wash, perhaps placing three drops in $\frac{1}{4}$ in. of water, and place a wash over the top segment. When this is dry, place a wash over the top two segments, then 3, 4, etc. The last segment, of course, will be covered by only one wash, and an excellent gradation will result. To make the gradation from light at the top to dark at the bottom, one would begin by rendering the bottom segment first, then proceeding as before.

Now that we have completed a practice sheet of washes, we might benefit by a constructive analysis. As in any other newly learned process, imperfections of various types can creep in. They may fall into any of the following categories:

Wash Failures

1. If horizontal brush strokes show, the wash was probably run too dry, or the pigment was not thoroughly mixed, or you may have used the wrong brush for making the wash.

2. If the edges of the wash dried with dark crusts, you probably used too large a puddle of water.

3. If the wash dried dark at the bottom, the puddle was not adequately removed.

4. If the wash dried with a light, uneven ending, too much of the puddle was removed, or the brush touched the paper when you were removing it.

5. If a jagged, fan-shaped imperfection formed at the bottom, the wash was permitted to dry with a puddle at the bottom and this puddle was drawn up into the dried area above it.

6. If white, uneven spots showed during the wash, there is a good chance that perspiration from your hands was absorbed by the paper, and those areas, being oily, resisted the wash.

7. Graded washes: If the gradation is uneven, you may not have made the mixture at a steady rate; that is, you may have added more water or wash at one place than at another.

Before attempting a rendering, it might be well to read the following helpful hints:

Hints

1. Keep all parts of every wash equally wet, and complete the wash to its conclusion, no matter how light it may seem to be.

2. Do not try to "feather off" the edge of a light wash.

3. Keep to the limiting lines of the wash, whether they are straight or curved, neither overrunning nor falling short of such lines. If, however, the washes somehow manage to run over the edges that they are meant to meet, they should be repaired immediately by blotting the overruns. If the overruns may still be seen after drying, they should be scraped with a small brush and clean, cold water, and blotted. This process should be repeated until they have disappeared. This removal process should be used whenever a single overrun is discovered, since if several overruns occur in the same area, it is almost impossible to remove the defect.

4. Once a wash has been started, do not let it stand for any time, since a horizontal line will always appear where applications overlap.

5. Do not touch the paper with the brush; touch only the surface of the wash.

6. Mix the wash thoroughly as you are drawing it along, with a rotary motion.

7. Limit the size of puddle that you render with, since too large a puddle may suddenly run to the bottom of the board, or may cause the wash to dry with a hard edge.

8. In running a graded wash by the French method, crusts may appear at the edge of each subsequent wash. These will disappear when additional washes are run over them, if the washes are run as described above. If an attempt is made to run such graded washes by giving each small area its proper number of washes separately, hard crusts will form between them.

9. In overlaying a previous wash with another, be sure that the first wash is thoroughly dry before proceeding.

10. If a drop of wash falls upon a drawing, blot it immediately, first with the corner of a blotter, being careful not to spread the blot. Wet the drop with clean water and blot it again. Repeat this process until the spot has been removed.

11. If the blot cannot be removed by the foregoing method, carefully erase it so that it is lighter than the adjoining areas, then shade it to match the surrounding tones by stippling or hatching with a fine brush. Be careful not to let the stippling or hatching run into the surrounding areas.

Fig. 13.3   Cutting the Stretch from the Board. See page 162

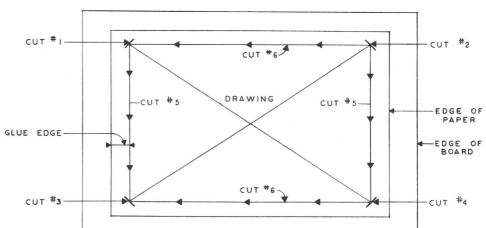

While making the charcoal study, it was decided to make the tower dark at the base and light at the top, so that the dark bells would stand out.

Before the rendering was started, the paper was given a wash of alum mixed in water in order to recalender the paper and neutralize any possible greasy perspiration spots. This alum wash was made of a tablespoon of alum in a quart of water.

The outlines of the building were reproduced on the sheet by the use of graphite pencil and each line was in turn drawn with a pale, thin, diluted waterproof ink line, using ruling pen with T-square and triangle. The shadows were cast and outlined in the same manner.

MATERIALS USED: *No. 4 and No. 10 brushes, the smaller for mixing and the larger for rendering.*

Fig. 13.4

A carillon tower rendered by James Stevenson Whitney Student project

It was decided to reverse the gradation at the sky so that it was light at the bottom and dark at the top. The framework of trees in the mid-distance beside the platform frames the tower and locates it, at the same time permitting and encouraging the eye to look around the tower into the distance. When the charcoal study was completed, another study to determine the number of washes for each area was made on tracing paper over the line drawing which had previously been inked as in the practice washes.

It was decided that the left sides, which were to receive the direct sunlight, would be given one wash. The bright side of the left fin and the edge of the fin facing the spectator would receive five washes, the shadows would be made of ten washes, the sky of four washes, the grass area in the foreground of four washes, the trees in the distance and the risers of the steps of three washes.

The trees were first textured with convolutions, using a freehand pen and dilute waterproof black ink (see Chapter 11), and were then modeled with washes and stippled to create the illusion of form. The grass areas were also stippled.

The first washes were put on the sky, the board being turned upside down for this purpose. Two pans were used, one with water, the other with a medium wash. The washes were begun at the ground line and were run over the trees. Because of the height of this wash, it was graded at 2-in. increments. The sky was completed before the tower was begun.

After the second and fourth washes, crusts around the tower were removed by sponging. This is an important part of Chinese ink rendering, because it permits the delineator to correct errors, get rid of crusts that have formed, and remove surface ink. When a Chinese ink rendering has been completed, the ink should look as if it is a part of the paper and should not stand on the surface. Sponging, as well as the transparency of the washes, contributes greatly to the atmospheric quality of this medium.

The tower was rendered in a manner similar to that for the sky, the light areas being rendered first. No two adjoining areas were rendered at the same time or in sequence, because to do so would have been to cause one wash to run into the other.

The shadows in the foreground and the trees were built up simultaneously until they had achieved the darkness indicated by the charcoal study. The bells were rendered individually—those at the top were made darker than those at the bottom in order to gain maximum contrast with adjoining areas. The bells were rounded by introducing a medium gray wash at the sides and front, then joining them into surrounding areas with a damp brush. The trees were then given additional form by stippling, and the scale figures were painted in.

When the rendering was completed, it was removed from the rest of the stretch by cutting along the border lines with a sharp knife. A short 45-degree cut was first made at each corner (Fig. 13.3). The top and bottom were first cut; then the sides were cut. A word of caution: If possible, the rendering should be cut by two people, one cutting one side while the other person cuts the opposite side. If the cut is made so that each person's knife is exactly opposite the other person's the pressure of the stretch will be gradually released. Large stretches especially sometimes crack if they are carelessly cut from the board. The author has seen this occur many times.

Fig. 13.5

Chapel of the Rosary
Vence, France
Henri Matisse, artist and
designer
Auguste Perret, architectural
supervisor
rendered by S. Amaru
Student project

While making the charcoal study it was decided to bathe the front of the facade in bright light for maximum contrast with the arch forms, scale figures, and fountain. The drawing was placed on the sheet and inked as previously described. The light source was taken to the right. A tracing paper "plan" similar to the one used in the previous rendering was next made, showing the approximate number of washes and location of gradations in each area. For example, the light wall surfaces would receive one wash, and the shade end of the building would receive about 15 washes; the roof shadow at the front would be given 12 washes; the light area of the sidewalk, two washes. The shadow upon the sidewalk would receive 20 washes, while the doorway shadow would require 10, the dark arcs in the arch openings would be made of pure mother wash, and these, as well as the arches themselves on the light side, would be graded from dark in the foreground to light toward the right side of the building.

The shadows were to be given washes of varying intensity. The darks of the building at the right were given 15 washes, the light side of the same building was given 10. The very dark areas of this adjoining building were built up of 15 medium graded washes. Scale figures and the fountain were built up gradually of the same medium graded wash. The fountain was formed by leaving a light, rounded lip, and dark underneath the lip. This dark then blended into the light area by wetting the light area and drawing the dark area up. The same process was used for the lower portion of the fountain.

The drawing was sponged after the first two work sessions to remove crusts and imperfections. As in the previous rendering, the work was not sponged until all washes were completely dry. The drawing was tilted in the sink, completely wetted by pouring a container of clean water over the entire surface, then sponged lightly with the clean wet sponge. In using the sponge, care was taken not to streak the drawing. Some delineators prefer to remove imperfections or lighten the drawing by running a water wash with a large brush over the entire drawing. No matter which method is used, the edges of the drawing should be blotted immediately to prevent the stretch from coming up from the board.

This rendering illustrates two important points of technique.

The drum of the building was rendered by the French method. Since it diminishes in diameter at the bottom, the diminishing of the various steps was achieved as indicated in Fig. 13.7. After the highlight and darkest dark had been located in Fig. 13.8, the rendering became a mere matter of applying washes from light at the highlight to dark at the right side, and from light at the highlight to dark at the left point of tangency of the drum and the darkest dark to a light gray at the extreme left (Fig. 13.6).

The small circular elements to the left of the drum were, on the other hand, graded by the method described in the experimental double graded washes (Fig. 13.2, Sketch 5). The small square areas in back of the drum on the upper part of the flat facade were rendered by applying mother wash to the top and right side of each opening, then cleaning the brush and placing clean water in the rest of the opening so that the mother wash blended with it. The darks were later reinforced.

Fig. 13.6

Guggenheim Museum
Frank Lloyd Wright, Architect
Philip Gordon McIntosh
Student project

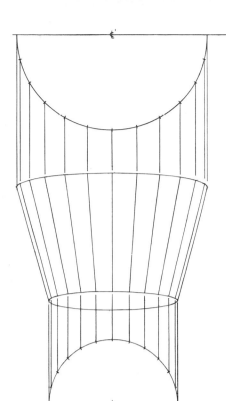

Fig. 13.7   Laying Out the Facets of the Drum for the French Method

Fig. 13.8   Determining Lights and Darks of the Drum

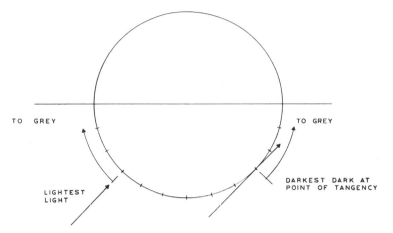

TO GREY

TO GREY

LIGHTEST
LIGHT

DARKEST DARK AT
POINT OF TANGENCY

The method used in rendering this problem was similar to that described for the previous renderings, but it is notable in several ways.

The sky, for instance, was made not by the wash method, but by wetting the surface, then dropping undiluted mother wash into the dark areas, creating an atmospheric cloud effect which complements the building,

Fig. 13.9

An exhibition building rendered by C. S. Fang Student project which is quite rectilinear. The light walls of the building were given a realistic appearance by the darkening of a number of stones to simulate the actual differentiation of value in such stone. The sculpture is in itself a triumph in wash rendering. Each section was rendered separately: an arm was completely executed, then the breast, stomach, drapery folds, etc. Nearly every portion of these figures is rounded, and that effect was obtained by the use of a number of sharply graded washes. The underside of the breast for the female figure at the left, for instance, received a medium wash which was then drawn upward to round the breast by the addition of a paler wash at the top side. The same process was used throughout.

This rendering is also noteworthy in that the delineator was so skillful in the use of wash that it was not necessary to sponge after the first base washes were applied.

Fig. 13.10

Chapel
Ronchamp, France
Le Corbusier, Architect
rendered by Frank Hollenbeck
Student project

A building with forms as subtle as those found in this rendering presents special problems. Since the walls are almost completely without texture, one must depend entirely upon a carefully graded wash and a delicate balance between the values of the building and the sky. Note that, for instance, the sunny side of the building is lighter than the sky, while the shade side is darker than it. Yet the sky itself is merely a straight graded sky—light at the horizon, dark at the top.

Regarding the building itself, it should be noted that the surface of the highest tower, while in shade, was given the illusion of reflected light which, no doubt, would result from the ricocheting of sunbeams from the roof deck below, the strongest beams, of course, hitting the lower portion of the tower, the weak beams the top of the shade side.

The subtlety of the rounded corners was obtained by a combination of the French method of "free" rendering; that is, after the curves were made by the French method, the difference between the increments was softened by running washes from light to dark to light over the same areas without regard for the increments themselves. Note also that reality was obtained in the shadow cast by the water spouts by making the shadow darker at the water spouts and lighter at the opposite end of the shadow. To further accentuate the projection of the water spouts, they were rendered lightly at the bottom so as to give the illusion of reflected light from the wall below.

Fig. 13.11

An interior
rendered by Robert Badia
Student project

This interior view is an excellent example of the simple expression of form by the use of carefully predetermined values and gradations. It is the kind of exercise which should be tried first by the beginner before he becomes involved with more complicated renderings. Notice that the rules of the workings of light are carefully followed. The wall and balconies at the left are graded from dark in the foreground to light in the distance. The pierced areas are left very light for maximum comparison with the wall areas. The right sides of the pierced areas were made dark because they were not receiving light rays from the glazed areas in the distance. The dark vertical wall area at the right completes this rendering. In addition to being a successful one, it forms a handsome abstract pattern which would be pleasing to look at even if subject matter were ignored.

We have mentioned several methods for rendering trees in wash: for instance, that in which the trees are first drawn and textured in dilute waterproof ink, and also that method in which the tree foliage masses are formed by flat washes or stippling. Another method, "looser" in appearance, is this:

The tree masses are "blocked out" in pencil. A pale wash of dilute Chinese ink is then put on each foliage area to approximate the shape of the tree mass. After this has dried, each tree is rendered by first wetting a spot about ¼ in. larger than the foliage mass with clear water. While this is still damp, the foliage mass is formed by dropping a brush of fairly dark wash on that part (usually near the center of the foliage mass) which is to be darkest. This spreads with a feathery edge which is controlled by the use of a blotter. When its movement has stopped, it is brushed rigorously with a 45-degree motion, pressing the brush on the surface of the paper, thus intensifying or decreasing value as desired. As each foliage mass dries, the process is repeated until the desired values are obtained. The tree trunks and branches are added after the foliage masses are dry, and these are varied in intensity according to their location, the darkest being in the foreground, the lightest in the distance.

To render trees in plan, first draw them in dilute waterproof ink, then dampen each tree with clean water. When this has almost entirely dried, place dark dilute Chinese ink wash on the shade sides of the trees, and grade to light at the opposite side by adding water to the wash as you proceed to the light side.

Wet-into-Wet Method for Trees

Rendering Trees in Plan

Chapter 14

Water color rendering

History of Water Color

THE MEDIUM that we now call water color is one of the oldest that we know. There are records of its use in China in the third century, and also of its use by Japanese and East Indian artists. Their brushes were of sable hair or pig bristles, and they were masters of the delicate and beautiful line in black ink, dark brown, or sepia. Wood bark was first used for painting upon, and later silk mounted upon paper in a manner similar to that used for making stretches today.

Few people realize that water color is centuries older than oil paint. It has always been highly regarded by artists because of its delicacy and great flexibility. Studies for many oil paintings have been made in water color because of the ease and speed with which it can be used, and some of the best known masterpieces in oil were influenced by the brilliance of water color studies. This water color brilliance is still apparent in the decoration of the caves of Altamira and Perigord, painted 20,000 years ago. Egyptian wall paintings (see Chapter 1), were executed in a form of tempera, or opaque water color. The Greeks used this medium, and the magnificent illuminated manuscripts of the Middle Ages were colored with water color or tempera.

The Middle Ages

For some reason, water color seems to have been forgotten between the Middle Ages and the beginning of the eighteenth century, when the English artists began to use it again. It had been used only to tint pencil or pen sketches with black, brown, or sepia, but soon it was employed in monochrome. During the early period in England, which lasted until about 1780, landscape began to be used as subject matter. It was painted in monochrome, since full color had not yet appeared. Paul Sandby (1725–1809) and Thomas Malton, whose work is illustrated in Chapter 1, were chiefly responsible for the use of this medium on landscapes and architectural subjects.

Painters who lived in the second half of the eighteenth century used a rich palette and sometimes brushed strong color on wet paper. The period they began lasted until the beginning of the twentieth century, when many additional colors and styles were developed.

Water color got off to a slow start in the United States, because in Paris, where most early American artists and architects studied, water color was not considered a serious medium, and most students worked in oil. However, several late nineteenth and early twentieth century American artists, such as Winslow Homer, George Inness, and John Singer Sargent, realized the possibilities of water color and developed its use in this country.

Today's architectural delineator inherits his knowledge of water color from these few Americans, from the English school of water color painting and rendering of the same period, from delineators on the European continent who used simplified water color, and from a number of American architects and delineators who have helped develop it to its present state. It comes to us in three basic forms:

1. That in which water color and water are mixed and applied as a transparent medium to white paper made especially for this purpose.

2. Tempera (or showcard colors), all of which are opaque.

3. A combination of transparent water colors with opaque, or Chinese, white.

When one speaks of water color today, he usually means transparent water color, or transparent water color combined with a minimum of tempera. This chapter is devoted to these two categories. When one speaks of tempera rendering, he usually means delineation in which all of the paints used are opaque, as described in Chapter 15, or in which opaque temperas are sprayed upon the paper by the use of an airbrush (Chapter 16).

There are a number of reasons why water color has survived for such a long time. To begin with, it is a clean, easily used medium, lacking the odorous quality of oil. It is possible to use it in small or large scale, even on the same painting or rendering, always giving an accurate illusion of reality. There is no problem that it cannot solve, and it can be used as easily to portray a beach viewed through an ocean mist as a gloriously sunny scene. If necessary, several atmospheres can be created on the same painting, and several techniques can be combined. Some delineators make an entire rendering by building values with a series of light washes, but others use the wash method on the building itself and the direct method (that is, painting directly from the palette) for the entourage. Because of the qualities that the various colors possess, the delineator is able to simulate practically any shade or texture he desires with a minimum of effort. With practice, water color becomes a fast medium. It produces results which appear to have been created by an effort much greater than that actually expended. A rendering in water color usually impresses a client favorably.

We have already mentioned palettes and pigments in a general way in Chapter 7, but we will now expand upon this data. As we have noted, Winsor & Newton's Artist's Colors are strongest and most predictable, while their Student Colors rank far below in quality. Many other colors are good, but are not always predictable. The foregoing are all sold in tubes. Water colors also are available in cakes or pans, and because they are usually neatly packaged in a metal box, frequently attract the novice. However, such dried colors are extremely hard on expensive water color brushes, as it is necessary to keep dabbing and grinding in the cake or pan in order to obtain enough pigment for a wash of any size. Such a box of dried water colors is helpful if held in reserve for mixing small washes, but it is wise to depend for the greater part on tube colors.

As mentioned, tubes are sold in a number of sizes. For example, standard size is No. 2, called a whole tube, and measures ½ x 2 in. The No. 5 size measures ¾ x 2½ in. Even the smaller tubes, however, contain enough water color for several jobs. Tube water colors tend to dry quickly, and unless constant use is anticipated, it may be better to purchase them in the smallest size possible.

The caps of water color tubes are often difficult to remove, particularly if the user has not cleaned all the paint from the threaded portion of the tube before replacing the cap. A stubborn cap can usually be removed by holding a match under it and rotating the tube until the cap is heated slightly, or by holding the cap under hot water for a few minutes. If the cap still refuses to budge, you have no recourse other than to unroll the bottom of the tube and make an opening through which to squeeze the paint.

Brushes

The same brushes used for Chinese ink rendering (see Chapter 13) are employed for rendering in water color. Winsor & Newton, Inc. No. 4 and No. 12 red sable "pencil" brushes were recommended. You will also find a No. 2 and a No. 8 useful. In addition, some delineators use flat brushes for certain purposes. These should be the kind made for oil paintings, of either sable or camel's hair. The smaller flat brushes should be about ¼ in. or ³⁄₁₆ in. wide; and a large, springy, flat brush, ¾ in. wide, will also be found helpful for running skies and other large areas. A hog bristle brush will be useful for "scrubbing" certain areas as the work progresses.

Although Winsor & Newton, Inc. Series No. 7 Albata red sable brushes are of the highest quality, the budget sometimes will not allow their purchase. In this case, a reasonably good brush, particularly in the smaller sizes, can be obtained in Winsor & Newton, Inc. Series No. 8, No. 9, No. 33, or No. 133. Other fairly good brushes are made by other manufacturers in tiger hair or camel's hair (made from the tail hair of Siberian squirrels). (Although "tiger hair" is merely a name which attracts attention, some Japanese artists have actually used brushes bristled with shredded bamboo, bear hair, or mouse whiskers!)

Care should be exercised in the purchase of brushes, as discussed in Chapter 13, and they should always be cleaned after use by swishing them around in clean water before they are put aside. They should never be allowed to stand in a container of water when they are not being used, since they will acquire a bend which you may never be able to correct. There are spring holders for brushes which suspend them so the bristles do not touch the bottom of the water container, and they may be found helpful, but the brushes may just as safely be placed upon your desk, or bristles up in a vase or other container, when not in use. Some delineators, such as Alan Davoll, occasionally bathe their brushes in vaseline, then wash them in soap and water.

Wash Dishes

The same white enamel or plastic wash dishes used for Chinese ink rendering will be found most helpful in mixing water color washes. At all costs avoid wash dishes that are not white, as it is impossible to see the color you are mixing in such pans. Some delineators prefer to use nests of china saucers, and these are useful for mixing small amounts of water color.

You will also require a container for clean water, and this should be large enough to hold a quart or more. A large china vase is excellent for large projects.

Palettes

An excellent, inexpensive palette, used for mixing colors in direct painting, can be made by using a 9-in. white dinner plate. Avoid using a plate with a colored pattern as this will be confusing. A small quantity of each color pigment should be placed on the rim of the plate (Fig. 14.1), with the colors in the same relationships as those in the chromatic circle (Plate II). If this is done, you will automatically reach for each color in the same position every time you need it. If, on the other hand, the colors are placed haphazardly upon the palette, you will spend a great deal of time hunting for the colors as you require them. The center of the plate provides a splendid place for the actual mixing of the colors.

More expensive palettes are sold in art materials stores, but these are usually flat and have no concavity for mixing the colors. In addition, some have depressions for the water color pigments which actually limit the accessibility of the colors. These are to be avoided.

Fig. 14.1   Placing Pigments on the Palette

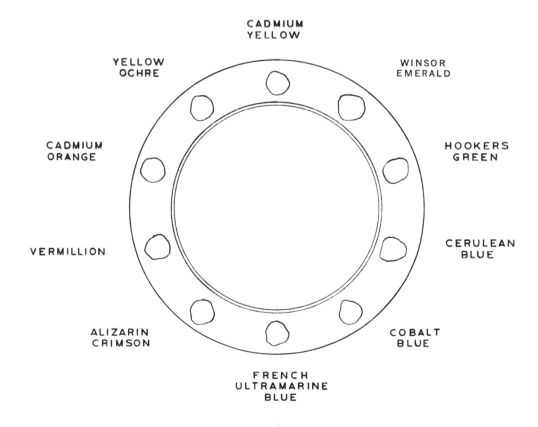

Paper or Illustration Board   The same qualities found in paper used for Chinese ink rendering (Chapter 13) are required for water color rendering. Be sure that the surface has a cold pressed finish.

Miscellaneous Items

1. 1 dozen white blotters, for correcting errors and blotting mistakes
2. 1 silk or baby sponge, for sponging, lightening areas, applying pigment, and creating highlights
3. 1 sponge brush, for creating highlights in small areas
4. 1 piece of cheesecloth and a box of cleansing tissues for producing special textures
5. Erasers: pink pearl, ruby and glass or steel erasers, and razor blade, for correcting errors and creating special effects
6. 1 small bottle of liquid latex for masking the main parts of tree structures while painting skies behind them

Getting Acquainted with Pigments

Palettes   As mentioned in Chapter 7 on the subject of color, the palette that you use will depend upon your own wishes. However, for discussion in this chapter we will conduct all operations with the palette that the author prefers. This does not mean that other colors are not helpful—it merely means that experience has shown that colors normally required in rendering can be mixed from these pigments. They are:

Cadmium yellow pale	French ultramarine blue
Yellow ochre	Cobalt blue
Cadmium orange	Cerulean blue
Vermilion	Hooker's green dark
Alizarin crimson (or rose madder)	Windsor emerald

Color Experimentation   After you have purchased these colors you will want to see them and to determine their characteristics when used alone or mixed with other colors. Some of the pigments, such as cadmium yellow pale, cadmium orange, alizarin crimson, and cobalt blue are relatively clear; some are opaque, and still others have the quality of settling—that is, they have particles that settle out when the wash dries. "Sediment" colors include yellow ochre, vermilion, French ultramarine blue, cerulean blue, and emerald green. There are also colors which resist mixture with others. All of these characteristics should be discovered by experimentation. The following exercise will assist you in determining the various qualities of your pigments.

On a piece of 140-lb inexpensive machine-made water color paper, about 15 x 20 in., squeeze about ½ in. of each of the ten pigments along the long edge of the sheet, being careful to keep each color several inches away from the others. Wet your large brush and draw it across each color in turn, being careful to wash the brush completely after each pigment is touched. Note the relative differences between the various pigments, and their relative intensity.

Now take another sheet of the same paper and experiment in color reaction. Mix a medium intensity wash of each pigment, and using a large brush, run a horizontal wash of each directly across the sheet of paper, leav-

Fig. 14.2   Flat Washes for Practice

Fig. 14.3   Graded Washes for Practice

ing a white space between each two washes so that they do not run together. When these washes are dry, repeat the process, running new washes vertically over the first washes, again being careful to leave sufficient space between them so that they do not run together. When the second washes are dry, analyze the results and you will see that some combinations blend to a new color, that others do not mix, and that still others create surprisingly beautiful textures by the settling out of one or both of the colors. An experimental sheet such as this should be kept for future reference.

Practice Washes

The same methods are used for laying washes in water color as in Chinese ink. In order to attain a correct value, it must be built up of several light washes, each applied after the previous one has dried. Using a sheet of the paper mentioned above, about 15 x 20 in., divide the upper portion into ten equal spaces with $\frac{1}{16}$ in.-spaces between, using an "H" pencil, T-square, and triangle. These will be used for practicing flat washes (Fig. 14.2). The lower portion of the sheet should be laid out in the same manner and will be used for practicing graded washes (Fig. 14.3).

Tilting the board at an angle of 10 or 15 degrees, and using a No. 12 brush, run each wash as described in Rendering with Chinese Ink, Chapter 13. About $\frac{1}{4}$ in. of wash in a wash pan, with a sufficient amount of pigment to stain the water to medium intensity, will be sufficient for each flat wash.

Graded washes should be practiced in the spaces at the bottom of the sheet, again following the method described for Chinese ink, using two wash dishes, one containing the medium intensity wash and the other plain water, and two different brushes. These washes should be run from light at the top to dark at the bottom. On still another sheet of paper, the washes should be run from dark at the top to light at the bottom. Gradations by the French method should also be practiced on this second sheet.

Textures   Perhaps no other medium accepts modifications for the creation of textures as does water color. The surface of the paper may be sandpapered, sandpapered and glazed, scratched with a razor and glazed, sponged, scrubbed with a bristle brush, blotted, dabbed, spattered, or erased.

The indications of textures of building materials explained and shown here are basic and will, of course, not fit every case because of the possible difference of the materials involved. However, they will serve as guideposts and should be practiced until you have mastered the techniques described. These techniques should be practiced on the cold pressed water color paper previously recommended, or on illustration board, ruling off rectangles with pencil, T-square and triangle (see Fig. 14.4, Sketches 1-5). The textures described herein are for surfaces considered to be in sunlight and color for similar textures in shade should be modified by the use of a richer, darker mixture of the same colors. The various textures should be drawn in with an "H" pencil at ¼-in. scale, making a careful line drawing.

Wood Siding and   Make a pale mixture of wash of yellow ochre and a small amount of alizarin
Clapboards   crimson and wash the surface of your practice square with this, using your No. 4 brush. When this has dried, the joints may be introduced by using a darker mixture of the same colors and drawing the joints with the same brush held against the side of the tilted T-square (see Fig. 14.4, Sketch 1). The same method may be used with the following modification:

After the base tone has been placed on the sheet, wood grain texture can be introduced with a wiping motion, using a fairly dry brush (from which the moisture has been partially removed by touching it against the blotter or cheesecloth). If the drawing is at a scale large enough to clearly see the grain in the wood, actual grain texture can be introduced freehand over the base wash with the use of the No. 4 brush before the joint lines have been put in.

To render redwood siding in natural finish (Fig. 14.4, Sketch 2), proceed as follows. *Step 1:* Draw the siding and battens in pencil, and then place a pale wash of yellow ochre and vermilion over the entire area. *Step 2:* Mix a slightly darker shade of the same color, dip a No. 4 brush into it, and draw the brush over a clean piece of paper, pressing down heavily enough to make the brush flat and relatively dry. Holding the ferrule of the brush against a tilted T-square placed parallel with the vertical siding, draw the brush lightly over each board, leaving a wood grain effect over the wash below. *Step 3:* Using a still darker mixture of the same colors, holding the T-square as in Step 2, and using a very small brush brought to a fine point, draw shade lines at the right side of each batten.

Wall and Roof Shingles   The actual color of the shingles, of course, will determine the mixture that is to be used. Considering, for instance, that a shade of brown is desired, it might be mixed with French ultramarine blue, alizarin crimson, cadmium

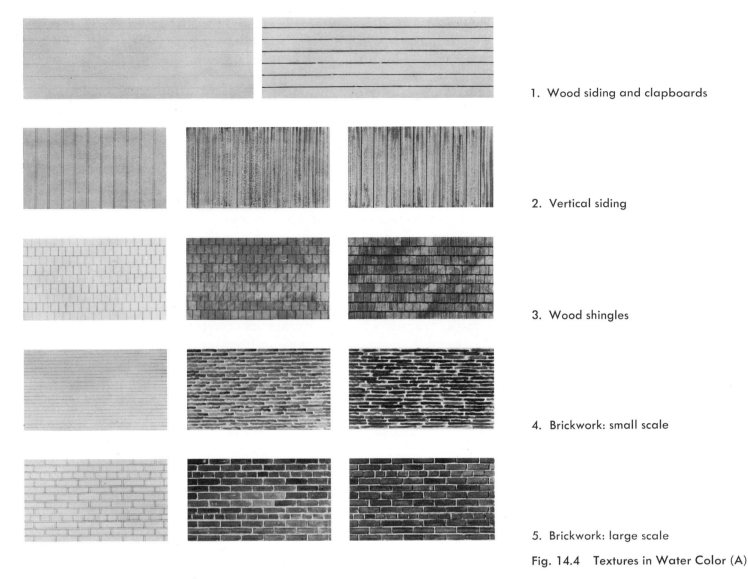

1. Wood siding and clapboards

2. Vertical siding

3. Wood shingles

4. Brickwork: small scale

5. Brickwork: large scale

Fig. 14.4   Textures in Water Color (A)

orange, and yellow ochre. Since shingles vary in shade a great deal, particularly after they are stained, the base tones are best made by placing a number of washes one upon the other, being careful not to mix the colors thoroughly in the wash pan but merely drawing them together. After the base washes are dry, the shadow lines can be introduced with a slightly wavy freehand stroke, see Fig. 14.4, Sketch 3.

Brickwork

The rendering of brick will vary according to the scale of the drawing, but no matter what the scale, the brick joints should first be drawn in with pencil. At a scale of 1/8 in. or less, a wash the color of the masonry between the bricks should first be passed over the paper. Another wash of the color of the brick, and fairly intense in value, is then used to show the courses of brickwork. Using a small brush and small wavy lines, the various courses are painted over the base wash (Fig. 14.4, Sketch 4). Finally some of the bricks are darkened by the use of additional washes.

At larger scale, such as 1/4 in. to 1 ft, the brickwork may be shown as follows: A wash of the joint color is passed over the area and permitted to dry. The various courses of the brick are then drawn by the use of a brick color applied with a ruling pen or small brush, guided by the edge of the T-square. Where it is not desirable to show a great deal of texture, brickwork may be indicated by giving the surface one or more washes of the brick color, then drawing in the joint lines with a sharp 2-H pencil, breaking the lines often to relieve monotony. At very large scale, as in a rendered detail, each brick must be carefully drawn, the joint wash then introduced, and the various bricks rendered individually, care being taken to get variations in tone by introducing more washes over some bricks than others, to show the natural color differentiations of the bricks themselves (Fig. 14.4, Sketch 5).

Stonework   Although there are dozens of different ways of laying stone, the delineator need only be interested in whether it is smooth or rough. The smooth, tooled stone, such as limestone, is rendered as follows:

Mix a warm gray from alizarin crimson, yellow ochre, and cobalt blue, and place one or more washes on the surface of a practice sheet. When these are dry, gently sponge the area, thereby introducing variations in tone. When the paper is again dry, create the natural differentiation of the various stones by introducing an additional wash or two over several of the stones. Then, using a fine brush, draw shadows on the underside and shade side of the stones (see Fig. 14.5, Sketch 1). If the stones have bevelled edges, the above method must be modified, as follows:

Place a base tone upon the sheet and when this is dry, paint each individual stone separately, leaving the light bevelled edges the color of the first

Fig. 14.5   Textures in Water Color (B)

1. Limestone

2. Limestone with bevelled edges

3. Smooth rubble stone walls

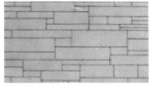

4. Rough rubble stone walls

wash. The shade sides of the bevelled edges should then be darkened by the addition of another wash (see Fig. 14.5, Sketch 2).

Rubble walls, rough in texture, may be rendered by first painting the surface the color of the stone joints. Then, using a second sheet of white paper as a palette, place a small amount of each of the pigments that you have used in the wash on this paper, several inches apart. Mix an average stone color by drawing the pigments together in a puddle with your brush, then apply this tone to about a half dozen widely dispersed stones. Now modify this average tone by adding more of the cool color, and paint several more widely dispersed stones. Modify it again by adding more of the warm color and paint several more stones. Repeat this process until the entire surface has been covered. When you have completed the process, the drawing should look like a unified wall surface with subtle variations, and not a series of stones widely different in value or color.

Shadows beneath and next to a number of stones may be painted with a fine brush, merely using a dark shade of the colors that you have been working with. Care must be taken to break these shadows (see Fig. 14.5, Sketch 3), or monotony will result. If it is desired to show the roughness of the stones, a number of them may be "shaped" by introducing shade areas on the underside and on the shade side, using a slightly darker tone than the general tone of the stone itself, and a fairly dry brush (see Fig. 14.5, Sketch 4).

Metal

An increasing amount of metal is being used in contemporary architecture and the color, of course, will depend upon the composition of the metal. Generally speaking, the color of this material is rather light. Since, for the most part, it is flat and lacking in texture, interest is best obtained by grading the washes, or placing the washes, letting them dry, and then scrubbing with a sponge to create differentiations in value.

Glass Openings

Small openings: Completely draw the type of window that you are to render in pencil, being careful at the same time to draw the curtains, shades, or blinds. Using a paper palette (as described above) and a small amount of each of the colors that you are working with, paint the opening left between the window shades and curtains so that there is a variation in tone throughout the small wash. When this is dry, paint the shades or blinds their proper colors, then put in shade and shadow areas such as the shadow cast by the window frame on the curtains and blinds. Finally, with a fine brush or ruling pen, and a fairly dark, grayish color, draw the shadows cast by the various members of the windows on the glass, etc. (see Fig. 14.6, Sketch 1).

Large glass openings: Glass openings that are large enough to allow one to see inside are painted as follows: If one is looking directly into the window, all of the interior furnishings, floor, walls, pictures, etc., must be painted, being careful to allow for the depth of values created by shadows in various parts of the room. Shadows cast on the glass by jamb and head, mullions and muntins, are then painted to indicate the glass (Fig. 14.6, Sketch 2). If the glass opening is being seen so that it reflects light and other

1. Small openings

2. Large openings

Fig. 14.6   Glass Openings

objects in it, the objects reflected must be drawn in in pencil (see "Reflections," Chapter 9), and these painted in tones usually darker than those of the objects being reflected. The upper portions of such glass areas sometimes reflect the color of the sky and should be painted a tone slightly deeper than that of the sky (Fig. 14.6, Sketch 2).

Entourage   **Foreground trees and bushes by the built-up method:**   Foreground trees and bushes must be accurately drawn down to the last detail with a soft pencil before the rendering is begun. Each leaf may be actually drawn in some cases. But whether the individual leaves or tree masses are drawn in detail or generalized, they must be located before the rendering is begun so that the tree structure itself is not painted over these areas. When this has been done, the light color—the color on the side of the tree receiving sunlight—can be painted over the entire wood structure of the tree as a flat wash. When this is dry, a light wash the approximate color of the foliage masses is mixed and washed over these areas. When they are dry, the modelling of the tree structure itself is begun by using short, but rather definite strokes to indicate the various shades of bark tonality. These small, dark areas will, of course, be for the most part on the shade side of each member with the darkest tones on the extreme shade side. The individual leaves of foliage masses are then modelled one by one, care being taken to obtain differentiation in color and value throughout. Finally, shadows cast by foliage masses and branches on branches and trunk must be carefully plotted and painted in (Fig. 14.7, Sketch 1).

A   B   C

1. Built-up method

2. Direct method

Fig. 14.7   Foreground Trees

Fig. 14.8   Mid-Distance Trees

A   B   C

A

B

Fig. 14.9 Background Trees

A

B

Fig. 14.10 Foreground Foliage

Foreground trees by the direct method: There are, of course, many different ways of painting trees by the direct method, but the easiest of these is as follows: Make an accurate drawing of the tree structure and, using a flat, dry, brush, draw the entire tree structure in an appropriate color. Draw from the ground up, just as the tree grows. The shade side of the tree can be darkened by using the same brush. The foliage can be introduced upon the tree structure with either a large "pencil" brush (Fig. 14.7, Sketch 2A), a flat brush (Fig. 14.7, Sketch 2B), or a small bit of sponge torn away from the silk sponge, held in the fingers, dipped in the paint and dabbed on the various areas (Fig. 14.7, Sketch 2C).

Trees in the mid-distance: These also can be rendered by either the built-up method or the direct method. The same process as for the foreground trees and bushes should be followed for the direct method, but the foliage masses may be applied in a generalized way by the use of small washes or stippling (Fig. 14.7).

In the direct method, the tree structure is usually drawn as for the foreground trees and the foliage is painted by the use of a smaller No. 4 brush in individual strokes (see Fig. 14.8B).

Background trees: An interesting method of painting background trees consists of drawing the trees in the distance and then painting them with a pale flat wash. While this wash is still damp, and with the board lying in a flat (not tilted) position, dip the brush into a strong (almost pure) pigment mixture of the same color and lightly drop it at the base line of the trees in the distance. This strong pigment will bleed into the damp surrounding areas and give the illusion of darker base trees (see Fig. 14.9).

Bushes: Foreground bushes as well as mid-distance ones are built up in much the same manner as foreground trees; that is, they are first given a light general wash, then modelled with a dabbing motion to add texture and form (see Fig. 14.10). Distant bushes can be shown with practically a flat wash.

Grass: Perhaps the most important thing to remember in painting grass is that there is a great differentiation in value and color throughout grass areas. A flat, even wash gives an unsatisfactory appearance. A lawn made of a series of different tones and values to show the actual variation in the

Fig. 14.11　Skies

1. and 2.　By graded washes
3.　By dropped-in pigments
4.　By airbrush

1

2

3

4

1

2

Fig. 14.12   Skies

1. By fixative atomizer
2. By toothbrush spatter

grass is much more interesting. Additional interest can also be given to grass areas that appear to be too plain by the use of short vertical, or nearly vertical, strokes placed close together to simulate grass blades. In building up the tones of grass areas, a great deal of interest can be obtained by failing to cover the undertones entirely in over-painting (Fig. 14.9).

Skies: There are four basic ways to render skies:

1. The first is that in which a graded wash, usually light at the horizon and dark at the top of the rendering, is made with no attempt to indicate clouds (Fig. 14.11, Sketch 1).

2. The second is by painting the same type of sky, then erasing clouds with a ruby eraser (Fig. 14.11, Sketch 2).

3. The third method is that in which the entire sky area is dampened with a wash of clear water and colors are dropped or stroked in to create the illusion of a broken, cloudy sky (Fig. 14.11, Sketch 3). In this method the board must be flat (not tilted) and the colors dropped in must be of a fairly deep intensity or they will dissipate into the damp sky and the cloudy textures will disappear. Frequently in this method it is also necessary to raise the board and tilt it first one way and then the other in order to "coax" the color to the areas desired.

4. Excellent skies, of course, can be painted in water color by the use of an airbrush (Fig. 14.11, Sketch 4), atomizer (Fig. 14.12, Sketch 1), or toothbrush spatter (Fig. 14.12, Sketch 2). Additional techniques will be explained as the following renderings are discussed.

Making a Rendering   The perspective line drawing should be transferred to the final sheet in the manner described in Chapter 4. All renderings discussed in the following pages were made on stretched paper, as suggested in Chapter 13, Rendering with Chinese Ink. In addition to the value study in charcoal, a color study was made on a piece of water color paper to determine the color scheme to be used. The various color schemes were described in Chapter 7, Color, and examples of each will be discussed in each section on color rendering. As each presentation is discussed the color scheme and the pigments used will be given.

PAPER: *Handmade, cold-pressed, stretched*
COLOR SCHEME: *Triadic*
PALETTE: *Alizarin crimson, cobalt blue, yellow ochre*

Finally the grayed blue trees and bushes were completed directly from the palette. The foreground was further darkened by spraying a deep mixture of the several colors, moving the airbrush to the left and right during the process. (See Chapter 16 for airbrush technique.)

Plate III

Beach house
rendered by Elaine Frank
Size: 14 x 21 in.
(see Fig 14.15)

Plate IV

St. Augustine's Church
Union City, New Jersey
Arthur Rigolo, Architect
rendered by Alan Davoll
Size: 17 x 18 ½ in.

Plate V

**Community Reformed Church
Baldwin, New York
Ryder, Struppman &
Neuman, Architects
rendered by Charles Spiess
Size: 19 x 16 in.
Medium: Water color**

COLOR SCHEME: *Triadic*
PALETTE: *Cadmium yellow pale, cobalt blue, alizarin crimson, white, black*
MATERIAL USED: *Handmade cold pressed paper, stretched*

Plate VI

A House in the Desert
Richard J. Neutra, Architect
rendered by Gordon Schenck
Size: 14 x 21 in.
Medium: Tempera

The style of this rendering is unusual in having building, background, and sky painted directly from a palette in the very loose style of water color landscape artists. The colors were painted wet-into-wet. The artist first applied the sky with horizontal strokes, beginning with a mixture of blue and white, and then added white and a small amount of red as the work neared the edges of the building. The building was painted bit by bit directly from the palette, with off-white for walls and fascias, and deep blues and orange for interior portions and with charcoal and color studies as value and color guides. Straight lines, such as those of columns and sash, were done by using a T-square and a small brush. The remote parts of the open glass areas were painted dark to create the illusion of depth, and the portions of the same rooms nearest the light source were purposely made lighter to create the illusion of reflected light. The blue, white, and orange water was painted wet-into-wet directly from the palette after the reflections were approximately located in pencil. A few blue and purple ripples and reflections were indicated after the water areas were dry.

PAPER: *Handmade, cold-pressed, stretched*
COLOR SCHEME: *Analogous with complementary accent*
PALETTE: *Vermilion, alizarin crimson, cadmium yellow, yellow ochre, cobalt blue*

The charcoal and color studies for this rendering indicated that a great deal of foliage would not be desirable, since it created a jungle-like, closed-in appearance. It was necessary to determine carefully where trees were to be placed for the best effect, in order to complement the building, rather than to draw attention away from it.

In this effective rendering the blue-gray sky was painted in as in the previous presentations, by turning the drawing upside-down and running a wash from the horizon line to the top limits of the picture. The various gray-orange graded tones of the wooden part of the building were then washed in, again by tilting the board as desired. The soffits were painted in a series of blue-gray washes. The tan base tone of the stonework was then introduced, after which the light gray-tan tones of the trees were painted in and the drawing was sponged as previously described.

When the rendering was dry, the various tones were again built up to their final intensity, and the shadows under the boards were drawn in by the use of a fine brush and a medium gray wash, using a T-square, care being taken to avoid monotony by varying the intensity of the lines.

The soffits were then darkened, the stonework was begun by painting individual stones using tan and gray-orange, and the drawing was again sponged. In the final phase, all of the tones were again reinforced, the stonework was completed, and the shadows on the stonework were put in.

Until this point the foliage had not even been started and this was painted directly from the palette by first placing the drawing in a flat position and dampening the entire area over which the foliage was to be placed with a large brush and clean water. Then spots of rather strong color ranging from yellow-green through blue, green, and purple were dropped into the dampened area and allowed to spread and mingle, giving the illusion of foliage rather than an actual delineation of it. The tree structures were completed by painting the dark sides, and a few leaves were added.

Fig. 14.13

John C. Pew House
Madison, Wis.
Frank Lloyd Wright, Architect
rendered by Isadore Wolf
Student project

PAPER: *Handmade, cold-pressed, stretched*
COLOR SCHEME: *Triadic*
PALETTE: *Alizarin crimson, cobalt blue, yellow ochre*

Fig. 14.14

Beach house
rendered by Elaine Frank
Student project

The color study for this rendering confirmed the fact that all of the colors required could be made from a triadic color scheme. An analysis of the presentation illustrates the fact that one or more of the colors in a scheme may not appear in pure form at all. The alizarin crimson, for instance, is not obvious.

Step No. 1, Fig. 14.14, Sketch 1: The sky was painted with a watery graded wash of pure cobalt blue with the drawing turned upside-down, as previously mentioned. Care was taken to paint the sky in those portions of the house through which it could be seen. When this was dry, pale washes of the various colors were put on the several parts of the house, and a light grayed background tone was put on the stone wall. The hillock and trees were begun by first applying a light gray-blue wash made of a mixture of the three colors. A light blue wash was put on the water area, working with the board upside-down. At this point the entire drawing was gently sponged and the process of building tones was resumed, leaving the base tones on the light side of the building alone, and darkening all others as required.

Step No. 2, Fig. 14.14, Sketch 2:   The underside of the roof was heavily reinforced by the use of a number of washes. The orange panels were painted in several washes and the trees, bushes, and water were again reinforced. The stones in the wall were painted individually tan, gray, and rust by using a small amount of the several colors as in Plate III, and shadows were put under some of the stones.

The gray shadows under the gravel stop and on the wood panel were next reinforced and the wood was given the appearance of graining by the use of a deeper yellow ochre wash and a fine brush.

Plate III: Finally the grayed-blue trees and bushes were completed directly from the palette. The foreground was further darkened by spraying a deep mixture of the several colors, moving the airbrush to the left and right during the process. (See Chapter 16 for airbrush technique.)

A triadic color scheme was chosen for this presentation, which is a rather classic example of the subtlety of tones that can be obtained with water color. As in the previous renderings, the various values in the building, foreground and background, were built up one wash at a time. The walls of the building are pale yellow, the foreground and background many tones of yellow, gray, violet, and blue. When the trees in the background were painted in detail, it became obvious that they did not appear to retreat into the distance as they should. After the tones had been put upon the entire

Fig. 14.15

Boat house
rendered by Kyunghan Kim
Student project

PAPER: *Handmade, cold-pressed, stretched*
COLOR SCHEME: *Triadic*
PALETTE: *Cobalt blue, alizarin crimson, yellow ochre*

drawing, it was gently sponged, and in this process the details of the trees in the background were obliterated. The tones in the rendering were then completed, and the reflections in the water were painted directly from the palette.

Fig. 14.16

Interior
rendered by
Emil Ferdinand Jettmar
Student project

An interior rendering such as this is done in a manner similar to that described for the previous exterior renderings. Each tone was made by mixing the three colors in different proportions. The ceiling, for instance, was made with a mixture of the three colors, but with cadmium yellow predominating. The chairs, in the same manner, were painted with a combination of the pigments, but with alizarin crimson predominating. The floor, of course, had a heavy proportion of French ultramarine blue in it, while the stonework of the fireplace was built up of a series of washes predominantly red and yellow in tone.

The various details such as the fire in the fireplace, plants, and books, as well as the pattern in the curtains, were painted last to insure crispness. The drawing was sponged twice during the process of rendering.

PAPER: *Handmade, cold-pressed, stretched*
COLOR SCHEME: *Triadic*
PALETTE: *French ultramarine blue, cadmium yellow, alizarin crimson*

PAPER: *Handmade, cold-pressed, stretched*
COLOR SCHEME: *Triadic*
PALETTE: *Alizarin crimson, yellow ochre, French ultramarine blue*

Fig. 14.17

A residence
rendered by
William Petchler, Jr.
Student project

Fig. 14.18

Color study for above

This fresh rendering was made in a crisp, sure style, in the same manner as described for previous illustrations. It is notable because of the treatment of the ground, stonework, and trees. The preliminary color study (Fig. 14.18) illustrates the amount of detail that such a study should contain. It was done spontaneously, direct from the palette—not built up as was the final rendering. It is quite usual for the final rendering to deviate somewhat from the color study, which, like a charcoal study, may show faults that can be eliminated, as well as the general direction that the rendering should take. In this rendering, for example, the pale yellow walls were made darker, the entrance door more vermilion than red, the glass openings were made bluer, the foreground a paler green, and the gray sky lighter.

PAPER: *Handmade, cold-pressed, stretched*
COLOR SCHEME: *Split complement*
PALETTE: *Vermilion, yellow ochre, cobalt blue*

Fig. 14.19

A residence
rendered by Michael H. Irving
Student project

This rendering illustrates a bold and interesting method of painting trees. Those in the background were first given a general pale yellow-green tone. When this wash was dry, the same area was dampened with water and the trees were modeled with strong color taken directly from the palette. This was then "scrubbed in" with the side of a No. 8 brush to avoid soft, ragged edges. The darkest trees in the background were painted with a brush that was quite dry, the dark sides being painted in single strokes, bled into surrounding areas by the addition of lighter and paler washes placed immediately next to them. The tree trunks and branches were added last.

The branch in the foreground was painted directly from the palette, dark green foliage being made in a series of short strokes, beginning at the branch and radiating outward. The wood walls of the building itself were painted in tones of orange, the windows in blue-gray, blue, and violet, and the stone walls in several shades of tan and blue-gray. The sky was rendered in cobalt blue.

This presentation is an excellent example of the use of a settling type of wash, as in the sky, and of the use of subtle colors. The entire rendering was built up of light tones of the various pigments, the walls of the building being tan and grayed orange, the foreground many shades of grayed green, the sky blue. The largest trees were built up of a purplish brown, while the small ones were painted directly, in yellow and brown. The leaves in the foreground were painted in a deep blue-green.

This rendering is also a splendid example of the successful determination of elements in the composition. During the making of the charcoal study it quickly became apparent that the foreground would have to contain many interesting fine elements in order to complement the enormous stone mass of the building. As a result, numerous trees, some quite small and others large in diameter, were strategically placed to form an interesting abstract pattern through which the building could be seen. The lawn area performs a similar function. It has many variations of tone and value, with numerous shadows cast by the various trees, providing an interesting pattern that helps to describe the slope of the terrain. When the drawing had been completed it became apparent that the trees should be lightened on the sunny side. This was done by scraping them with a razor blade. The plain, rather deep tone of the sky is effective because it tends to push the building forward.

Fig. 14.20

Sol Friedman House
Pleasantville, N. Y.
Frank Lloyd Wright, Architect
rendered by
George Nicholas Van Geldern
Student project

Fig. 14.21

Color study for 14.20

PAPER: *Handmade, cold-pressed, stretched*
COLOR SCHEME: *Split complement*
PALETTE: *Vermilion, cadmium yellow, French ultramarine blue*

PAPER: *Handmade, cold-pressed, stretched*
COLOR SCHEME: *Triadic*
PALETTE: *Alizarin crimson, cadmium yellow pale, cobalt blue*

Fig. 14.22

Hopewell Baptist Church
Bruce Goff, Architect
Edmond, Okla.
rendered by S. Amaru
Student project

This difficult problem, which entailed a great deal of meticulous work, is well worth analyzing, since it contains many problems not mentioned before. The steel structure was first drawn in ink lines with a ruling pen. Then these areas were shaded in water color as desired. The several sides of the roof were first given yellowish base tones in shades of varying intensity. The stone walls were lightly rendered in gray, the windows in dark gray, the background in gray and orange, and the sky in pale blue. When the entire drawing was dry, it was gently sponged and a number of individual shingles were then picked out in light shades of blue, purple, orange, and red. The joints and butts of the shingles were applied with a small brush, using a dark wash of the pigments employed.

Although it is usual to limit the palette to three, or at most four colors, there are times when an additional color is used for special effects. In this interior, the extra color was raw umber, mixed with the other colors of the palette in order to create the illusion of deep texture in the round rug on the floor. True, both vermilion and French ultramarine blue give a settling effect, but in this case, the delineator wanted even more than he could get with them. If the extra color is limited to one or two areas, fine; but if a color like raw

PAPER: *Handmade, cold-pressed, stretched*
COLOR SCHEME: *Split complement*
PALETTE: *Yellow ochre, vermilion, French ultramarine blue, cobalt blue, raw umber*

umber is indiscriminately mixed with other colors, it will give too much texture in smooth areas, and "muddy" colors that should be kept clean, clear, and bright.

The order of procedure was as follows: The round rug was given a graded wash of yellow ochre and vermilion; then one of yellow ochre, vermilion and raw umber for extra texture. The table was rendered with a soft mixture of vermilion, yellow ochre and cobalt blue. The floor around the carpet was given a graded wash of yellow ochre, French ultramarine blue and a small amount of vermilion. The sides of the chairs were rendered next, the webbing of the one on the right receiving graded washes of pure but watered-down vermilion, the left chair several graded washes of yellow ochre, French ultramarine blue, and a small amount of vermilion. The stone wall was first given a wash of cement gray, the stones were then rendered individually in varying shades of medium gray, rust, and reddish gray. The inside of the fireplace was rendered in brown. The field of the ceiling was graded in pale tan, then jointed with a small brush, straightedge and brown paint. The undersides of the beams were washed with a more vermilion tone, the sides of the beams a pale mixture of the same color.

The sofa under the window was given graded tones of a mixture made of vermilion and a small amount of cobalt blue and yellow ochre.

The bookcase was then rendered; the background a deep brown, the books and shelf-edges light tones of white, blue, yellow and vermilion. After the outside landscape was painted, the wall areas around the windows were made a rather deep brown, the curtain grayed orange.

Finally such details as lamps and flowers were carefully painted, directly from the palette.

Professional Technique

Alan Davoll, well known for his magnificent water color renderings, uses a number of tricks that are well worth mentioning, since he produces such excellent results with them. To begin with, he uses Whatman rough finish illustration board because it gives interesting settling effects. He masks all borders with drafting tape 202 before he begins so that he obtains sharp border lines; this makes a mat unnecessary.

Detailed leaves are drawn with black chalk, and these are "fixed" by washing them with water.

Sky areas are prepared for rendering by masking tree trunks and branches with Maskoid Liquid Frisket, wetting the entire sky area with a house paint brush 2-in. wide, and permitting it to soak for 15 or 20 minutes. The paints for the sky are then mixed (he uses Antwerp blue or mixes it with cobalt blue), the sky area is blotted, and the rendering begins on a moist, but not wet, surface. A sufficient amount of water has been absorbed by the paper so that no streaks or uneven dry edges occur. While the sky washes are still wet, sky areas and clouds that are to be light in tone are wiped out with a bristle brush, cellulose sponge, or blotter (see Fig. 14.28, Montclair High School Auditorium Addition). If necessary, clouds are erased after the sky washes have dried, and for this purpose Mr. Davoll prefers to use a Blaisdell New Way Eraser (one covered with twisted paper).

Fig. 14.24
Women's Dormitory,
Newark State College,
Union, N.J.
Scrimenti/Swackhamer/
Perantoni, Architects
rendered by Alan Davoll

Fig. 14.25
Notre Dame Jr.-Sr.
High School,
East Stroudsburg, Pa.
William A. Rake, Partner
in charge,
Rinker, Kiefer & Rake,
Architects-Engineers
rendered by Alan Davoll

Fig. 14.26
Nativity Lutheran Church
East Brunswick, N.J.
George E. McDowell,
A.I.A.
McDowell-Goldstein,
Architects,
rendered by Alan Davoll

Mr. Davoll usually renders in realistic colors that are prepared from the following palette:

Reds	**Orange**
Vermilion	Cadmium orange
Rose madder	
Alizarin crimson	**Yellows**
Indian red	Yellow ochre
Burnt sienna	Chrome yellow
	Lemon yellow
Greens	
Olive green	**Brownish gray**
Hooker's green No. 1	Sepia
Hooker's green No. 2	
Veridian	**Earth colors**
Emerald green	Burnt umber
	Raw umber
Blues	
Cerulean blue	**Black**
Antwerp blue	Ivory black
New blue	
Cobalt blue	**White**
	Luma bleed-proof Chinese
	white (Steig products)

Two different sets of colors are used for mixing grays. The first—cobalt blue, alizarin crimson, and yellow ochre—will produce either warm or cool grays. The second—French ultramarine blue, burnt sienna, and alizarin crimson—produce cool, luminous grays such as those required for whitish areas (like doors) that are on the shade side of the building. Although painted gray with a wash of the second combination, they actually appear to be white.

Mr. Davoll uses a casein paint (which is similar to tempera) for scale figures, which he paints after all transparent water color work is finished. Those in the foreground are painted drab colors, and those in the mid-distance warm colors, while those near the building are painted yellow or white. Red is not used because it photographs black in a black and white photograph.

Looking at Mr. Davoll's renderings, one cannot fail to notice that each problem is handled in an individual way. There is no "pat" solution into which all renderings are pressed. Usually the buildings are left quite light, as compared with surrounding green lawn and foliage areas (Fig. 14.25, and Plate IV). Occasionally, in order to make the building stand out, unusually dark trees are placed behind the building (Fig. 14.24), but to keep these from appearing "heavy," they are broken up with lighter green mid-distance trees and minimized by use of a relatively dark blue sky. Plate IV illustrates some of the points regarding the use of wet streets for reflections mentioned in Chapter 9. Notice that the reflection is approximate; not an exact reproduction of the precisely rendered architectural forms. Notice also here that the light is thrown upon the building very unevenly: that there is more on the left side than the right. This very difference contributes enormously to the illusion of reality. It imitates the individual differences of all things in nature.

Fig. 14.27
Lehigh County Courthouse
Wolf, Hendrix &
Associates, Architects &
Engineers
rendered by Alan Davoll

Fig. 14.28

Montclair High School
Auditorium Addition
Montclair, N.J.
Alfonso Alvarez, A.I.A.,
Architect
rendered by Alan Davoll

Water Color Variations

The methods described thus far in this chapter for water color are those used by the purist. He will never countenance the use, for example, of any opaque color in his water color work. Yet, from a practical standpoint, it must be admitted that many of the most successful professional renderers combine Chinese white with water colors for portions of their renderings. As a delineator practices, he sometimes finds it expedient and more to his personal liking to render in a manner slightly different from that which he was taught. This is a natural phenomenon. As we mentioned in Chapter 3, one must develop his own style, and as long as satisfactory results can be obtained, departure from the usual methods can be justified, and even considered desirable. The medium must be moulded to the individual, and until this has been done the delineator may not reach maximum success.

In the general method used by most renderers, all parts of the rendering are built up concurrently. But there are those, like Charles Spiess, who work differently. Mr. Spiess begins by "killing" the white of the paper with a light wash of cadmium yellow pale over the whole sheet. He does this to produce the illusion of the warmth of natural sunlight in his drawings. Then he renders the sky and foreground completely before beginning the building. Before painting the sky, Mr. Spiess masks, i.e. covers, the edge of the building itself with drafting tape and paper to insure a sharp edge. The type of sky he uses varies according to the kind of building at hand; sometimes it is a smooth, domed sky such as we have described. But often it will be a sort of "planned accident" obtained by first running a water wash over the entire sky area with the board lying flat, and then dropping strong pigment into the various parts of the sky. The pigment spreads and is encouraged to go to any portion of the sky desired by lifting the board and tilting it first one way and then another (Fig. 14.29 and Plate V). The colors dropped in for the sky will vary according to the color scheme being used. However, one satisfactory combination is French ultramarine blue and emerald green, with perhaps vermilion added to the French ultramarine blue for darker portions of the sky and cloud shadows. There is no limit to the colors that can be used, of course. If the color scheme permits, interesting cloud effects can be obtained by using a mixture of cobalt blue, yellow ochre, and alizarin crimson.

Fig. 14.29

Arthur Poole Residence
Schuman & Lichtenstein,
Architects
rendered by Charles Spiess

Fig. 14.30

St. Agnes Academic School
College Point, N.Y.
William J. Boegel, Architect
rendered by Charles Spiess

For the base tone in the immediate foreground, Mr. Spiess uses a mixture of French ultramarine blue and alizarin crimson. Near the building his base tone is of raw sienna, while in the distance his base tone is a mixture of burnt sienna and cobalt blue.

When the ground and sky areas have dried, he renders his building completely. Then he paints all of his background trees, and finally his foreground trees, with thick water color and an oil brush. He prefers the chisel type of oil brushes, No. 7 to No. 20 (Grumbacher or Winsor & Newton) because they produce a crispness not obtainable with heavy color if a conventional water color brush is used. In pure water color, white spaces must be left for trees and bushes, but when they are painted with heavy water color

Fig. 14.31

A house for farm
or suburban living (Plan 9556)
Rudolph A. Matern, Architect
rendered by Charles Spiess

pigment, or with an even more opaque mixture of water color and Chinese white, they may be applied over any previously rendered area.

While some of Mr. Spiess's renderings are done entirely of transparent water color, others run the gamut from completely transparent water color washes to completely opaque washes of Chinese white mixed with water color (Fig. 14.31). In rendering brickwork, he always uses Chinese white with water color. All window openings are rendered with transparent water color washes, but the frames, mullions and muntins are applied with a thick mixture of Chinese white and water color, using a small brush and a straight edge. This gives the rendering a precise quality, particularly if the scale is small, and it must be admitted that it is difficult to obtain this result with the use of transparent washes alone (see Figs. 14.30 and 14.31). These two renderings also illustrate two general principles: in aerial views, in order to obtain the illusion of depth—that is, of distance—the rendering is built up of a series of transparent washes. In a ground view, in which the building is silhouetted, Mr. Spiess usually paints direct from the palette. For dark trees and small background buildings in an aerial view, he uses a combination of water color and Chinese white. Another interesting rule used by Mr. Spiess is this: If a drawing is to be vignetted (finished with uneven picture edges) and not matted, he leaves as much white as possible in and around the rendering. On the other hand, if a mat is to be used, all white areas are tinted to differ from the color of the mat.

Mr. Spiess's palette is vitally different from the author's. He keeps ready at all times three china containers with concavities, and fills them as follows:

No. 1 (used most often)
    Well No. 1: Mixture of French ultramarine blue and alizarin crimson
    Well No. 2: Burnt sienna
    Well No. 3: Raw sienna
    Well No. 4: Antwerp blue
    Well No. 5: Combination of Indian red and vermilion

No. 2 (greens)
    Well No. 1: Cadmium orange
    Well No. 2: Aurelian
    Well No. 3: Raw sienna
    Well No. 4: Viridian
    Well No. 5: Windsor green

No. 3 (for infrequent combinations)
    Well No. 1: Cobalt blue
    Well No. 2: Yellow ochre
    Well No. 3: Raw umber
    Well No. 4: Combination of sepia and alizarin crimson
    Well No. 5: Ivory black

With this palette, Mr. Spiess can obtain a wide variety of colors, yet his work is subtle in quality, and the colors used on his renderings relate to each other rather closely. Garish colors are never used.

Chapter 15

Tempera rendering

TEMPERA is a water-soluble paint that becomes sufficiently insoluble when dry to allow overpainting with more tempera. Imperfect washes and errors can be eliminated by sponging, or they can be repaired by merely covering with more paint. Tempera can be used on white or colored paper or illustration board, and is excellent for night as well as day renderings. Almost any project can be rendered with this medium; notice the varied types presented in this chapter.

Tempera is made in shades of gray, for renderings that are to be reproduced in black and white, as well as in most of the colors in which transparent water colors are made, plus a few more. Whether in black and white or in color, tempera photographs in a precise, sculptural way and gives such a realistic appearance that a photograph of a tempera rendering is often mistaken for a photograph of a finished building. The colors themselves are strong and brilliant and must be mixed with a great deal of white (and sometimes a small amount of black) before they can be used.

Since tempera colors are mixed with a white base, the hues that result can be duplicated in actual job finishes, and the final color scheme for a project can be determined during the rendering project.

The most subtle hues, tints, and shades can be mixed with tempera, but because the colors obtainable are subtle, they are difficult for the novice to duplicate. Therefore it is advisable to mix more of each color than one intends to use, and to keep the excess for damage repair, or for use on other parts of the rendering, until it has been completed.

Paper: Tempera can be used on cold-pressed or hot-pressed handmade paper that has been stretched, on illustration boards with the same finishes, or on stretched, colored charcoal paper. The better grades of boards are recommended because they have hard tough surfaces that withstand such hazards as sponging and drafting tape, which frequently destroy the surface of the less expensive board.

Tempera is available in ready-mixed sets of grays. The numbers of the shades in sets vary according to make. Some, for instance, are numbered 0, 1, 2, 3; others 1, 2, 3, 4 and 5; but the lightest shade usually bears the lowest number, the darkest the highest number. Gray tempera is available in warm or cool colors. The author recommends warm grays for architectural work.

Tempera pigments, whether gray or colored, are produced in tubes, jars, and cakes. The tube colors have more "body"; those sold in jars usually contain a large amount of water. It is not advisable to use the cake tempera for rendering. The tube colors are slightly more expensive than those in jars. All tempera dries if not used within a reasonable time; therefore, as with water color, it is advisable to buy the smaller sizes in tubes or jars. Jars of color can be kept moist by adding water and a little glycerin periodically before they have dried.

A thin line indeed separates the various kinds of opaque paint. Some are sold as tempera, others as designer's opaque water colors, poster colors, and showcard colors. Winsor & Newton, Inc. Designer's Opaque Water Colors, while they are especially made for gouache painting, are excellent for opaque renderings, as are Grumbacher's Designer's Colors, Weber Malfa, Shiva "Nu-Tempera," and Rich Art Poster Colors.

Like transparent water colors (Chapter 14), opaque water colors are made in a great many hues and usually vary in price according to the pigment desired. Nearly all the colors recommended for transparent water color are available, but in addition such colors as the following can be had in tempera, designer's, or showcard paints:

Marigold yellow	Brilliant green
Mistletoe green	Magenta
Burgundy lake	Cadmium primrose
Rose malmaison	Permanent orange
Peacock blue	Permanent green
Persian orange	Flame red
Forest green	

One could become very confused in buying such colors if he depended entirely upon the name, particularly if he is purchasing tube colors, so the author again recommends limiting the palette and dabbling only occasionally in the unknown. In any case, before purchasing a tube of an unfamiliar color it is advisable to take off the cap and examine the contents.

The following palette of tube colors is recommended:

Cadmium yellow pale	Cobalt blue
Yellow ochre	Cerulean blue
Cadmium orange	Viridian
Vermilion	Windsor emerald
Flame red	Ivory black
Alizarin crimson	Permanent white (or any
Ultramarine blue	opaque white, commonly
	known as Chinese white)

If jar colors are used the following palette is recommended. (This list was selected from Rich Art Colors.)

Yellow (spectrum)	Light blue
Dark yellow	Blue (spectrum)
Yellow ochre	Ultramarine blue
Orange (spectrum)	Emerald green
Vermilion	Green (spectrum)
Red (spectrum)	Poster white
Dark red	Poster black

In addition to the above, whether they are purchased as tube or jar colors, it is recommended that small jars or cakes of gold and silver be obtained.

Since tempera colors dry hard, it frequently becomes a problem to remove tube caps and covers, particularly if excess paint has not been removed before they have been replaced. It is, of course, advisable to wipe any such excess paint away before the covers or caps are replaced. If it will not open, a tube cap may be removed by placing a lighted match under the cap while the tube is rotated (do not burn your fingers), and a jar cover may be loosened by holding it under warm or hot water.

Brushes

Expensive water color brushes used for transparent water color or Chinese ink wash drawing will quickly be ruined by tempera. In general four types of brushes are used for tempera painting:

1. *Red Sable, Bright Shape:* Like water color brushes, tempera brushes made by different manufacturers vary greatly in number and size. Winsor & Newton, Inc. Bright Shape Series 52, Nos. 3, 4 and 6, or Series 807, Nos. 1, 2, 4, and 6, are excellent, as are Crumbacher Series 320, Nos. 3, 6 and 14. Tempera brushes should also be examined carefully when purchased (see Chapter 14) to make certain that there are no loose ferrules or loose hairs. After being bent, as for use, they should immediately spring back into a straight position. (Note: Be sure that you purchase short hair, thin "brights" with square, straight edges—not "longs.")

2. *Round "pencil" brushes:* These are water color–type brushes which should be reserved for tempera work. Nos. 1, 4, and 6 in sable or camel's hair will be found useful.

3. *Flat bristle oil color brushes:* Because tempera is a thick paint, rendering brushes should never be used for mixing. Bristle brushes are excellent for this purpose and are available in many makes, all quite inexpensive. A No. 4 is about the right size, but a No. 7 will also be found helpful.

4. *Stipple (Stencil) brushes:* Flat-ended stipple brushes, Winsor & Newton, Inc., or equal, Nos. 0 and 1, are helpful for texturing.

Every brush should be washed out in clean water immediately after it has been used. Brushes which are permitted to dry with paint in the bristles quickly become useless. As suggested in Chapter 14, they should be stored dry in boxes with moth balls.

Mixing and Storing Equipment

Because tempera is an opaque paint (unlike transparent water color) it can be mixed in metallic (unpainted) containers. Wash dishes of enamel, iron, or plastic, of course, may be used, but since it is necessary to keep a small quantity of each color until the rendering has been completed, it is advisable to obtain an aluminum muffin tin with as many large cups as possible—preferably at least a dozen.

Palette: An excellent large size palette can be made of a flat, white enamel tray (one with slightly turned-up edges) similar to those used in butcher shops. Tempera palettes may also be made of opaque white pad paper or white illustration board.

Water container: The same type of water container recommended for water color rendering can be used for tempera work. It should contain at least a quart of water, preferably more.

Miscellaneous Items

Additional equipment for tempera rendering should include:
1. 1 doz. white blotters
2. 1 silk or "baby" sponge
3. 1 doz. or more wooden spoons or wooden tongue depressors for removing paint from jars
4. Ruling pen
Artist's cabinet (as described in Chapter 8)

Color Experimentation

If you have not used tempera before, you should become familiar with the colors that you have purchased. Place a small amount of each pigment on an inexpensive illustration board or a piece of water color paper. Look at each color, and compare it with its neighbors. Now mix each one with an increasing amount of white and notice the changes that take place. Add a small amount of black and note the changes that this produces. You will observe that the addition of white sometimes changes the color instead of merely lightening it, while the addition of black frequently produces a surprising new color. Black added to yellow, for instance, produces a kind of green, because there is a great deal of blue in the black. For the same reason, black tempera added to red or orange produces a purplish color. All of these things must be taken into consideration in mixing tempera.

Practice Washes

In general it may be said that the building is usually rendered in a series of flat base washes which are modified by lines or textures placed over them. Therefore, before proceeding further it is advisable to practice making washes. To begin with, tempera should be mixed with just enough water to produce a mixture of a creamy consistency. It is meant to be opaque and should, if the wash is applied correctly, completely cover the surface of the paper so that none of it will show through. Washes are best applied with flat brushes.

Using a sheet of 15- x 20-in. illustration board, draw a ½-in. border around the outside edge in pencil and divide the upper half into ten equal spaces with ⅟₁₆ in. between them, using an "H" pencil, T-square, and triangle. Divide the lower portion in the same way, with a 2-in. space between the upper and lower rectangles (Fig. 15.1). Label each rectangle with the name of a color. The top rectangles will receive flat washes in full intensity, the lower rectangles will receive graded washes.

Beginning with spectrum yellow, for instance, one would proceed as follows: Place the desired amount of Chinese white in one of the

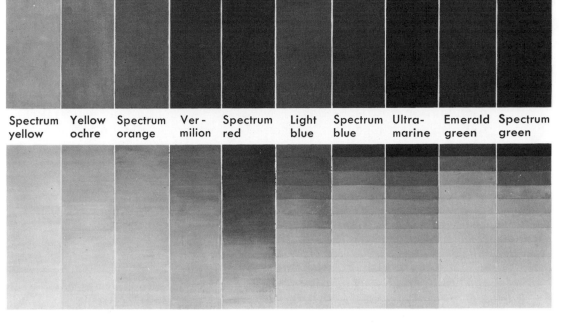

Spectrum yellow	Yellow ochre	Spectrum orange	Ver-milion	Spectrum red	Light blue	Spectrum blue	Ultra-marine	Emerald green	Spectrum green

A. Flat

B. Graded

Fig. 15.1   Practice Washes in Tempera

cups of your muffin tin and add the color to it drop by drop, mixing as you do with the bristle brush until you think you have achieved the shade that you want. Because tempera colors are very strong, only a few drops, or a small bit from a tube, will stain a large amount of white to the value that you wish. If you were to begin with the color and add Chinese white, it might be necessary to use an entire jar of white before the right color was obtained. The author remembers several occasions when enough color to paint a small house was mixed by a student in this way, and almost everyone in the class made use of the color.

Using the raised edge of a T-square and one of the smaller conical brushes, or a ruling pen, surround each area with a fine line in its proper color. This assures straight edges. Then, dipping a flat brush into the tempera, and removing the excess on the edge of the cup, begin to paint at the top with short (¼- to ½-in.) vertical overlapping brush strokes, brushing the thick paint out as you do so. Brush hard, as if this were your last bit of paint. Work from left to right, and when you have covered the entire upper edge, add more paint to your brush and repeat the procedure, overlapping the first strokes with those of the second row. Repeat this process until the bottom of the rectangle has been reached. Leave no white spaces, but also refrain from touching surfaces that have been painted before they dry, since this will result in a scarred surface. It will take a few minutes for each rectangle to dry, and when it does it should be completely opaque and smooth. Do not be surprised if some of the washes are not completely opaque; this takes some practice and experience. The fault may be corrected by placing a second wash over the first, identical except for the addition of a little more water.

The building-up process can be repeated to produce an opaque quality or to correct mistakes in rendering until about three coats have been placed upon the sheet. After that the paint will probably begin to crack and flake off the paper. If such a problem occurs, mask the area with drafting tape and paper, making sure that the tape is securely fastened, and then sponge the tempera from the paper with a damp sponge. It may be necessary to wash the sponge several times, but almost all of the tempera can be removed in this way. When the area has dried it may be rendered upon as before.

By this time you will probably have noticed that tempera dries darker than it appears in the liquid state. This can be quite a problem, since the success of a rendering depends heavily upon obtaining the right shades for each portion of it. Therefore it is advisable, before using any tempera paint, to brush a small amount of it on a piece of white paper and to dry it quickly —by lighting a match and passing it back and forth under the paint. The edges of the paint usually dry first and the true color may be seen here. Be careful not to burn the paint and change its color; a hair dryer is safer.

Graded Washes For the most part, tempera is not meant to be graded when used on the building itself. It can, however, be used in this way, perhaps not so successfully as transparent water color, by the wet-into-wet method and the French method. The first five rectangles at the bottom of Fig. 15.1 should be used for practicing the wet-into-wet method, the second five for the French method. For the wet-into-wet method, proceed as follows:

Surround a rectangle with drafting tape and paper, making sure that the tape is firmly in place (Fig. 15.2). Place an amount of color, say spectrum yellow, for the first rectangle, in a cup. Place a similar amount of Chinese white in another cup, using a wooden spoon to handle the color if jar color is being used. Using a bristle brush, mix a sufficient amount of water with the pure color so that it is of a creamy consistency. Take a brushful of this, and, using a horizontal stroke, cover about ¾ in. at the top of the rectangle. Using a mixing brush, take a small amount of Chinese white and mix it with the yellow that you have just used (in the cup). After it has been mixed thoroughly, add a brushful to the first wash, and again in horizontal strokes brush it gently into the bottom edge of the first wash. Repeat this process about every ¾ in. until you have reached the bottom of the rectangle. Now do the same for the remaining four colors.

Note: Be sure that the paint is dry before the drafting tape is removed, and remove each piece gently and slowly by pulling it downward and to the side at the same time so that you do not scar the surface of the board.

Fig. 15.2 Framing the Wash

Fig. 15.3 Washes by the French Method

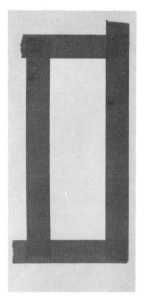

For the French method, proceed as follows:

Prepare a creamy mixture of a color—say light blue—to begin with, in one cup, and an equal amount of Chinese white in another. Divide each rectangle into ½-in. increments, and draw lines at these points with a pencil and T-square (Fig. 15.3). To grade from dark to light, introduce a small amount of blue into the white and stir with the bristle mixing brush until it has been mixed thoroughly. Surround the upper increment with this color by resting a small conical brush on the edge of a T-square as a guide, and then fill in the surrounding space with the same color. Add another small amount of blue to the mixture, stir it thoroughly and repeat the process for the second increment, but not before the first increment is dry. Repeat the process for the entire height of the rectangle and you will achieve an excellent gradation. Repeat the process for the remaining four colors.

After this exercise is completed, clean your brushes immediately; otherwise the paint will dry so hard that it will be almost impossible to remove it. Take the muffin tin and brushes to a sink and dump out all of the liquid paint, then run clean cold water into each cup in turn, scrubbing with the largest bristle brush that you have. (Note: Do not use warm water; it does not soften the pigment so well as cold water.) Now clean each brush in turn, swishing it around in clean water and then squeezing the excess from the brush gently with your fingers.

As mentioned earlier, it is advisable to preserve some of each color for damage repair until the rendering has been completed. Tempera dries quickly and becomes a hard, cracked substance in the bottom of the container that it is in. It cannot easily be returned to a liquid state by adding water to it. Therefore, after each work session, add a few drops of water to each color (no more), mix it in with a clean bristle brush, then wet the area around the top of each cup with some of the paint. Finally, press a piece of heavy tracing paper over the top of the entire muffin tin. The paint will dry between the muffin tin and the tracing paper, forming a seal. This will keep the color for about one day. When you are ready to use it again, merely puncture the tracing paper and tear it away from each cup.

The textures described herein are for surfaces in sunlight. Generally speaking, the color that is used for a surface in sunlight is darkened for shade and shadow by adding more of each pigment, and in particular, more of the darker colors in the palette being used.

Using a 20- x 30-in. piece of white illustration board, draw a ½-in. border around the outside edge in pencil and divide the remaining 29-in. width into 11 equal spaces, with ⅛-in. space between each two. If a line is drawn 8½ in. down from the top border this will produce 11 equal rectangles in which textures can be practiced (see Fig. 15.4). Beneath each rectangle letter one of the following: wood siding made with ruling pen, wood siding made with small brush, wall shingles, stucco and concrete, brick at small scale, brick at large scale, brick at very large scale, cut stone, rubble coursed, rubble uncoursed, metal.

The color of the wood, of course, will vary with its finish, but for a natural finish wood, make a pale mixture of white, yellow, green, and a small amount of alizarin crimson. Lay a flat, opaque wash of this color in the first

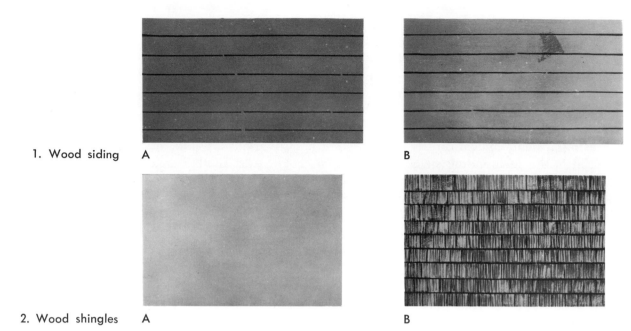

1. Wood siding   A   B

2. Wood shingles   A   B

Fig. 15.4   Textures in Tempera

rectangle. When it is dry, using ¼-in. scale and a graphite pencil, draw the siding across the wash at 8 in. to weather (8 in. exposure of each board). Now mix a darker wash using the same pigment with perhaps a small amount of cobalt blue. With a ruling pen draw the shadows under the butts in the upper half of the rectangle (see Fig. 15.4, Sketch 1A). For practice, draw the shadows in another rectangle with your smallest conical brush, guided by the raised edge of your T-square (Fig. 15.4, Sketch 1B).

Clapboards

Clapboards can be indicated in the same manner as siding in the second rectangle, but should be drawn to indicate 5 in. of exposure.

Wall Shingles

While the actual color of the shingles to be rendered will vary according to the job, an adequate base color for this exercise can be made by mixing ultramarine blue, alizarin crimson, cadmium orange, and yellow ochre with white. Place a base tone upon the paper as described above, then draw the wood shingles at ¼-in. scale upon this with a sharp "HB" pencil. Using a small brush and a darker mixture of the same paint used for the base tone, draw the butts of the shingles with short, broken, wavy lines (Fig. 15.4, Sketch 2). Then draw occasional vertical spaces between the shingles with straight freehand lines or straight lines drawn with the aid of the raised edge of a T-square. If additional variation in color and value seems desirable, these may be introduced by mixing small amounts of the same colors used in the base tone on a paper palette, picking out a few shingles in lighter and darker tones.

Stucco, Concrete, and Dressed Stone Ashlar

An excellent color for stucco, concrete, or cut stone in sunlight can be made by mixing a small amount of white with No. 2 gray. If this gray is unavailable, it can easily be mixed by adding yellow ochre, cobalt blue, and alizarin crimson to white. A flat tone of this color will suffice for stucco or concrete. For cut stone, the joints should be lined in with a graphite pencil, T-square, and triangle, and these then covered with an off-white tempera in a ruling pen or with a small brush used with the raised edge of the T-square as a guide (Fig. 15.4, Sketch 3).

A

B

C　　　　　　　　　　　3. Stone ashlar

The type of indication for brickwork will depend upon the scale of the drawing. At small scale (⅛ in. or less, Fig. 15.5, Sketch 1) a wash of the brick color is first applied to the area and the joints ruled over it in pencil at about four courses to 11 in. Brick, of course, varies in color, but for this exercise make a pale terra cotta mixture using white, yellow ochre, vermilion, and cobalt blue. The joint color will be a pale gray, mixed with white and a small amount of the same colors.

At larger scale (¼ in. = 1 ft) place a wash of light, warm gray over the entire rectangle, then with a T-square and pencil draw all of the courses at four courses to 11 in. Now, using a ruling pen or fine brush, and with a T-square as a guide, brush or rule in each course of brick, breaking the lines of each course fairly even, by leaving the width of a joint between them (Fig. 15.5, Sketch 2).

For very large scale brickwork (½ in. or larger) give the area a wash of joint color, draw the individual bricks in pencil with T-square and triangle, then mix an average color for the brick and paint most of them individually. Modify this color by adding more pigment or more white, painting in the remaining bricks in varying tones (Fig. 15.5, Sketch 3).

Brickwork

Fig. 15.5　Other Textures in Tempera

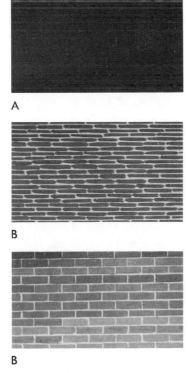

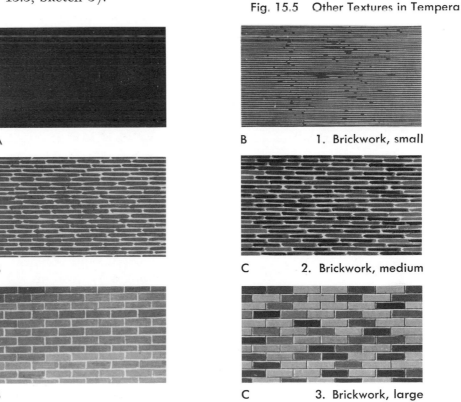

A　　　B　　　1. Brickwork, small

A　　　B　　　2. Brickwork, medium

A　　　B　　　3. Brickwork, large

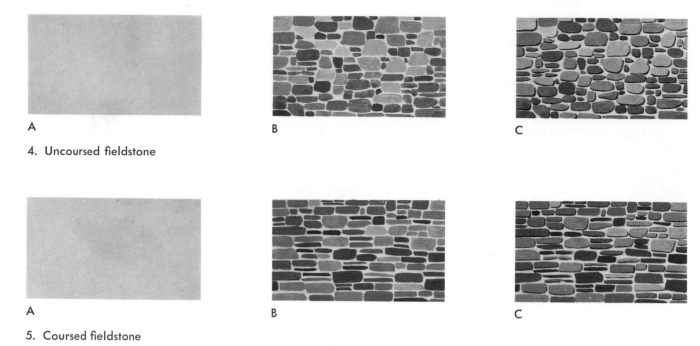

A

4. Uncoursed fieldstone

B

C

A

5. Coursed fieldstone

B

C

Fig. 15.5   Other Textures in Tempera

Rubble (Coursed and Uncoursed)

Place a wash of pale gray (the joint color) over the entire area. Then carefully draw every stone in pencil, using horizontal pencil lines as a general guide. Place a small amount of each of the colors in your palette—in this case, those used for cut stone—on a piece of *white* illustration board, and, with a medium-sized conical brush, draw the several colors and white together to form an average stone color. Place this color upon half a dozen widely dispersed stones. Now modify the average color by adding more of one pigment than the other so that the next wash is warmer than the first, and paint another half dozen stones. Vary the color again and repeat the process. Continue until every stone has been covered. Now mix a darker tone than any that you have used, and with the smallest conical brush draw an occasional shadow under and next to a number of stones (Fig. 15.5, Sketches 4 and 5).

Metal

Like all building materials, metals vary in color. Aluminum usually has a warm gray tone; stainless steel a tone that is more bluish. For this exercise mix a small amount of cobalt blue with some Chinese white and water and place a base tone upon the rectangle. Then make another mixture of white, blue, and a *small* amount of black, and apply the joints with a fine brush or ruling pen, using a T-square as a guide.

Multiple Glass Openings

Small glass openings are painted exactly as described in Chapter 14 for water color. Large openings are painted as for water color, except that when there are large banks of windows the entire glass area is first painted a general tone, or for skyscrapers, a graded tone, and when this is dry, the mullions, muntins, and spandrels are superimposed upon it (Fig. 15.6).

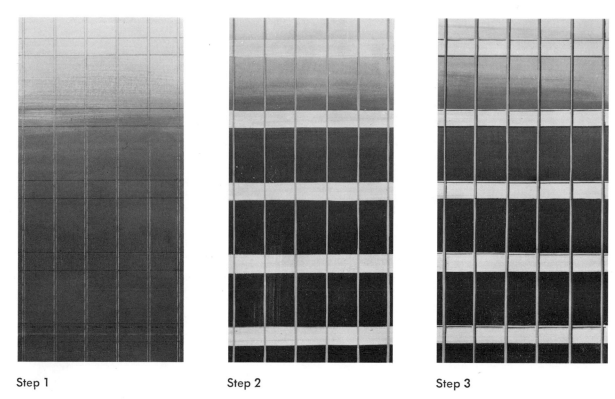

Step 1   Step 2   Step 3

Fig. 15.6   Multiple Glass Openings

Entourage

Whereas in transparent water color rendering it is necessary to leave white spaces wherever trees and bushes are to be placed, tempera trees and bushes may be painted over areas that have previously been painted. All trees and bushes are painted from a palette. Small amounts of each of the several colors being used are placed so that they may be drawn together with a wet brush, and this thick color is then applied directly to previously pencilled trees and bushes. The opaque quality of the paint allows for a building-up process.

Background trees are generally painted in light, flat, pale washes with soft edges to suggest leaves (Fig. 15.7, Sketch 1). These are always painted in first. The tops of the background trees should be of irregular shape. Mid-distance trees are next applied. These are detailed in structure, darker in value, and darker in hue (Fig. 15.7, Sketch 2). The foliage masses are carefully drawn, then painted with flat washes, again with soft edges. Some delineators prefer to stipple this color on with a flat brush.

Fig. 15.7   Trees in Tempera

1. Background trees

Wet-into-wet   Separate planes

| 2. Mid-distance trees | Foliage dabbed with 3/16″ flat dry brush | Flat wash | Foliage painted on damp paper with ½″ flat charged brush |

| 3. Foreground trees | Overhanging branches | Framing foreground trees |

Fig. 15.7   Trees in Tempera

As in transparent water color rendering, the foreground trees and bushes are painted quite completely in detail (Fig. 15.7, Sketch 3). The structure and bark texture are shown in considerable detail; branches and twigs are shown completely and as realistically as possible to help create the illusion of reality. As in all media, it is important not to hide the design of the building with foliage masses, but rather to arrange them so that the building is either framed by them or seen through them.

The trunks of large trees can be rounded by working wet-into-wet: first paint the light side of the tree its proper pale color, and then add darker color on the opposite side and blend it into the light color. It is sometimes desirable to paint several branches of a tree as if they are hanging from a tree located behind the spectator. These are usually painted quite dark and help to push the building back into the mid-distance. In all trees in tempera one should use several different shades of the same color in foliage masses so as to relieve monotony and to create the illusion of light, local color, shade and shadow.

Grass   Grass is generally given a sunny quality. It may be painted wet-into-wet, by starting at the horizon and painting forward, changing the color now and then in order to relieve the monotony, and to create the illusion of perspective (Fig. 15.11). The spaces between these variations should be graduated so that they are smallest near the horizon and largest near the spectator. Usually grass is darkest in the foreground and lightest in the distance. Tree shadows upon it will add to the illusion of reality, and describe the rise and fall of the ground. These should be relatively pale in value, except in the immediate foreground, where they should be quite dark.

In tempera work skies are used only when they enhance the design being studied. There are many occasions when a sky is not necessary, or when it is insignificant in its plainness. Basically there are four different types of skies:

(a) Flat: This is made with a wash of a single tone or color (Fig. 15.9 and Plate VII).

(b) Flat sky with clouds (Fig. 15.11).

(c) Graded or domed (Fig. 15.10 and Plate VI). Graded skies such as these can be painted in the same way as described for wet-into-wet graded washes, or by a series of rough-edged flat washes as in Plate XI, with the lightest flat wash at the horizon, and the darkest at the top of the picture. It is advisable when painting in a sky other than that for a flat wash to mask the top edge of the building with drafting tape and paper to assure a clean line at the top of the building.

(d) Airbrush: By masking in the same way as described above and covering the entire building as described in Chapter 16, skies may easily be sprayed with an airbrush, but more about this later.

Making a Tempera Rendering

The perspective line drawing is applied to the paper or illustration board by the method described in Chapter 4. A value study and a color study must be made for each project, and an exploration of the color scheme selected should be made before the rendering is begun, as described in Chapter 14. With the exception of buildings on colored paper, it is advisable to cover all portions of the paper with tempera, even though some areas are apparently white, since the portions not covered in such drawings have a different appearance than the tempera.

Generally speaking, a tempera rendering should proceed in the following way:

1. The sunny walls of the building should be given their main wash.

2. The shade side of each building should be given its main wash.

3. Shadow areas should be applied.

4. The interior furniture, furnishings, wall and ceiling colors should be applied in glass areas. The general tone of curtains is painted as a flat wash and then the shaping of the curtains is done.

5. Mullions and muntins are painted over glass areas.

6. Doors, louvers, and grilles are painted in.

7. Wall textures are applied with brush or ruling pen.

8. Crooked edges are corrected and straightened.

9. The sky is applied.

10. The grass areas are indicated.

11. The background trees are painted.

12. Trees and foliage in the mid-distance are applied.

13. Foreground trees, bushes, and shadows are painted and tree and building shadows on the ground are indicated.

14. Scale figures and automobiles are indicated last. The following renderings illustrate various techniques developed for tempera rendering.

Fig. 15.8

An apartment house
rendered by Ralph Medcalfe
Student project

All parts of the building were rendered with flat washes. In this case the entire building was rendered first. The sash areas were painted in several shades of grayed blue so as to provide the illusion of light reflection. Because the fins between the sash were so large, each sash area was rendered separately. Some of these were painted dark, some medium blue, others light blue so as to relieve monotony. The face and the front edges of the fins were next painted with a mixture of off-white. The sides of the fins were given a tone of light gray, and the shade and shadow areas of the fins were painted in shades of blue-gray.

After the canopy and columns were painted, the window mullions and muntins were drawn in with a ruling pen and white, while the texture of the concrete was drawn with a ruling pen and dark color. The pale blue, slightly domed, sky was sprayed with an airbrush after the entire building had been masked with drafting tape and tracing paper. The foreground was painted directly from a palette with horizontal strokes, and the small amount of shrubbery was also painted directly by brush.

Fig. 15.9
A church
rendered by Robert Burley
Student project

Fig. 15.10

Office building
rendered by Rishon S. Rosen
Student project

Mr. Rosen's rendering is particularly successful because of the contrast between the precise handling of the building and the freely painted graded sky and surrounding buildings. It was rendered as follows:

The general tan tones of the light and shade sides of the building were mixed and applied as flat washes. The light tan color of the fins was next painted, then the shade and shadow areas between and on the fins were applied in gray. The shadows on the light side were next painted rather freely in gray and the lettering and shadows were applied.

The surrounding buildings were painted directly from the palette, in tones of blue, green and deep orange, the general light tone being first applied, before the shade and shadow areas. The same method was used for the blue and green automobiles in the foreground. The sky was applied wet-into-wet after the building had been masked with drafting tape and tracing paper. Using the widest brush available, a mixture was made on the palette of blue with a small amount of white, and this was applied at the top of the picture in long, horizontal strokes. It was carried down approximately to the top of the building and then additional white was added to the blue on the palette. It was mixed with the blue and again applied into the edge of the first wash and carried down for several inches. During this process some of the white of the paper was allowed to show through the paint. Finally more white was added, and the mixture was brushed into the still wet medium graded wash and carried down again with horizontal strokes, finally being scrubbed with the almost dry brush into the bottom portion of the sky. In this particular case the white of the sky received no color at all.

The building was rendered by a series of washes mixed in pans. Some areas, such as those on the light brown underside of the building, were later graded by the application of slightly darker washes near the front edge. The white front of the building surround was applied first, then the gray shade side of the building was indicated. The green and brown walls, warm gray ceiling, yellow and vermilion furniture and scale figures were painted in the open glass area; then the general pale yellow tone of the curtains was applied with a flat wash. Pale orange mullions were next drawn in with a ruling pen, and the shadow cast by the roof overhangs was applied to mullions, curtains, and wood panel. Of course the shadows were dark tones of the materials they fell upon, dark yellow on yellow curtains, dark orange on light maize mullions etc. The drape of the curtains was next painted by using a T-square and a fine brush. Finally the entire wooden and brick structure under the building was painted and textured. The brick wall, in this case, was first given a general light red brick color and the joints were applied with a ruling pen and a darker tone of the same color.

The grass areas were painted with a mixture of yellow, black, and white to obtain the various shades of green. The background trees were indicated in light uneven washes, later stippled with darker tones. The trees and bushes in the mid-distance were next indicated in yellow green. The foliage on the white birch trees was stippled with a fairly dry brush. The foliage in the mid-distance was painted directly from the palette with a series of short stippling strokes, using a flat brush. Flat, or nearly flat, washes and short grasslike strokes were used for making the lawn, and flowers were painted with a small "pencil" brush in a rather loose way.

Plate VII

A residence
rendered by **Harry B. Mahler**
Size: 14 x 21 in.
Student project

COLOR SCHEME: *Analogous*
PALETTE: *Vermilion, cadmium yellow pale, black, white—plus the green of the paper*
MATERIAL USED: *Dark green charcoal paper*

KEMPA AND SCHWARTZ · ARCHITECTS · J. H. LIVINGSTONE · ASSOCIATE

Plate VIII

A study for the American
Baptist Denomination
rendered by Robert Schwartz
Architects: Kempa & Schwartz;
J. H. Livingstone, Associate
Size: 26 x 16 in.

Plate IX

Passenger facilities for
Iberia and Icelandic
Airlines, New York Inter-
national Airport
Kempa & Schwartz, Architects
rendered by Emil Kempa
Size: 30 x 19½ in.

Plate X

**United Fuel & Gas Co.,
Charleston, W. Va.
Architect: Douglas Orr
rendered by George Cooper
Rudolph
Size: 40 x 26 in.**

Mr. Rudolph's rendering creates a sunny quality by presenting a sharp contrast between the light of the building and the dark of the sky. Notice that the brilliance of the many colored sunny side of the building is echoed by light cloud edges. Notice also the cloud reflections in the large glass area, which add to the realism and break the monotony of the sash pattern. See how the eye is drawn to the entrance by the red automobile placed near it. The reflections in the canal of the shrubs on the bank, together with a dark ripple in the water, help to create a magnificently transparent, liquid feeling in contrast with the sharp, realistic quality of the building.

This gay rendering is full of excitement and anticipation of the building's interior. Since the inside of the building is the most important part of the presentation, such a project can best be rendered as a night scene. Yellowish light is allowed to spill over the sidewalks, and numerous figures walking by are silhouetted against it. The exciting variation of tone and color helps to create the illusion of reality. To give it one final realistic touch, the building is reflected in a wet street. Searchlight beams help to suggest movement and excitement.

In order to achieve a concentration of light in the showroom, colors and values are muted in surrounding areas. The farther a surface is from the light area, the darker it is. Surrounding buildings are shown gray or dull reddish brown so that they look old compared to the proposed new building. Generally speaking, these colors are made by mixing all of the colors of the palette together. Such dull colors form a splendid foil for the bright colors in the new building.

Plate XI

Proposed auto showroom for Park Avenue office building Carson & Lundin and Kahn & Jacobs, Associated architects rendered by Pierre Lutz Size: 40 x 30 in.

Plate XII

**The Seagram Building
New York City
Mies van der Rohe and
Philip Johnson, Architects
Kahn & Jacobs, Associate
Architects
rendered by Elliot Glushak
Size: 25 x 35½ in.**

This rendering illustrates a number of problems typical of skyscraper presentations. To obtain an illusion of reality, one must take into consideration not only the difference in the way that glass is seen in various parts of the building (Chapter 6) but also reflections of other buildings, clouds, and cloud shadows. The lines of the building must be clearly expressed without monotony, and it must be shown in its setting in as believable a manner as possible. This requires an extremely careful study of the site and the buildings around it. Note that the light source places the buildings to the right

This is an example of quite a successful vignetted rendering. It was made as follows: The light side of the building was applied with a flat wash of warm gray. The shade (wood) side was first given a base coat of light brown. When this was dry, the boards were applied, in dark brown with a small, flat brush used on the edge of a T-square. The brush was dipped into the darker paint before each stroke; sometimes the brush was allowed to be almost dry, creating the effect of wood. Portions of the undercoat were purposely not covered.

The light blue glass areas were painted in a combination of pan-mixed and palette-mixed colors. Each area was given a general tone, which was later modified by a lighter or darker tone. The area inside the open windows was purposely painted dark blue (it always is dark when one can "see" inside such a small opening). The underside of the building was next given its shade tone—a grayish brown—and the foreground, with varying shades of a pale yellowish green and dark green, was painted in horizontal strokes.

The sky was painted before the background trees were applied by first wetting the area over which clouds were to be applied, then dropping pigment into it, and when dry scrubbing blue and white areas to simulate clouds and open sky.

The background trees were purposely constructed so that they did not parallel the shape of the building. They were applied in three steps:

1. A medium green tone was applied in a dabbing motion over the entire tree area with water color brush of the pencil type, leaving open areas between the various spots of foliage.

2. The tree at the left was applied in the same way in a darker tone of green.

3. Finally, light leaves in pale yellow and greenish white were dabbed in with a small pencil water color brush over the previously applied areas. The blue-green background trees were done in much the same way, while the foreground bush was applied with a flat brush, using a dabbing motion, and the three different tones described above.

---

of the new structure in shade, while the buildings behind the new structure are in shadow, the two dark areas forming a frame for the light building. The structures in the background are kept extremely light so that they will not become confused with the block under consideration. The foreground is shown as meticulously as possible and includes groups of figures moving toward the entranceway, and automobiles passing by it. Again, tire tracks are shown in the streets to add realism. The sky is painted in varying shades of blue and given a cloudy, busy appearance to offset the otherwise plain quality of the building.

Fig. 15.11

A residence
rendered by Samuel C. Wang
Student project

Fig. 15.12

Living room
rendered by John MacRerry
Student project

It is usual in rendering an interior view to assume that the room is generally lighted by interior illumination as well as by an outside source. When glass areas are present, landscape that can be seen through these glass areas should be painted in first, remembering that anything seen through glass becomes lighter in value than it really is. In addition, it is usual to assume that a landscape seen through such glass areas is darkest in the foreground and lightest in the distance. In this rendering the stone area of the wall was first given a general wash of the joint color, pale gray. The stones were then painted directly from a palette, by mixing first an average grayed blue stone color and applying this over a number of stones, then varying the general tone, making it now warmer and now cooler (Fig. 15.5, Sketch 5), so that an interesting variation occurs.

Some dark gray shadows were applied on the underside of a number of stones in order to create the illusion of depth and form.

Ceiling areas: A flat wash of the lightest tone of the grayed orange ceiling was applied over the entire ceiling area. The color of the roof boards was then varied by masking the roof area with tape and brushing the various boards on with a flat brush, working directly from the palette, and using a T-square to guide the brush. The roof rafters were then drawn in place with pencil, and their sides were given a medium tone of orange brown. The undersides of the rafters were made lighter because they would normally receive reflected light from the floor. It should be noticed that the rafters were purposely graded so that those in the foreground are darkest and those in the background lightest.

The floor was painted with a flat wash of medium brown, carefully painted around the furniture. The furniture (deep red, medium blue, and off-white) was rendered by painting the general values first, with careful value distinctions between the sides and tops of the pieces. Where necessary, the furniture was "modeled" by using a slightly lighter or darker tone of the main color and a rather dry brush. When this had been completed, buttons, stripes, nail patterns, etc. were applied with a small pencil water color brush. The light wood table, orange-gray book, ashtray, and a red cigarette box were added after the general table values had been applied. The yellow flowers and blue lamp were painted directly from the palette. The shadows of the furniture on the floor were applied last.

A successful rendering is usually full of comparisons—of value, color, and texture. The three are almost inseparable—each makes the others important by its own presence. In this rendering, warm autumn colors within the room itself were contrasted with the cool blue sky and green and blue hills outside. After the pencil drawing had been placed upon the paper, a charcoal study was made, and in this stage it was decided that reflected light should bathe the interior.

Before the sky and mountains were painted, the edge of the fireplace, columns and roof were masked with drafting tape and paper. Then the sky was painted long continuous sweeping strokes from left to right. The same sense of continuity was obtained in the mountains because of the masking. Without it, of course, it would have been necessary to paint the sky and mountains in pieces, and the landscape would have lacked cohesion.

The left portion underside of the roof deck was given a flat wash of warm brown, the right side a slightly deeper tone of the same. The undersides of the beams were made quite light since a great deal of light would ricochet from the floor. The sides of the girder and beams were painted varying shades of deep brown. Joints between the roof boards were drawn over the base tone with brown and a ruling pen. The floor was painted around the furniture—very light near the glass area to simulate sunlight, quite dark for the rest—the joints being drawn over the base coat with brown and a small pointed brush. The various sides of the sofa were rendered in flat washes, and the seat and top were textured by dabbing with a pale yellow and a small brush. The stone fireplace was given a coat of gray, then a number of stones were painted in darker grays and browns over it. The copper hood was painted wet-into-wet directly from a paper palette, using shades of yellow, orange, vermilion and brown. Finally, the curtain was painted in a grayed yellow with a dry-brush technique, stroking from top to bottom.

Fig. 15.13

A Living Room
rendered by Robert Burley
Student project

Fig. 15.14

Lobby of Building for
The United Nations
New York City
Architects: United Nations
Headquarters Planning Staff,
Wallace K. Harrison, Director
rendered by Frederick Nugent
Student project

When rendering an interior such as this lobby, the architectural elements within the building should be treated in a sharp, precise manner, and those outside (such as surrounding buildings, trees, grass, and plant areas), should be low in value and soft in hue. This keeps the spectator's interest where it belongs—inside the building. In this case, the entire area outside was rendered before the interior was begun. The end wall was given a wash of light gray obtained by mixing a little of each of the colors with plenty of white. When this was dry the stone coursing was expressed by painting a number of stones over the base tone, leaving some of it to show as a joint color. The glass area on the side of the building was painted loosely direct from a palette, varying the glass area from gray-blue to greenish blue to gray, etc. When this was dry, glass and spandrel joints were ruled and brushed over the glass area. Sky, planting areas, lawn, and walks were next painted, purposely keeping them pale.

The interior was begun by painting the columns (a thick mixture of vermilion and white) directly over the outside work, with a quarter inch flat sable brush. Two coats were necessary to obtain complete opacity. The inside edges of the columns, the shadows on the columns and the window mullions were painted with a fairly dark mixture of vermilion, yellow and blue. The ceiling and steps were given a coat of light brown; the columns were painted darker tones of the same color. The marble graining was painted over the base color with a small conical brush, using white and brown. The floor was made pale yellow; the column and wall shadows on it were a deep tone of grayed yellow.

Where several people are working with the same media and materials, it is always interesting to observe that each one will develop a style vitally different from the style of his fellows. Robert Schwartz, of the firm of Kempa and Schwartz, has developed a style which is singularly his own. His work is sharp and crisp, and he obtains a reality that is impressive. He achieves a luminosity in his buildings by a sharp contrast between the rather light values of his buildings and the much darker values of the entourage. His skies are usually domed from light at the horizon to dark at the top. Some have a horizontal quality, with long clouds; others have wispy, whitish clouds painted over the sky. His trees are always very realistic—quite dark in the foreground, lighter in the mid-distance, and still lighter in the distance. His foregrounds are carefully detailed. He varies color and value of grass areas and roadways by streaking them with lighter and darker tones of yellow green and green. For additional realism, brush strokes are used to simulate tire tracks. All of the relatively dark blue and green surrounding areas are closely related in tone so that they form a frame in which the light, brilliant building is displayed, a setting which displays the building as a brilliant jewel.

The beauty of Mr. Schwartz's renderings is far from accidental. It is the result of a calculated study of value and color. An analysis of his various presentations displayed in this book shows this. All of the renderings, even

Fig. 15.15

Residence
Blue Harbor Colony
Bright Waters, N.Y.
Kempa & Schwartz, Architects
rendered by Robert Schwartz

the finest lines, are painted by Mr. Schwartz with a brush and straightedge; the ruling pen is never used. His palette:

Spectrum yellow	Prussian blue
Yellow ochre	Thald green
Burnt sienna	Black
Red (spectrum)	White
Designer's magenta	

Emil Kempa, of the firm of Kempa and Schwartz, also works with a similar palette and technique. The same kind of luminosity is present in his work (Plate IX and Fig. 15.16).

Fig. 15.16

Ticket offices for
Iberia Airlines
Kempa & Schwartz, Architects
rendered by Emil Kempa

Notice that the design under consideration has been carefully framed by darkened surrounding tones. In the ticket offices for Iberia Airlines, it is further enhanced by an exciting street scene with silhouetted figures moving about and gay reflections in the street. All these things, together with the bright colors of the office interior, create a mood designed to remind one instantly of the pleasures of holiday travel and adventure. Imagine how ordinary this presentation could have been had it not been so brilliantly planned and executed!

George Cooper Rudolph of Rudolph Associates is known for the brilliance and sunny quality of his renderings and for the free watercolorlike technique used in his trees, bushes and skies. He believes that no element in a project is more important than the presentation of the design to the client, and that specialists in delineation are as necessary as specialists in the various categories of design.

This rendering illustrates the method for executing an aerial view. The building occupies the major portion of the rendering and its off-white and warm gray tones are generally the lightest in the picture. One is "allowed" to look into the glazed areas, to see things inside, and is encouraged by the nearby scale figures to look at the entrance. The automobiles and trees are distributed with an eye to variety in location and color, while the building itself is separated from the background by the use of a deep purple-gray shadow and dark green trees. The shadow across the foreground forces the building back into the mid-distance, and the background shadow holds it firmly in place.

Fig. 15.17
An aerial view of development for Abraham & Straus Babylon, N.Y.
John Graham & Co., architects and engineers
Daniel Schwartzman, Architect
rendered by
George Cooper Rudolph

Fig. 15.18

A house
Eldridge Snyder, Architect
rendered by
George Cooper Rudolph

An analysis of this rendering illustrates a purposeful comparison of values. Dark green trees are used behind light building areas, light trees behind dark areas. Notice the way that the windows are handled: they are a combination of reflected sky, interior furnishings, and darkness, to indicate inner space. The lawn, for the greater part, is yellow-green, with yellow streaks to add interest and relieve monotony. The sky is off-white with gray-blue clouds.

One of the simplest, yet most sophisticated color schemes—one color, plus black, gray, and white—was used by Mr. Rudolph in this excellent study. The color, of course, is that of the paper itself, which is golden in hue. Time and effort were saved by using the paper color for the paving, a great portion of the furniture, for the roof in sunlight, the underside of the roof overhang, and for the sky. This technique is similar to that described in Chapter 10, in which carbon pencil and Chinese white are combined.

A great deal of charm was obtained by skillful selection of the point of view, the spectator's eye being led from the outdoor furniture to the planting behind it, thence to the interior of the building at the rear, and finally to the right wing. What appears at first to be a sketchy presentation turns out, upon closer analysis, to be a carefully conceived design study.

Fig. 15.19

A residence reprinted by permission of *Good Housekeeping* Cliff May, designer rendered by George Cooper Rudolph

Comparative Renderings

It is sometimes necessary to prepare a number of comparative renderings to illustrate variations in a basic design. See Plate XIII and Plate XIV.

These renderings are particularly meritorious in that the buildings are all shown in rich, colorful autumn settings. It is interesting to note that clients are attracted to buildings that are bathed in bright sunlight. The foregrounds in all cases are dark yet somewhat transparent. The grass surrounding the houses seems full of sunlight; the trees vary from dark green through red-orange and autumn yellow. Where skies are shown, they are a clear blue. Note that as a result of Mr. Rahill's careful planning, the colors of the trees near the house, in each case, vary in order to complement the building. For example, in Plate XIII, top, the cool gray mansard roof is complemented by reddish brown and dark green trees immediately in back of the house. In Plate XIII, bottom, where the second story of the building is of a dark brown material, it is complemented by the use of brilliant yellow trees around and in back of it. Invariably light is used against dark and dark against light, for contrast.

Casein Paints

Similar to tempera in many ways, casein paints, which are made from skimmed milk, are often used for rendering. They are water soluble and remain moist and pliable while they are being used, but dry quickly and soon become water resistant. They can be used as gouache, tempera, or transparent water color and are available in miniature sets in as many as 40 different colors and white. Generally speaking, they can be used in the same manner as tempera colors.

A meticulous quality that is obtained by superb draftsmanship is illustrated by Fig. 15.20 and Fig. 15.21. After first carefully constructing his perspective, Mr. Morgan selects the direction of the sun and, as may be seen here, thus provides a minimum amount of shade area so that the majority of the buildings are bathed in sunlight. He is most faithful in the representation of textures and uses pencil, washes, opaque paint, and dry-brush paint to achieve this.

When the building has been completely rendered, the sky, entourage, foreground, and background are painted directly, using "Japan" edged brushes and a straightedge. For long vertical lines, Mr. Morgan uses colored paint in a ruling pen. Whenever possible, he paints from dark to light.

Both Fig. 15.20 and Fig. 15.21 are rendered on Crescent gray illustration board.

This delineator prefers to use a limited palette due to the necessity of matching colors when revisions are called for. His palette includes the following Shiva casein paints:

Cadmium red extra scarlet
Cadmium orange
Cadmium yellow medium
Cadmium yellow light
Yellow ochre
Naples yellow
Cerulean blue
Shiva (Thalo) blue

Plate XIII

Designs for
Leisure Time Developers, Ltd.,
Rock Hill, N.Y.
Dennis Jurow, A.I.A., Architect,
Middletown, N.Y.
rendered by Peter Rahill
Central Valley, N.Y. 10917

Plate XIV

Designs for
Leisure Time Developers, Ltd.,
Rock Hill, N.Y.
Dennis Jurow, A.I.A., Architect,
Middletown, N.Y.
rendered by Peter Rahill
Central Valley, N.Y. 10917

Fig. 15.20

Proposed Center for
Marine Environmental
Studies
College of the Virgin
Islands
St. Thomas, V.I.
Erdman-Tafel, Architects
and Engineers
rendered by Dave Morgan

Fig. 15.21

Library and classroom
building
Union College,
Cranford, N.J.
Hamby, Kennerly,
Slomanson and Smith,
Architects
rendered by Dave Morgan

Fig. 15.22

Hamilton Walk, Hospital
University of Pennsylvania,
Philadelphia, Pa.
Vincent G. Kling
Associates, Architects
rendered by Art
Associates, Inc.
Ronald W. Rose, Jr.
and Rod Dullum

Fig. 15.23

Center Square,
Philadelphia, Pa.
Vincent G. Kling
Associates, Architects
rendered by
Art Associates, Inc.
Ronald W. Rose, Jr.

When introducing a proposed new building into "existing surroundings," it is frequently desirable to vignette the picture, making the new building brilliant and light in color while surrounding it with darker existing buildings. See Fig. 15.22, rendered on blue-green illustration board.

Figure 15.23 illustrates the importance of selecting a correct light source. The structural members on the light side are the color of concrete in sunlight, while the shade side is a much deeper tone of the same color. Trees, hedges, and lawns are relatively grayed in tone and seem to support the building in its setting. A brilliant blue sky completes the rendering, which was done on colored illustration board.

Chapter 16

Airbrush rendering

History and Properties of Airbrush

THE AIRBRUSH was developed about 1882 by the Airbrush Manufacturing Company of Rockford, Ill. It is an instrument roughly resembling a fountain pen, through which may be sprayed a mixture of air and paint. The air source can be either a compressor or a tank of carbonic gas. The earliest mechanical compressors were hand pumps. Later hand pumps resembled those for bicycles, while early electric pumps were similar to those used for the dispensing of beer.

The chief advantage of the airbrush is that rounded forms which are difficult to render by the wash method may be easily represented. Another advantage is that the paint dries almost immediately upon application. Properly applied, airbrush washes are transparent, and excellent atmospheric effects can be obtained. Airbrush is particularly suitable for the rendering of projects which are architecturally very smooth or glassy in appearance.

Masking

In order to localize an area that is to be sprayed it is necessary to cover or "mask" all other portions of the rendering. The airbrush is equally effective on very small or very large areas, and once the process of masking is mastered, airbrush becomes a quick medium. Simple gradations can be made with one quick spray, and even the most difficult gradations call for little investment in time. Reflected light in shade and shadow, curved and round planes are rendered almost as easily as flat planes. As mentioned in Chapter 15, the airbrush is often used for spraying skies in brush tempera work, and it may also be used to soften or modify renderings in transparent water color or brush tempera.

Of course, because the masking usually prevents the renderer from seeing more than the one small area that he is working on, he must possess a rather thorough knowledge of rendering and the ability to imagine what the whole rendering will look like when it is finished. The delineator also needs a good memory, so that he can remember what each portion that he has already rendered will look like in conjunction with the area that he is spraying at the moment. As in all other techniques, a charcoal study and a color study are necessary before an airbrush rendering can be started.

There are a number of airbrushes on the market, but the best results in rendering can be obtained by using a Thayer & Chandler Model A or B; Wold, Model A-1 or A-2; or Paasche, Model F or Model V—all of which are relatively small.

The above brushes are made with both single and double action. The single action brush, usually used by beginners and students, sprays a mixture of paint and air when a trigger is pressed downward. The double action brush, on the other hand, permits control of the amount of air and paint so that a very small amount or a large amount of either can be sprayed by manipulation of the trigger; which, when pressed down, sprays air alone, and when pulled back sprays paint and air in increasing amounts. This, of course, is the better brush. The buyer must take care to select the kind of brush that he needs. Wold Model A-1, for instance, has a one-piece tip with an air cap that is not adjustable, while Wold Model A-2, which is a finer brush, has an adjustable cap. Paasche Model F is a single action brush, while Model V is a double action brush comparable to Thayer & Chandler or Wold A-2. If an airbrush is kept clean and not dropped, and if it is serviced regularly, it should last for many years.

Two basic air sources are used: the compressor or a tank of carbonic gas. For a single airbrush, the simplest compressor is a Paasche (D ¼ HP) oil-less single diaphragm air compressor which is light, portable, and quiet in operation. It delivers up to 30 lb of pressure and provides approximately 500 hours' service before the diaphragm must be replaced. A larger compressor for general usage requiring air pressure to 2 cfm at a uniform, continuous flow is also available. The pump in this unit operates automatically. When it is connected to electricity, the unit will pump up to 60-lb pressure. A regulator may be set at the desired air pressure. When the air pressure is reduced to 10 lb by use, the unit starts again automatically and pumps up to 60 lb into the storage tank.

Now, if for some reason you do not wish to purchase a compressor, tanks of compressed *carbonic* gas are available. *Do not* use a tank of oxygen by mistake, because oxygen is an explosive gas. Tanks of carbonic gas may be rented in 20-lb and 50-lb sizes. In order to control the release of the carbonic gas pressure, it is necessary to purchase a regulator and gage, which are fastened to each new tank in turn. The 20-lb tank is quite small in diameter, while the 50-lb tank is much bulkier. The renting of a tank of gas usually entails payment for the gas itself plus a daily rental for the tank. Because this can be quite an expense, many delineators purchase a "stubbie" 10-lb tank, which is about 22 in. high and lasts about 30 working hours. This is sold with a regulator gage and petcock. When the carbonic gas is used up, the stubbie tank can be refilled by any carbonic gas company.

A spray can of air may be purchased for small, simple renderings. Each can of air lasts about half an hour and is relatively expensive. In addition, a valve and hose must be purchased, which, of course, are used on each new can of air. One disadvantage of this type of air source is that it may be turned off and on only. The pressure varies between 25 and 30 pounds.

Air Hose

The air hose of fabric-covered rubber, which connects the tank or compressor to the airbrush, should be about 10 ft long. Be sure that you obtain the proper fittings for your particular air source and airbrush since these fittings vary according to the airbrush and air source used.

Airbrush Hanger

Most airbrushes are sold complete with a hanger that can be fastened to the edge of a drawing board. When not in use, the airbrush is hooked into the hanger, where it is relatively safe from harm.

Frisket Paper

The pressure of air emitted by an airbrush is sufficiently strong so that all areas except that being sprayed must be firmly masked. There are two basic types of frisket paper: (1) gumless, transparent, relatively waterproof paper, which may be fastened by the use of rubber cement thinned to half consistency with rubber cement thinner, and (2) gummed, transparent paper, such as E-Z Frisket, which is made with a removable backing. This is available in rolls 24 in. x 15 ft, 24 in. x 60 ft, or in sheets 18 x 24 in., or 9 x 12 in. Many art materials stores sell this paper by the yard.

No gummed paper can be stored for any length of time, because the gum undergoes a change in consistency which sometimes makes it useless. In addition, gummed frisket paper should never be stored near heat, which will dry it out. Therefore, it is advisable to purchase only enough for the job at hand.

The gumless frisket paper sold in art materials stores is quite transparent, and so the drawing can be seen beneath it. Any substitute that you can find, such as Saran Wrap, will also do. Before these items appeared on the market, tracing paper was employed, but this had two grave disadvantages: it was neither transparent nor waterproof.

Frisket Knives

When an area is to be sprayed, the entire drawing is covered with frisket paper, and that portion over the area to be sprayed is meticulously and accurately cut out and removed. Gummed frisket paper may or may not leave a small residue, which can be removed by rubbing with a clean finger. If rubber cement is used for the gumless type of frisket paper, this may be allowed to dry and can then be removed by rubbing with the finger.

Since only the thickness of the frisket paper is being cut, great care must be taken in cutting each mask. For this purpose special frisket knives are sold. They have metal holders, usually of aluminum, which resemble penholders and hold small, replaceable, razor-sharp blades. The least expensive type holds the blade in a fixed position, which is excellent for cutting straight lines. For cutting curves, however, pivoted frisket knives are best. Both types are made so that the knives may be replaced when necessary.

The same papers or illustration boards suggested for use in brush tempera rendering in Chapter 15 are suitable for airbrush rendering.

Paper or Illustration Board

Drafting tape: In addition to frisket paper, it is frequently necessary to use 1-in. drafting tape for holding pieces of frisket paper or other masking paper in place.

Other Materials

Pins: There are occasions when the frisket paper, even though it is carefully applied, will start to curl from the moisture of the paint. These curling spots can be held in place temporarily by the use of a pin stuck through the frisket paper and into the drawing itself. A handful of coins will also be found helpful for holding the frisket in place.

Silk sponge: Corrections in airbrush cannot be made by spraying color over areas which have been damaged or which are wrong in color. Since airbrush is a transparent medium, the damaged area, or any color below, will only be emphasized by attempts to cover it. Therefore, such areas must be carefully and tightly masked with drafting tape and paper and sponged gently with a damp sponge. If the tape and paper mask are fastened tightly enough, no water will get under to damage surrounding areas, and the same mask may be left in place for the spraying of the new tone. The paper must be entirely dry before the next tone is sprayed.

Newspapers: A pile of newspapers should be kept at hand for covering areas outside the edge of the frisket mask. The newspaper should be fastened to the edge of the frisket paper with drafting tape.

Brushes: Tempera brushes are used to supplement airbrush work (see Chapter 15).

Although transparent water color can be sprayed through an airbrush, tempera is most often used because of its fast-drying quality.

Paint

Note: Do not use a small airbrush for spraying fixative, lacquer, oil paint, waterproof ink, glue, liquid plastic, or metallic paint, since it will clog the brush. If you wish to spray any of the above substances, you should use a large airbrush such as Paasche H, VL, Thayer & Chandler C, or Wold W-9. It will be necessary, of course, to clean any of these large airbrushes with the solvent of the material you have sprayed.

Mixing and storing equipment will be similar to that for brush tempera (Chapter 15). A water container like that described in Chapter 15—or larger, if possible—will be required.

Mixing and Storing Equipment

One doz. white blotters.
Tools for paint handling: wooden spoons or tongue depressors, as described in Chapter 15.
Palette, also as described in Chapter 15.

Miscellaneous Equipment

Cleaning the Airbrush   Like the pen, the airbrush is a means for applying a medium. Also like the pen, it must be kept clean if it is to produce good results. The passages through which paint and air pass are so small that they easily become clogged, and therefore the airbrush should be cleaned after every spray. Dip a clean water color brush into clean water and drop the water from the brush into the cup of the airbrush. Then, while pressing the lever of the airbrush, hold your fingers over the nozzle so that the water that you are spraying must pass between your slightly constricted fingers. The back pressure will cause the water to force its way under pressure into the passages of the airbrush and break any crusts that have dried therein. This process should be repeated several times until the brush sprays clean water, smoothly and evenly. Be sure not to perform this chore where droplets of water can damage sprayed areas of your rendering.

Consistency of Paint   Tempera sprayed through an airbrush should be about the consistency of milk. If it is thicker it will clog the brush; if it is thinner, it will spray droplets.

Practice Washes   Before practice washes are made, fill the cup of your airbrush with clean water and spray it into the air so that you can watch the spray. By adjusting the nozzle at the tip of the brush with your thumb and forefinger, you can control the width of the spray. Wide sprays are used for large areas, narrow sprays for small areas. The airbrush should be adjusted so that it produces a medium-wide fine spray for general use. Do this several times so that you become familiar with the method for adjusting your brush. Now, provided you are using a double-action brush, fill it again with water, press the lever down, and pull it back slightly so that you may see the potential your brush has. Now you are ready to practice with tempera.

Mix a small quantity of any three colors, say dark green, spectrum orange, and spectrum red, in wash dishes, and tack a 20- x 30-in. illustration board or sheet of machine made water color paper over a drawing board. Draw several rectangles, each about 2½ x 5 in., on the upper portion of the sheet. These rectangles will receive flat washes. Three similar rectangles on the lower portion of the sheet will receive graded washes (Fig. 16.1).

Flat Washes   Before beginning, letter the names of the colors under each of the rectangles. Each of the colors should be mixed with white so that it is about half intensity. If you are using plain (ungummed) frisket paper and rubber cement, lift the brush out of the container and paint over the lines surrounding the first rectangle. The brush strokes should be at least ½ in. wide. When this is slightly dry, take a piece of frisket paper and press it firmly in place over the first rectangle. It should cover the rest of your drawing, or if it does not, complete the masking by fastening newspapers with drafting tape to the edges of the frisket paper so that the entire drawing is covered.

After a few moments the rubber cement will be sufficiently dry so that you can cut along the border lines of the first rectangle with a frisket knife. Press gently but firmly so as not to cut into the paper or illustration board below. When you have cut all four sides, with the point of the frisket knife gently raise a corner of the portion that you have cut out, and lift it slowly

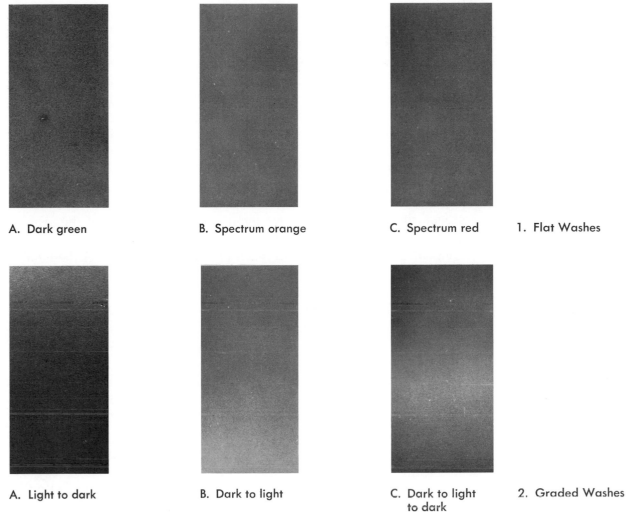

| A. Dark green | B. Spectrum orange | C. Spectrum red | 1. Flat Washes |

| A. Light to dark | B. Dark to light | C. Dark to light to dark | 2. Graded Washes |

Fig. 16.1 Practice Washes in Airbrush

from the drawing. Then rub a clean finger gently back and forth over the rubber cement that is left in the masked area until every trace of cement has been removed.

If gummed frisket paper is used, first remove it from its backing by prying one corner loose, and gently pulling it free while the backing is held flat on the desk or drawing board. When the backing has been removed, drop the frisket paper in place, gummed side down, over the area that is to be masked, making sure that no air bubbles form during the process. Then fasten it as tightly as possible by rubbing the frisket paper with a clean triangle, working from the center toward the edge to remove air bubbles. The corners of gummed frisket paper often begin to curl, and if they are not fastened with pins or tape the entire frisket mask may lift itself from the paper below. The gummed paper is cut from the area to be sprayed in the same manner as described above. Both the gummed and ungummed papers are sufficiently transparent to allow the cutting lines below to be seen.

Now that the mask is in place, you are ready to spray your first flat wash. Mix a small amount of dark green paint in a wash dish. Make sure that it is of a fairly thin consistency. Fill the cup of the airbrush with the paint, using a large bristle brush. Now, before applying the paint, press the trigger and watch the paint spray into the air. If it is spraying smoothly, proceed as follows:

Hold the hose in your left hand about 2 ft from the airbrush, so that the brush may be manipulated without the weight of the hose upon it. Now, moving your hand constantly from right to left and back again, press the lever of the brush down and back so that it begins to spray. Starting at the top of the first rectangle, move your hand back and forth slowly downward, holding the airbrush about 12 in. away from the paper. Keep the airbrush moving at all times or dark spots will occur. When you have reached the bottom of the rectangle, if you have moved your hand at an even pace throughout the process, you should have a flat wash. If any areas seem to have been slighted, you may, *after the first wash is dry*, repeat the process, giving the light areas a little more paint.

Repeat this entire process for each of the upper rectangles, being sure that each in turn is dry before removing the old mask and applying the new one, and also being sure to clean the brush with which you are handling paint before each new color is used.

Now look at the rectangles. If they are even in tone, you have been successful. If they are streaked, perhaps you should practice again. Chances are that they will be quite beautiful, but perhaps a few will have too much paint upon them. Every beginner makes this error; because the paint is sprayed upon the drawing and frisket paper mask at the same time he has no comparison, and before he knows it he has sprayed too much paint. The beauty of airbrush work lies in its transparency and delicacy, and the artist should not forget that a relatively thin layer of paint is required. The exact amount of paint to be sprayed will, of course, vary with the value required, and proficiency will develop with practice. However, it is safe to advise that when you begin, it is better to spray less rather than more paint upon any given surface. You can always repeat the process and darken a wash, but you cannot lighten it by spraying white over it, because this changes the wash to another color entirely. For the same reason, each area of the drawing must be masked while a single area is being sprayed. One cannot, for instance, spray a wall color on a sash area, hoping to cover the color when spraying the sash. The wall color will always show through.

Graded Washes

Each rectangle at the lower half of the sheet reserved for graded washes should be labeled with the proper color as for the upper half. Each rectangle will be masked as described above. Now you are ready to discover how easily gradations may be made with an airbrush. Using the same left and right movement with your hand, begin at the top and move downward with decreasing speed so that the wash is lightest at the top and darkest at the bottom. By gradually decreasing the speed of your hand, you can leave more paint on various parts of the wash. While it is slightly more difficult to repair any unevenness in a graded wash, this may be done by beginning again at the top of the wash and giving light areas a slightly larger amount of paint in order to correct the unevenness. With a small amount of practice, washes can be beautifully graded.

For practice, render the first color light at the top to dark at the bottom, the second dark at the top to light at the bottom, and the third dark at the top and bottom and light in the center. Now remove the frisket paper and look at your practice sheet, but before you do so, clean the airbrush by running water through it several times and place it in its hanger. You will notice that the washes you have sprayed have a fine, transparent, and atmospheric quality which reminds you of the results obtained with a Chinese ink wash. The same lightness and delicacy is present, but the brilliance of the color gives it a new dimension.

Using another piece of water color paper or illustration board (this one 15 x 20 in.) held horizontally, prepare it as follows: Draw a ½-in. border around the outside and divide the width into two halves with a 1-in. space between. This leaves two rectangles 14 in. high and 9 in. wide. Now divide the left rectangle so that it contains two rectangles which will be rendered as a concave and a convex wall in elevation, as follows: Using a scale vertically, mark off 2 in. from the lower border, 4 in. more for the height of the lower wall, 2 in. for the space between walls, and another 4 in. for the height of the upper wall. That will leave 2 in. to the upper border. Measuring horizontally, mark off 2 in. from the left border to the left edge of the bottom wall, and 5 in. more for its width. The upper wall should be located in the same way.

Divide the right-hand portion of the sheet as follows: At a point 4⅝ in. from the bottom border place a dot; then draw a light horizontal line which will be located on the horizontal axis of a sphere. Repeat the process from the top border. The center of the sphere at the bottom of the sheet and the center of the hemisphere at the top may be located along these axes by placing a dot 4½ in. from the right border on each axis. Now, using a large compass, draw a circle 5 in. in diameter at the bottom, and a half circle at the top, using the points that you have just located as centers (Fig. 16.2).

Mix a quantity of a color, perhaps dark green and Chinese white, for these exercises, and proceed as follows: Assuming that the upper wall in the

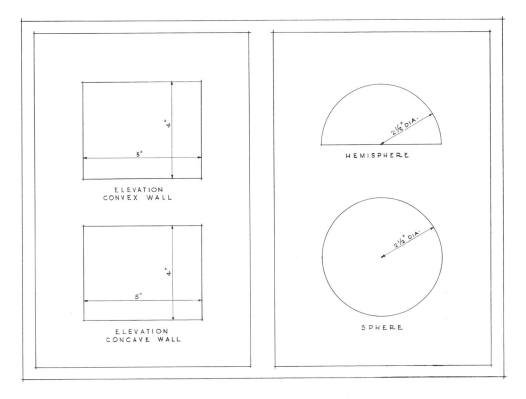

Fig. 16.2 Rendering Curved or Spherical Shapes

left-hand portion of the sheet is convex, draw above it, or on a piece of tracing paper placed over it, a plan of the wall, which will, of course, be a half circle 2½ in. in diameter. Now rest a 45-degree triangle on the horizontal T-square and draw the point of tangency on the right side of the half circle. Reverse the 45-degree triangle and find the point of tangency on the opposite side. Assuming that the light is coming from the left, at a 45-degree angle, the highlight of the curve will be at the left point of tangency. The darkest dark will be at the right point of tangency. Locate the highlight and the darkest dark by projecting them vertically upon the top rectangle, then mask as previously described (see Fig. 16.3).

Fig. 16.3A   Locating Highlight and Darkest Dark on a Concave Wall

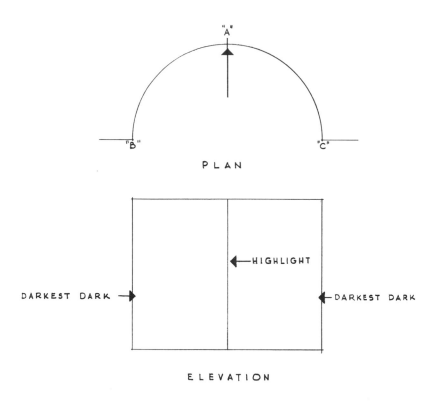

Double-graded Wash (Convex Wall)

Now, turning the board so that its short dimension is toward you, fill the cup of your airbrush with paint. Begin spraying at the top of the rectangle, moving rather quickly until you are in the neighborhood of the darkest dark —there move the brush more slowly and proceed downward at an increasingly rapid rate until the highlight area is reached. Then slowly proceed toward the bottom of the rectangle (Fig. 16.4). Now look at the gradation and see if it is smooth; if not, repeat the process, being sure to get the darkest dark in its proper place, grading toward the highlight at an accelerated rate.

The concave wall in elevation at the lower portion of the sheet may be rendered by drawing a plan similar to that used above, but this time drawing it so that it is concave. If the light source is assumed to be perpendicular to Point "A" in plan (for the sake of simplicity), the highlight will be at "A." The darkest darks will be at the extreme front edges of the wall at "B" and "C," and the values between these points and the highlight will grade gradually.

Now, again turning the drawing board so that the narrow edge of the board is toward you, and placing the mask in position, fill the cup of your airbrush, and moving it left and right, begin at the top of the rectangle and make a quick gradation from quite dark at the top to a highlight at the previously located point. Then, without interruption, proceed downward at a gradually decreasing rate so that the lower portion of the rectangle is darkest. Repeat the process until a smooth gradation of sufficient value results (Fig. 16.5).

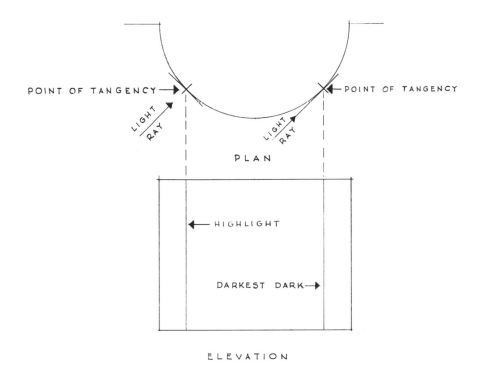

Fig. 16.3B Locating Highlight and Darkest Dark on a Convex Wall

Rendering the Sphere

The sphere at the right side of the paper may be rendered as follows: Fasten a sheet of frisket paper over the area of the sphere (and of course larger). Cut an opening in it the exact shape of the sphere. The darkest dark of the sphere, which can be accurately determined by the rules of shades and shadows, will be located on the underside and to the right of the sphere, slightly off the bottom, so that light will seem to be reflected there. Now fill the airbrush cup with paint, and with a circular motion proceed to spray a small amount of paint around the circumference of the sphere. Then, with a rocking, curved motion along the lower right and upper right portions of the sphere, spray more paint upon the lower right portion of the dark side and less on the left side and on the upper right side. Moving at an increasingly rapid rate toward the center of the sphere, smooth the wash from the darkest portion to the light face where the wash will disappear entirely (Fig. 16.6).

Fig. 16.4   Elevation: Convex Wall

Fig. 16.5   Elevation: Concave Wall

Fig. 16.6   Rendering the Sphere

Fig. 16.7   Rendering the Hemisphere

Spraying the Hemisphere   To spray the hemisphere, proceed as follows: Cut a mask to cover both the hemisphere and the area below the base line. Spray a small amount of paint around the hemisphere, using a left to right motion. Remove the mask when the paint is dry, and after fastening a new sheet of frisket paper over the same area, cut the exact shape of the hemisphere and lift that portion of the frisket paper which will expose the hemisphere for painting. Assuming that the light is coming from the left and above at 45 degrees, the highlight and the darkest dark can easily be determined in plan; as in Fig. 16.3A. Fill the airbrush cup with paint, and with a continuous back and forth motion spray a small amount of paint to the right, decreasing the amount of paint as you do so; so that the right side of the hemisphere receives a small amount of paint. Now repeat the process, starting at the darkest dark, and move to the left until the highlight is reached. This will receive no paint at all. Finally, spray the left side, from dark at the left edge to the white of the paper at the highlight (Fig. 16.7).

The textures described herein are for surfaces in sunlight. Generally speaking, the color used for such surfaces is darkened for shade and shadow by adding more of each pigment, particularly of the dark colors of the palette being used.

Form is easily obtained by the use of the airbrush; textures are not. They are indicated as conventions rather than as realistic imitations of the actual textures.

Fig. 16.8   Textures in Airbrush

1. Wood

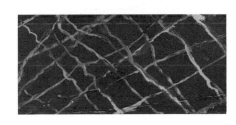

2. Marble

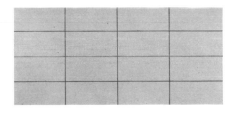

3. Stucco or concrete
   Stone ashlar

4. Brick

5. Metal

Preparing the Practice Sheet for Textures

Using a 10- x 15-in. piece of white illustration board or machine made water color paper, draw a ½-in. border around the outside in pencil. Now lightly draw a 1-in. space inside the border on all four sides. This will produce a rectangle 12 in. wide and 7 in. high. Divide the 12-in. width into six equal parts with ⅛-in. spaces left between them. Now turn the board so that the narrow end is toward you, and you will have six rectangles approximately 2 in. high and 6 in. wide. Label these as follows, in the ⅛-in. spaces: (1) Wood siding or clapboards, (2) marble texture, (3) stucco or concrete, (4) cut stone, (5) brickwork, (6) metal. Before proceeding further, draw the various textures in pencil in each rectangle at ¼-in. scale.

Natural-finished Wood

Mask the entire sheet and cut out the area for this rectangle. Make a mixture of yellow ochre, white, and alizarin crimson, and spray a flat or graded base tone over the entire area. Graining may be painted freehand over the base tone with a small pencil brush and fairly thick paint. Light reflections are made by spraying a small amount of white on the background color before the graining is applied, using the edge of a piece of stiff paper as mask.

Marble

To give the effect of marble, spray the background color first. Then place some of the same color and some Chinese white on a paper palette. Mixing these together in various shades, from quite dark to almost white, apply the graining with a small, fairly dry, brush.

Stucco or Concrete

Mask the area to be sprayed and cut the frisket paper for this rectangle. The color of this material may vary, but for this exercise make a mixture of white, yellow ochre, alizarin crimson and cobalt blue. The base tone is usually sufficient to indicate these materials.

Cut Stone

Cut stone or architectural terra cotta may be indicated by using the same colors as for stucco or concrete. The base tone is sprayed, then the lines are drawn with a fine brush or ruling pen and T-square. For light stone use dark joints; for dark terra cotta use light joints.

Brickwork

After masking, spray the base tone with a light mixture of white, yellow ochre, vermilion and a small amount of cobalt blue. The joint lines can then be drawn with a 3-H pencil or with brush or ruling pen, using a slightly darker tone of the same paint.

Metal

Spray the base tone with a color as described under "Metal" in Chapter 15, and rule in the joints with a ruling pen or small brush.

Glass Openings

Glass openings are rendered as described for tempera rendering in Chapter 15. Each small area, such as those for the blinds, curtains, furniture and furnishings, must be separately masked and sprayed. No attempt should be made to give the glass area a film of paint to simulate glass. If the glass area is large enough so that the spectator can see into it, the only indication that glass is present is made by casting shadows from mullions or overhang upon the glass.

Although it is possible to airbrush foliage masses for trees and bushes, it is most usual to paint them directly from a palette, as described for brush tempera in Chapter 15. Grass is usually shown by masking the areas and spraying graded washes, dark at the front and light at the rear; then painting variations in tone, as well as tree and building shadows, over the general spray. Large ground shadows are sprayed, but small shadows are usually painted directly with a brush and thin tempera. Scale figures are best painted directly from the palette as in brush tempera.

The airbrush excels in the rendering of skies. They can easily be domed, clouded, or mottled. Before spraying the sky, however, the entire rendering, including the building and ground areas, must be carefully masked so that the sky color will not seep under the masking paper onto any other portion of the drawing. Because the sky sometimes receives a lot of paint, the edges of the frisket paper are inclined to lift; therefore, wherever possible, it is more satisfactory to use drafting tape and paper for masking sky areas. In addition to the building and ground areas, the borders of the drawing should also be masked so that the drawing will have sharp edges.

Skies

Fig. 16.9   Skies in Airbrush

1. Domed sky

2. Domed sky with light clouds

Domed Sky

The simplest kind of sky is, of course, the domed sky, which is darkest at the top and lightest at the horizon (see Fig. 16.9, Sketch A). This is sprayed in the same horizontal left to right stroke described for the practice washes. The sky area is usually quite large, and the wash may take quite a lot of time to spray. Great care must be taken to simulate accurately the values predetermined in the value study, since there is no way to judge how it will look against the rest of the building when it is covered with frisket paper. It is wise to spray less paint rather than more, since a flat, opaque sky is not at all handsome. The sky in Fig. 16.16 is excellent.

Domed Sky with Clouds

It is quite usual to show light clouds in a domed sky, and this is done by sprinkling bird gravel over the cloud areas, then spraying as for a domed sky (see Fig. 16.9, Sketch 2). When the paint is dry, brush the gravel off the sky and into a waste basket, and you will find clouds that look quite atmospheric. Dark clouds can be made in this medium by narrowing the spray and passing the airbrush back and forth from the top of the sky down, painting a dark cloud now and again, with spaces between the clouds, becoming smaller toward the horizon (see Plate XV and Fig. 16.10).

Making a Rendering

Preparation for an airbrush rendering is similar to that for brush tempera. The perspective line drawing is applied to the sheet or illustration board with a clean pencil line, making certain that the drawing is entirely clean before any work is begun. If any dirt—such as a fingermark—is present, it will show through the airbrush washes. As mentioned before, the value study and color study are both of the utmost importance and must be relied upon heavily in the course of working with this medium.

Now you may ask "What do I do first?" Of course, there are many ways to proceed. The author prefers to render the entire building first, then the sky, and finally the ground, trees and bushes, scale figures, and automobiles. Since in airbrush work one can only see a small portion of the rendering at a time, one may just as well complete the building before proceeding with the sky and foreground. If any difficulty is going to be encountered, it will probably be met in working on the building, and if the difficulty is going to develop into a catastrophe, one has not wasted a lot of time on the foreground and sky. Also, there are times when a client finds that he needs the rendering before it is completed and if the building, at least, has been rendered, the presentation is of some value to him.

Before beginning any airbrush rendering, one must first carefully plan the order of masks and washes so that trouble can be foreseen before it is met. Careful planning can result, of course, in less masking than if the problem is attacked in a haphazard way. The author, in describing all of the renderings in this chapter, gives a step-by-step description of the masking in order to provide the reader with an insight into the use of this medium.

This project, almost identical with Plate XV, was rendered by the same method, but notice the difference in the shadows created by a different light source, as well as the different effect achieved by the use of another palette. Here we have a midday scene as contrasted with the early morning flavor of the previous rendering. The walls are a lighter shade of orange, the trees are lighter in color, and the sky less intense in value and more purple in hue. This proves once more that the character of a rendering is determined in the charcoal study and color study stages.

Fig. 16.10

A church
rendered by Pierre Lutz
Student project

Fig. 16.11

A church
rendered by Donald L. Dimick
Student project

The value and color studies showed that the shell-like quality of this building would require the use of very pale washes; therefore it was decided to make the sky unusually dark for comparison.

Mask No. 1: Walls in light on the building and bell tower were sprayed first, masking around the crosses. A coral mixture of white, vermilion, and yellow ochre was used.

Mask No. 2: The walls in shade and also the shade side of the canopy at the right were sprayed by using the same colors, with more pigment and less white.

Masks No. 3 to 8 inclusive: The six curved segments of the coral-colored roof were rendered separately, masking all other areas in the drawing in succession. Form was obtained by varying the spray of the airbrush and spraying more paint at the rear of each wash in turn.

Mask No. 9: The blue-gray shadow cast by the roof projection on the front wall was sprayed with a mixture of cobalt blue, vermilion, yellow ochre, and white.

Mask No. 10: The light sides of the canopy and supports at the entrance were sprayed with an off-white.

Mask No. 11: The shade side elements were sprayed using a mixture of blue, white, and vermilion.

Mask No. 12: A yellow graded tone was sprayed on the ground area.

Mask No. 13: The entire building and bell tower were masked and the dark gray-green sky was sprayed darkest at the horizon to lightest at the top of the picture, reversing the usual process in order to accent the building sharply. All of the colors of the palette were mixed together for this wash.

Brushwork The convolutions of the front wall were painted on with a small brush, using the edge of a T-square as a guide. The foreground was darkened and given texture by the use of paint brushed directly from a palette. The marble slab was then textured with a fine brush and the gray-green bushes were painted in.

This is an interesting rendering in that the building is dramatically framed and pointed out to the spectator by the use of a dark edge of the building, shadow in the foreground, and a dark wall beneath the building, which is itself rendered in pale tones. The color throughout is muted. This is another rendering where one or more of the colors used is not plainly seen in any part of the rendering. Yellow ochre, for example, is not obvious, but was used in mixing the warm grays.

Mask No. 1: The light upper face of the building, including the shadow area, was sprayed with a gray mixed of all of the colors being used, with the exception of black. Now we have seen, as in Fig. 16.11, that shadows can be sprayed directly on white paper by the use of a color that is darker than the wall color itself. In this case the shadow on the wall area as well as in other parts of the drawing was sprayed over a previously applied tone by using a neutral color mixed of blue and black. In this method, the shadow spray must be transparent so that the color beneath it shows through. This simplifies the spraying of shadows, since all shadows throughout the entire rendering can be sprayed at one time.

Mask No. 2: The light area of the concrete bent at the front of the building, including the shadow area, was next sprayed with a pale warm gray, using the same colors as above except for the addition of more white.

Mask No. 3: The shade tone on the underside of the roof overhang was next sprayed in the same colors, but with the amount of each varied so as to obtain a medium gray.

Mask No. 4: The front half of the roof arch was painted and formed by spraying it with gray as if for a concave wall.

Mask No. 5: The rear half of the roof was graded in the same way.

Mask No. 6: The convolutions of the materials in the gray upper portion of the front wall were next formed by first spraying the darkest portions of them as dark stripes.

Fig. 16.12

Laboratory
University of Mexico
Mexico City
Felix Candela,
Structural Designer
Jorge Gonzales,
Architectural Associate
rendered by
Edward G. Schildbach
Student project

Mask No. 7: The lighter stripes were sprayed on each side of each center stripe.

Mask No. 8: Still lighter stripes were sprayed on each side of the previous stripes. All corresponding stripes, of course, were done at the same time.

Mask No. 9: The general tone of the wall under the building was sprayed with a medium dark gray, darkest at the foreground and lightest in the distance.

Mask No. 10: The left rear portion of the building next to the main structure was next sprayed, using a great deal of white so as not to compete with the strong tones in the main structure.

Mask No. 11: The wall at the left was given a general spray of dark gray.

Masks No. 12 to 16 inclusive: Various stones were darkened by spraying several shades of darker gray upon the wall to represent the natural differentiation of the stone tones.

Mask No. 17: The general tone was sprayed on the paved areas.

Mask No. 18: A medium tone was sprayed upon a portion of the foreground for differentiation.

Mask No. 19: A dark strong tone was sprayed under the building.

Mask No. 20: The entire drawing except for the sky area was masked. The sky was blown first with a mixture of white and crimson, and then with a mixture of white and blue, with some of the undertone showing through.

Mask No. 21—scale figures: All of the scale figures were cut out of a single mask and sprayed at the same time with the same dark gray paint.

Mask No. 22: The shadows of the people on the ground were sprayed with a lighter tone of gray than that used for the scale figures.

Mask No. 23: All other shadows on the building, on the wall below the building, and on the ground were then sprayed with a mixture of blue and black. Incidentally, a water color similar to this color in shade can be purchased under the name "neutral tint."

Fig. 16.13

A church in Holland rendered by Theodore Boosten Student project

In a building such as this, where there are several similarly shaped—in this case, round—elements, they are all sprayed with cutouts made in a single mask.

Mask No. 1: The most difficult parts of the project, the tan drum-shaped elements, were sprayed first, on the assumption that if difficulty was going to be encountered and the drawing spoiled, the delineator would know it quickly and little time would be lost. The principles described for rendering concave walls (Fig. 16.2) were used here, the highlights being

toward the left side and the darkest darks toward the right. Before spraying, the drawing was turned so that the long dimension faced the delineator, and while each element was sprayed separately, the others were covered with sheets of paper laid upon them and held in place by tubes of paint.

Mask No. 2: The tan flat walls in light were sprayed next, with a slightly lighter mixture of the paint used for the first spray.

Mask No. 3: The general yellow color of the roof was sprayed.

Mask No. 4: All of the light sides of the steeples were sprayed simultaneously with one mask and a mixture of white and blue.

Mask No. 5: The shade sides of the steeples were then rendered with a deeper mixture of the same colors.

Mask No. 6: Finally the front face of the main steeple was given an intermediate tone of blue.

Mask No. 7: The low portion of the roof was rounded in a medium shade of blue.

Mask No. 8: The entire drawing was masked and all sash were exposed for simultaneous spraying with grayed blue. This was done with a mixture of blue and white, with a small amount of vermilion to gray the color. Note that sash on the sunny side of the building are dark and those on the shade side are light because of reflected light.

Mask No. 9: All window sills and the underside of the roof overhang were next sprayed with a whiter shade of grayed blue. The standing seams of the lower roof were painted with a fine brush and a straightedge.

Mask No. 10: The entire drawing was masked and all shadows were cut and exposed and sprayed at the same time with a mixture of blue and black.

Mask No. 11: The sky was painted next, after the entire building had been masked, and was generally domed with a mixture of white and blue. The cloud interest was obtained by spraying more of the same color in almost horizontal streaks.

Trees and bushes were painted with a gray-green mixture of yellow ochre and cobalt blue, using a flat brush and a dabbing motion.

Brushwork

Plate XV

A church
rendered by William
Petchler, Jr.
Size: 17 x 22½ in.
Student project

I t was decided to try to create the illusion of early morning light in rendering this church, as the building would be used mostly for early services. The colors are generally muted.

Mask No. 1: All areas but the walls in early morning sunlight were masked, and these light areas were sprayed with a mixture of Chinese white and vermilion.

Mask No. 2: All brick areas excepting walls in shade were masked, and these dark areas were sprayed with a mixture of white, cobalt blue, and vermilion. After the main color had been sprayed, it was graded while the same mask was in place by adding a small amount of black to the shade color. Note that the square openings and cross at the upper portion of the bell tower were masked when the shade brick area was sprayed, since wall color on these areas would have shown through the later dark spray for these openings.

Mask No. 3: The stone areas in shade were sprayed with a warm gray mixed of white, cobalt blue, vermilion and black.

Mask No. 4: The entire drawing except for glass areas and for small openings in the bell tower was masked, and these areas were sprayed with a blue-gray mixture of black and cobalt blue. They were graded dark at the top to light at the bottom to give the illusion of reflected light.

Mask No. 5—Sky: The first spray, a pale orange mixture of white, vermilion, and cobalt blue, was given to the lower portion of the sky to simulate early morning light. The gray blue upper portion of the sky was sprayed with a mixture of white, cobalt blue and black, using a horizontal motion and doming the sky, occasionally rendering a band of clouds by lingering longer over certain areas and permitting the light under-color to show in others.

Mask No. 6—Foreground spray: A general tan tone was given to the foreground by the use of white, vermilion, and a small amount of cobalt blue. It was purposely made dark at the front and light at the back.

Brushwork: Brushwork was applied directly from the palette, using a small amount of each color in the palette, plus white and black, as described for brush tempera in Chapter 15. The ground area was varied in tone so as to relieve the monotony. The gray trees and gray and brown scale figures were next painted with a small conical brush. The grass was painted with a small brush held against a T-square.

PAPER: *Handmade, cold-pressed, stretched*
COLOR SCHEME: *Complementary*
PALETTE: *Cobalt blue, vermilion, black, white*

Plate XV

A church
rendered by William
Petchler, Jr.
Size: 17 x 22 ½ in.
Student project

Plate XVI

End of a Viaduct
rendered by Samuel C. Wang
Size: 18 x 24 in.
Student project

PAPER: *Handmade, cold-pressed, stretched*
COLOR SCHEME: *Split complement*
PALETTE: *Cobalt blue, yellow ochre, red-orange,*
white, black

In this illustration a rather intricate structure is simplified for rendering in airbrush by limiting the number of colors, and therefore the number of spray masks.

Mask No. 1: For example, the entire light portion of the structure—walls and piers in sunlight—was first sprayed with a very light gray green.

Mask No. 2: All of the piers and upper part of the structure in shade were sprayed with a darker gray-green mixture of yellow ochre, cobalt blue, red-orange, and white.

Mask No. 3: The underside of the structure was sprayed with the same colors, but with the use of more blue than in Mask No. 2.

Mask No. 4: The shade areas on the bottom and side of the longitudinal structural member, a small amount of which can be seen, were sprayed with varying shades of the same colors.

Mask No. 5: All gray-green shadows on the viaduct were sprayed by masking for them at the same time. The shadows were graded so that they were dark at the front of the picture and light at the rear.

The front lateral beam of the structure in shadow was textured by rubbing lightly with a ruby eraser and a straightedge. After the main structure was painted, approximately the same procedure was followed for the surrounding buildings.

Mask No. 6: The sky was painted with a blue mixture of white and cobalt blue and was varied in tone.

Orange and green building, blue and black people, and blue and green ground shadows, as well as blue and white planting, were painted freely from the palette.

Plate XVI

End of a Viaduct
rendered by Samuel C. Wang
Size: 18 x 24 in.
Student project

Eraser Work

Brushwork

Fig. 16.14

Detail of a shopping center
rendered by Elaine Frank
Student project

By a careful arrangement of composition, the building in this rendering was interestingly related to the space around it. While the usual viewpoint is quite a distance away from the structure itself, this viewpoint was taken close to one corner of the building, which in turn frames another portion of it. This is an interesting trick in composition.

Mask No. 1: The sunny face of the upper wall and the two front columns were painted with an off-white color.

Mask No. 2: The entire drawing, with the exception of the ceiling area, was masked. In addition, all of the ceiling lights were covered, and the ceiling was sprayed with a warm brown mixture of yellow ochre, red-orange, spectrum blue and white.

Mask No. 3: The "out" lighting fixtures were sprayed a tone darker than the ceiling.

Mask No. 4: The floor, including the shadow area, was sprayed with a tan mixture of white, yellow ochre and red-orange.

Mask No. 5: The shadow areas on the columns and on the floor, as well as the shadow on the rear wall, were sprayed with a brown mixture of yellow ochre, red-orange, spectrum blue, and a small amount of black. The shadow cast by the roof overhang at the front was sprayed with a mixture of the same color.

Mask No. 6: The sash in the rear wall were painted with a light blue mixture of spectrum blue and white.

Mask No. 7: The edge of the rear canopy was painted with a warm brown mixture of yellow ochre, red-orange, and a small amount of spectrum blue.

Mask No. 8: The sky was prepared by masking the entire drawing, with the exception of this area, to the horizon line and then painting it with a gray-blue mixture of white and spectrum blue.

Mask No. 9: The ground in the mid-distance was rendered in a warm gray mixture of yellow ochre, red-orange, and white.

The following were painted directly from the palette as for brush tempera:

Brushwork

The yellow stone wall at the left

Green trees, bushes and gray and violet mountains

Blue and orange scale figures

The foreground texture was stippled with a small brush.

This rendering is of the same general type as Fig. 16.14. One is encouraged to look out into the distance—in this case to the blue sea—while standing under a dark blue enclosure. We will not attempt to describe the execution step by step, since it is so similar to the previous rendering. Not only is this rendering colorful and full of atmosphere (one can almost smell the sea), but its composition appeals to the spectator because it is full of small, interesting obstacles that he must observe and "look past" in order to see other interesting details in the distance.

Fig. 16.15

Seaside hotel
rendered by Robert Packard
Student project

Fig. 16.16

Detail of a desert house
rendered by Justo Gordo Jr.
Student project

The number of round and curved elements in this project, plus the plainness of the surrounding area, make it an ideal building for airbrush work. As in the case of Figs. 16.13 and 16.14 one is allowed to look through and around parts of the building. The color scheme is muted in a manner somewhat similar to that shown in Fig. 16.14. The walls and columns are gray. The ceiling and underside of the first floor slab are gray violet, the curtains a lighter shade of the same violet. Perhaps more color is used, but it is employed with restraint. Notice that the light source was taken so that the tones of the building itself, being in shade, are deep and strong, and that these are contrasted with light orange sky, tan ground tones, and green mountains.

Mask No. 1: All walls, floor slab, and side columns were given a light gray tone, and rounded and formed when the base tone was dry with a darker mixture of the same color.

Mask No. 2: The columns were rounded by spraying a deeper tone of gray at the sides of each column, leaving the light tone previously sprayed to act as a highlight.

Mask No. 3: The partition inside the building above and below the floor was sprayed with gray and gray-violet.

Mask No. 4: Ceiling and soffit of the overhang, together with the soffit of the floor slab, were painted in a mixture of violet, orange, and white, care being taken to grade the value so that it was darkest at the edges and lightest in the center.

Mask No. 5: The curtains were painted with a combination of white and violet.

Mask No. 6: The risers of the steps were sprayed; the treads were so narrow that they were drawn in a darker color with a ruling pen.

Mask No. 7: Since the sky could be seen through a large portion of the glass area, it was sprayed before the window mullions were drawn, in a mixture of white and orange. This was done by masking the entire building with the exception of these glass areas.

Mask No. 8: After the mullions were drawn, by using a ruling pen and T-square with an off-white shade (mixture of white and violet), the foreground, including that in shadow, was sprayed.

Mask No. 9: The shadow of the building on the light ground area was sprayed with a darker tone.

Mask No. 10: The distant mountains were sprayed in three stages, using three different masks: The lightest mountains in the distance, the medium value in the mid-distance, and the darkest values in the mountains closest to the spectator. These were all painted in various shades mixed of white, deep green, and a small amount of orange.

The few green blades of desert grass were applied directly from the palette, first with strokes of green, orange, and white. Highlights were then painted on some with pure white. The stair railing was drawn with a ruling pen, with a T-square and triangle as a guide.

Plate XVII

US Embassy
New Delhi, India
Edward D. Stone, Architect
rendered by Bernard Harland
Size: 21 x 14 in.
Student project

This delicate rendering illustrates once again the sophistication and charm that can be obtained with the airbrush.

Mask No. 1: The light face of the building, including the area in shadow, was first given a pale wash of white mixed with a small amount of yellow. It was then textured with the tip of a small brush and a gray tone.

Mask No. 2: A deeper version of the same tone was then sprayed on the face so as to indicate the shadow. The doorway motif and the dark line under the roof were sprayed at the same time, in a deep green.

Mask No. 3: The roof soffit, together with the plant pockets, were next sprayed a cool shade of gray.

Mask No. 4: The light sides of the columns were given a coat of light yellow.

Mask No. 5: The dark sides of the columns were given a darker shade of the same color.

Mask No. 6: The face of the pedestal upon which the building stands was sprayed next with a mixture of white, yellow, and vermilion, and the steps were ruled in with the same color over a previously sprayed tone.

Mask No. 7: The design motif over the entranceway was applied with an ink compass.

Mask No. 8: The blue sky was sprayed with a mixture of white and blue.

Mask No. 9: At the same time that the various washes were being sprayed on the building itself, they were being sprayed in reflection in the pool. After the building and reflections had been completed, the entire water area was given a coat of cobalt blue and black, care being taken to allow the reflections of the building to show through. Ripples in the water were put on by two means—white in the airbrush, which was adjusted to a relatively fine spray for this purpose, and used in horizontal strokes—and cobalt blue, which was applied freehand with a brush.

Mask No. 10: All edges of the building were masked with drafting tape and newspaper, and the immediate foreground was darkened with a dark spray of cobalt blue and black in order to further the illusion of perspective. The flowers of the water lilies were painted on top of the last spray so that they would shine brilliantly.

Plate XVII

US Embassy
New Delhi, India
Edward D. Stone, Architect
rendered by Bernard Harland
Size: 21 x 14 in.
Student project

PAPER: *Handmade, cold pressed, stretched*
COLOR SCHEME: *Split complement*
POSTER COLORS: *Yellow, vermilion, cobalt blue, white, and black*

Trees, bushes, and the leaves of water lilies were painted directly from the palette, in a green mixture of yellow, cobalt blue and white, with an occasional touch of vermilion.

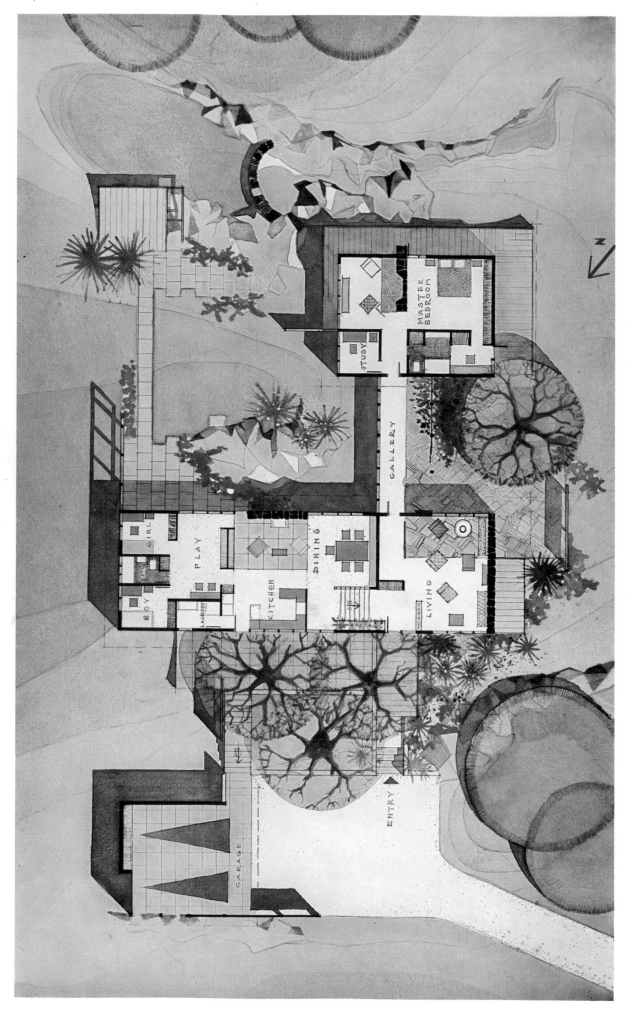

Plate XVIII

**Plan of a country home
rendered by Heino Kart
Student project
Size: 26 x 17 in.**

Chapter 17

Pastels

WHEN ONE WISHES to use color for rendering but does not have the time to use water color or tempera, a dry medium such as pastels can be used. Pastels have a number of advantages: they can be used alone or with other opaque media; they are fast, produce a delicacy of tone, are good for impressions rather than detailed renderings, and need relatively few accessories. In addition, pastel renderings can be made on various kinds of paper without the necessity of making a stretch.

Pastels are sold in sets or by the stick. There are two basic types: half-hard, usually available in square sticks, and soft, usually available in round sticks. Both half-hard and soft pastels are available in sets containing as few as 12 assorted colors and as many as, say, 360 assorted pure hues, tints, and shades. Half-hard pastels are also available in eight graded grays.

Materials Required

Like smudge charcoal, pastels require a rather rough surface for file action. Ordinary pastel papers, 19 x 25 in., have already been described in Chapter 10 on carbon pencil rendering. In addition, pastel drawing books of similar paper are made in the following sizes: 9 x 12 in., 12 x 18 in., and 18 x 24 in. These may be used for outdoor sketching or studies.

Pastel Papers

In addition to the pastel papers described above, there are available sand surface pastel paper, velour pastel paper, and pastel board made with the same surfaces. Generally speaking these do not lend themselves very well to architectural work. On the other hand, ordinary charcoal paper, white or colored, white rag tracing paper, buff detail paper, or even brown wrapping paper will do. Water color paper gives an interesting texture.

Pastel Holders Sticks of pastel (particularly in the soft grade) are easily broken, and holders are sold for small pieces.

Pastel Fixative Pastel fixative has been described in Chapter 12. This is the clearest type of fixative sold.

Shading Devices **Tortillons:** Although pastel is frequently smoothed with the finger, there are occasions when tortillons are required. They are small, round, paper stomps, pointed at one end and available in lengths of 2¾ in., 3 in., and 3¼ in. Gray paper stomps, which are larger (¼ x 4¾ in., ⅜ x 5⅛ in., ½ x 5½ in., ¹¹⁄₁₆ x 6 in.) are also helpful for smoothing pastel washes.

Powdering devices: Like smudge charcoal, pastels are often powdered for application. This is done by rubbing them on a sandpaper pad or a metal pencil pointer.

Absorbent cotton: A box of absorbent cotton for applying pastel in a manner similar to that for smudge charcoal is required.

Masking paper: A number of 8½- x 11-in. sheets of thin white bond paper will be found helpful (see Chapter 12).

Powder masking devices: It is often necessary to mix several powdered colors. This can best be done with a pen knife, or even better a palette knife.

Erasers: A kneaded eraser and a pink pearl eraser.

Palette: As in all colored media, a palette must be selected from the many colors at hand before a rendering is begun. The same set of color principles is used for pastel as for any other color medium (see Chapter 7, Color—Fact and Theory). While the names may differ, a palette roughly comparable to that used for transparent water color can be selected. Such a palette might consist of:

1. Cadmium yellow deep
2. Light or deep ochre
3. Cadmium orange
4. Permanent red
5. Madder lake
6. Ultramarine blue deep
7. Indigo
8. Gray-blue
9. Permanent green deep
10. Moss green

Pastels are so simple to use that it is not necessary to make a carefully drawn sheet of exercises as for water colors. Flat and graded washes may be practiced by powdering a small amount of any color, say blue, on a piece of white pad paper, dipping a small piece of absorbent cotton into it and rubbing this back and forth on a sheet of pastel paper. It will be found that by overlapping the strokes and crossing the first strokes with a second series of strokes a smooth wash can easily be made. As with smudge charcoal, areas to be shaded must be masked. This is done with the 8½- x 11-in. white bond paper, as described in Chapter 12.

Graded washes are easily made by the same process, but with the addition of more pastel powder and an additional number of strokes in the darker areas.

In addition to washes of powdered pastel, textures, foliage, etc. are frequently obtained by the use of a sharp corner of half-hard pastel or a sharp piece of soft pastel broken off for the purpose. Because pastel is an opaque medium it will be found that tones can be built up of a series of powder washes, by a series of strokes, or a combination of both. One color can be mixed with another directly on the paper.

Textures of building materials are made in a manner similar to that used in brush tempera; a base wash of powder pastel is applied, and the various textures and shadows are applied over these washes by the use of stick pastel or pieces of stick pastel.

Glass openings are rendered in the same manner as for water color. Each small wash, as that for blinds, curtains, furniture, carpets, flooring, etc., is made with a separate mask.

Bushes and trees can be applied in the same way as are the washes for buildings; the foliage can be generally applied by the use of cotton and powdered pastel, and the tree structure drawn directly with a stick of pastel. Detailed leaves in foreground and trees in mid-distance can be applied directly with the stick.

Entourage

Grass and roadways can be applied with flat washes, and later modified with stick strokes for shadows and tonal variations.

Flat, graded, or graded and clouded skies are usually applied with long horizontal strokes of powdered pastel. Clouds can be added with a light colored stick of pastel applied directly over the undercoat. In addition, cloud streaks can be erased with a kneaded or pink pearl eraser in a manner similar to that used in water color rendering.

Skies

Because of the nature of pastels, the value study and the color study may be combined, using the sticks directly on a sheet of the same type of paper as will be used for the presentation. The linear perspective is transferred to the paper as described in Chapter 4, using a graphite pencil.

Procedure

Fig. 17.1

A country house
rendered by Paul Hilary Pinter
Student project

The various shades used for this presentation were mixed by powdering the several required colors in separate piles on a single sheet of white pad paper. These were then mixed together much as a druggist mixes powders, by the use of a palette knife, first drawing them together in a single pile and then stirring and mixing them until the colors were blended.

An approximately correct base tone was rubbed on each surface of the building; glass areas were assumed to be in glare because of the wood roof overhang. Each line forming the squares on the underside of the roof was made over a previously rendered dark gray pastel wash by placing two sheets of 8½- x 11-in. paper close together and erasing between them with a kneaded eraser, in a manner similar to that used in smudge charcoal. Wall texture was obtained by dabbing the general washes with a corner of a rolled piece of kneaded eraser, while the vertical folds in the gray curtains were made by the use of a rolled, pointed piece of kneaded eraser and a straightedge, using a vertical wiping motion.

Reflections in the terrace floor were also made with a kneaded eraser in the previously rendered blue-gray wash. The yellow and green grass areas were indicated by directly applying strokes in perspective, leaving a number of areas—particularly those near the building—white for maximum comparison. The dark green shadow on the ground was applied in the same way, but was rubbed smooth with the finger. The light green background trees and those in the mid-distance were drawn by first applying general base washes for the foliage, this being darkened and modified by the use of streak strokes which were then lightly rubbed with the finger. The tree structure was applied directly with the corner of a piece of pastel broken from the stick.

The drawing was then lightly fixed with pastel fixative blown from a mouth spray.

The entire rendering with the exception of scale figures was applied by the use of paper masks and powdered pastel. The light blue sides of the building received values that were lightened by mixing a great deal of white pastel with cobalt blue. The medium blue shade sides, as well as the shadow cast by the sculpture, were a mixture of cobalt blue, white, and a small amount of symphonic orange. By using some 45-degree strokes, streaks of light which relieve the monotony of the large shade areas were used.

The sculpture was formed by carefully locating and drawing shade areas and rendering these individually in shades of blue. The tan promenade around the pool was rendered by a mixture of symphonic red and white, with a small amount of yellow, and the foliage was rendered by using cotton, powder pastel and paper cutouts. Some of the sharp top edges were then rubbed down with the finger. Joints in the stonework at the left and in the promenade were erased, as described for the foregoing rendering. Scale figures were drawn directly by using a broken piece of pastel.

The drawing was then lightly fixed with pastel fixative blown from a mouth spray.

Fig. 17.2

An exhibition building rendered by Lawrence Braverman Student project

Chapter 18

Mixed media

WHILE THE PURIST uses one medium only, many delineators mix various media for striking results. Among the combinations illustrated in this chapter are:

1. Pen and black ink plus black water color sprayed with airbrush.
2. Pen and black ink with colored water color sprayed or hand brushed.
3. Pen and ink (Rapidograph type pens) with water color sprayed with airbrush.
4. Pen and ink and aniline dyes sprayed with airbrush.
5. Pen and ink plus tempera sprayed with airbrush.
6. Black and colored inks, using pen and/or airbrush, plus ink spatter.
7. Pen and ink plus gouache.
8. Pen and ink plus Magic Markers.
9. Pencil and Magic Markers.
10. Pen and ink, Pentel, and Magic Markers.
11. Pentel and graphite pencil.
12. Tempera and Flex-Opaque on photograph.
13. Chinese ink, Chinese white tempera, and charcoal.
14. Casein and colored pencil.
15. Casein and acrylic paints.
16. Water color, tempera, and ink.
17. Graphite pencil plus water color washes.
18. Pentel and Magic Markers.

Fig. 18.1

Entrance to an office building
rendered by Joseph King
Student project
Media: Pen and ink
and water color

Fig. 18.2

Study for a domed building
rendered by
Edward G. Schildbach
Student project
Media: Pen and ink
and water color

Fig. 18.3

Study for a building
and a bridge
rendered by Sylvan L. Joseph
Student project
Media: Pen and ink
and water color

Fig. 18.4
John Hancock Center,
Chicago, Ill.
Skidmore, Owings & Merrill,
Architects
rendered by Helmut Jacoby
Size: 35½ x 12¼ in.
Media: Ink and colored
water color spray

The name of Helmut Jacoby is practically synonymous with a technique which combines pen, black ink, and airbrush. This combination produces an extremely articulate result. (See Fig. 18.4 and Fig. 18.5.) Small-scale building detail, textures, foliage, automobiles, and scale figures are first drawn in pen and ink. Sash, spandrels, structural elements, as well as shades and shadows in general, and trees, bushes, and sky are sprayed with the airbrush. The result is an extremely photographic description of the building and site, superb for reproduction and tasteful. Although most of Mr. Jacoby's works are in black and white, he occasionally adds a small amount of color to his black water color for use in the airbrush. The success of Mr. Jacoby's works lies for a great part in the carefully determined station point, his meticulous draftsmanship, and skillful rendering.

Fig. 18.5
BMW Headquarters, Munich, Germany
Karl Schwanzer, Architect
rendered by Helmut Jacoby
Media: Ink and water color spray, black and white

Fig. 18.6A
Fig. 18.6B

The New Family Court
Building of The City of
New York
Haines, Lundberg & Waehler,
Architects
rendered by Juri Kirsimagi
Size: 30 x 33 in.
Media: Airbrush, liquid
water colors

The ink outline drawings for Fig. 18.6A and B were made on Albanene prepared tracing paper. Since it was necessary to save time for the final rendering, the line drawings were silk-screened on Strathmore illustration boards. In this process the line drawing is a little darker and heavier than ink drawing would have been on an illustration board. In large work, particularly if there are no details or small-scale line work, this process seems to work well.

The actual rendering of Fig. 18.6A and B was done with airbrush using Dr. Ph. Martin's Radiant Concentrated Liquid Water Colors. Frisket film was used for masking. Areas to be sprayed were cut out of the frisket film. Darkest areas were rendered first, lighter areas were sprayed second, etc. The upper portions of the trunks and branches of the foreground tree were painted with a hand brush.

In general the new building was rendered in grays, while the surrounding buildings and street were rendered in soft browns and beiges. Male scale figures were painted in muted tones, i.e., soft shades of gray-green, and some of the female scale figures were painted in bright yellow-orange. Because of the relation of this new building to other buildings in the area, it was necessary to make two renderings to adequately describe the project.

In Fig. 18.7 the line drawing, wood graining, floor textures, and lighting fixtures were drawn in pen and ink. The wood grain walls, lighting fixtures, entrance door, and curtains, as well as the floor, were rendered with airbrush. The walls are a rich walnut tone, the door bronze, the floor a pale yellow, and the curtains white. The furniture was rendered with a hand brush and water color, as were the decorative flower pots and scale figures.

Fig. 18.7
National Westminster Bank Ltd., New York, N.Y.
Bonsignore, Brignati, Goldstein & Mazzotta, Architects
rendered by Juri Kirsimagi
Size: 28 x 19 in.
Media: Airbrush, hand brush, and water color

Fig. 18.8

Lufthansa German Airlines
Cargo Terminal
J.F.K. International Airport,
New York, N.Y.
Robert C. Mock & Associates,
Architects and Engineers
rendered by Al Lorenz
Size: 24 x 36 in.
Media: Pen and ink,
transparent water color,
airbrush
Photo: Gil Amiaga

The amount of airbrush work in a pen and ink–airbrush rendering depends, of course, upon the desire of the delineator. Figure 18.8, by Al Lorenz, contains a great deal of pen and ink texture and only a small amount of airbrush. Interestingly, the clouds in the sky were indicated by hatching with a crow-quill pen and ink, and the hatched areas were given a light tone by the use of the airbrush. The original was rendered in black and white with some parts of the building in color, while the entourage was accomplished in full water color, but in muted tones.

Each delineator develops his own approach to airbrush work. Mr. Kenneth Sailor, for instance, uses a double-weight white Strathmore (hot-pressed) illustration board. A pencil perspective layout is made directly on the board, then inked in using a variety of Rapidograph pens. Interior details seen through glass are usually rendered in gray ink. When the inking has been completed, clear E-Z Frisket is applied. Shadow areas are cut out first and airbrushed; shade areas are then sprayed, with shadow areas done again. The lighter areas are sprayed last, with both shade and shadow areas sprayed once more. A new frisket is applied for each color used.

In general, the major colors of the building are applied first and are used to determine the colors of the surrounding buildings and entourage.

In order to ensure that his rendering will reproduce as anticipated in black and white, Mr. Sailor takes Polaroid photographs at regular intervals during the course of a rendering. Water color used by Mr. Sailor is mixed to the consistency of colored ink in order to ensure transparency. All colors used are Winsor & Newton, Inc. Professional Grade.

Figure 18.9 is notable in that the main building, including plant pockets, terrace, and sculpture, is given importance by the use of a relatively strong bronze color, while other elements in the picture are much lighter in value. Note that the cars are presented in line only, so as not to compete with the building being illustrated.

Fig. 18.9
Martin Luther King
High School,
Board of Education,
City of New York
Frost Associates, Architects
rendered by Kenneth J. Sailor
Size: 25 x 36 in.
Media: Pen and ink,
water color, airbrush
Photo: Gil Amiaga

The technique used in this rendering is similar to that in Fig. 18.9. Maximum attention is given to the brick pylons and the lower elements nearby, which are the color of sepia brick, while the rest of the building is left white. Again, all elements that are fine in detail, such as foliage, scale figures, grass areas, and the tree in the foreground, are drawn with pen and ink, then sprayed with the airbrush. The foliage is lightly sprayed with gray-green. The pale sky is sepia in color.

Fig. 18.10
Psychology Building,
University of Connecticut
Storrs, Conn.
Frederick G. Frost, Jr.,
Architect
P. Whitney Webb, Architect
rendered by Kenneth J. Sailor
Size: 24 x 30 in.
Media: Pen and ink,
water color, airbrush
Photo: Gil Amiaga

Typically, in Fig. 18.11 the brick was drawn with a dark mixture of sepia. The concrete remained the color of the illustration board (white), while concrete in shade and shadow was made of a mixture of ochre and lamp black. Trees and grass were sprayed with terra verte (green earth). Background buildings, with the exception of those at the right, were sprayed with a mixture of burnt sienna and lamp black. Street windows, sky, and the large building in the background were painted with a mixture of yellow ochre, ultramarine blue, alizarin crimson, cadmium yellow light, red earth (terra rose), cerulean blue, and lamp black, which produced gray-yellow tones.

Fig. 18.11
Henry Phipps Plaza North
Bellevue South
Urban Renewal Project
City of New York
Frost Associates, Architects
rendered by Kenneth J. Sailor
Size: 20 x 30 in.
Media: Pen and ink,
water color, airbrush
Photo: Gil Amiaga

Fig. 18.12
Student Union,
State University College at
Oneonta for the State
University Construction Fund
Oneonta, N.Y.
Francis X. Gina' and Partners,
Architects
rendered by Arnold Prato
Size: 17 x 28 in.
Media: Pen and ink
(black and white)

This rendering by Mr. Prato illustrates the manner in which pen, ink, and airbrush complement each other. They are, indeed, a small but powerful vocabulary. Note that details such as stonework, brickwork, trees, bushes, scale figures, boats, and interior details, all of which are fine in scale, were drawn with pen and ink. They were complemented by using the airbrush for general tones, shades, shadows, and the reflection of the building in the water in the foreground.

Figures 18.13A and B illustrate the striking results that can be obtained by the use of pen, ink, and airbrush. No two delineators use a medium or combination of media in the same way. Here, Mr. Toscano not only selected striking views of the building, but provided maximum contrasts between light and dark so that the building seems so real one feels that he could walk around it and into it. Interestingly, limited color was used. For example, about 85 percent of the rendering was done in grays and tones of gray. The sky was painted very light blue. Railings were executed in a bright blue, and some of the doorways were made red. Interestingly also, Mr. Toscano uses Dr. Ph. Martin's Aniline Dye Colors in his airbrush to keep it from clogging.

Fig. 18.13A Fig. 18.13B
Two views: Hall of Science,
Flushing, N.Y.
Max O. Urbahn Associates,
Inc., Architects
rendered by
Wallace J. Toscano
Size: 27 x 37 in.
        20 x 20 in.
Media: Pen and ink, airbrush

The combination of pen, ink, and tempera (or opaque water color) sprayed with an airbrush is used by many delineators, particularly for reproduction in black and white. Mr. Hoftyzer's method of procedure is as follows:

1. He makes a perspective drawing on tracing paper.

2. When the perspective has been critically analyzed by Mr. Hoftyzer and his client, it is transferred to illustration board by a sheet of tracing paper coated with graphite. This leaves a faint line copy of the perspective on the illustration board.

3. This line copy is then inked in, producing an inked version of the original perspective.

4. A value study is made to determine light and dark areas, shades and shadows.

5. Textures, such as tree and plant foliage, grass, shadows on grass, and scale figures, are applied with pen and ink.

6. Areas to be airbrushed, which have been determined in the value study, are then prepared for spraying by masking each area in turn. Mr. Hoftyzer uses a clear plastic film adhesive, coated on one side. The drawing is covered with the film, and the areas to be sprayed are uncovered by carefully cutting the film with a sharp knife. When the proper areas are exposed, spraying can begin. When spraying is completed, the remaining film is removed from the drawing and the procedure is repeated until every area in the drawing has its proper value.

For example, the first spray might be the dark tones of walls, leaving the light walls white or the color of the illustration board. Sky, if any, is sprayed after masking the rest of the drawing. Rounded forms, if any, and shadows are sprayed. The leaves of trees may be lightly sprayed in order to give them a cohesive quality, leaving the tree structure white in some cases, dark in others.

Fig. 18.14

John Hancock Parking Garage
Boston, Mass.
I. M. Pei & Partners, Architects
rendered by Peter Hoftyzer
Size: 22 x 28 in.
Media: Pen and ink, airbrush
(black and white)

Fig. 18.15

Proposed design for church
Kenneth Kassler (Dec.)
Architect
rendered by Kenneth A. Licht
Media: Pen, ink, and
brush tempera

Figure 18.15 depicts an effective combination of media and technique. In order to create an autumn scene, Mr. Licht proceeded as follows:

1. The outline drawing of the building was drawn on 140-lb hot-pressed water color paper which had previously been stretched.

2. All white areas were masked out with white tempera.

3. The various parts of the building and the background trees were rendered in colored inks, using pen and/or hand brush. Mr. Licht used Pelikan waterproof ink in colors of yellow, orange, burnt sienna, ultra-marine blue, and dilute black.

4. The building was marked out and the sky, foreground, and background were spattered with black and dilute black inks, using a toothbrush.

5. In order to create a great deal of variation in the colors and tones of the trees, columns, and spire, the entire drawing was taken to the sink and *cold* water was allowed to run gently across its entire surface. With a small hog bristle brush and a small piece of sponge, the major trees in the foreground were sponged and/or partially sponged, allowing the white of the paper to show through in most places.

6. When the drawing was entirely dry, white areas were reinforced where necessary with paint; variations in the trees were obtained by modelling them with hand brush, ink, and white tempera. Tree shadows and foreground shadow were applied with a brush and colored ink.

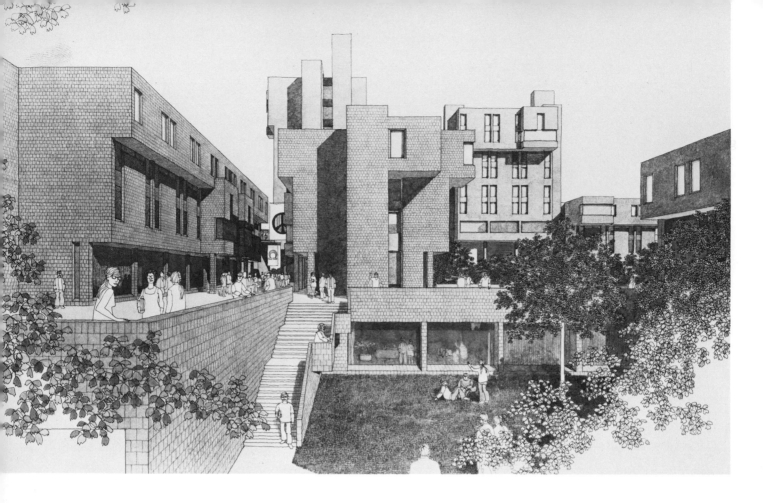

Fig. 18.16

Six colleges, State University
of New York, Buffalo, N.Y.
Davis, Brody & Associates,
Architects
rendered by A. C. Bergmann
Size: 20 x 30 in.
Media: Pen, ink, and
Magic Markers

Fig. 18.17

Dormitory & dining hall
State University of New York,
New Paltz, N.Y.
Davis, Brody & Associates,
Architects
rendered by A. C. Bergmann
Size: 20 x 30 in.
Media: Pen, ink, and
Magic Marker

Figures 18.16 and 18.17 illustrate the personal approach of Mr. A. C. Bergmann. Examining his drawings, one discovers that he uses wide cones of vision and the vignette. His works are purposely left incomplete and gain a great deal of individuality because of this. It has often been said that what is omitted from a drawing is as important as that which is included.

Mr. Bergmann works with freehand ink drawing and color washes of colored Magic Markers built up over gray Magic Marker. The inking precedes the coloring. It is next to impossible to remove the color once applied, so great care must be taken while using the Magic Marker.

Figure 18.18 was drawn on tracing paper which was mounted on an illustration board. A light pencil outline drawing was first made; then various elements were covered with relatively broad strokes by the use of gray Magic Markers. Fine details, including scale figures, were delineated by the use of a Prismacolor pencil. The original was black and white.

Fig. 18.18
PATH Journal Square
Transportation Center
Jersey City, N.J.
The Port of New York
Authority
Leibowitz/Bodouva
Associates, Architects
Robert H. Fava Associates,
Assoc. Architects
rendered by Arnold Prato
Size: 18 x 24 in.
Media: Magic Marker and
Prismacolor

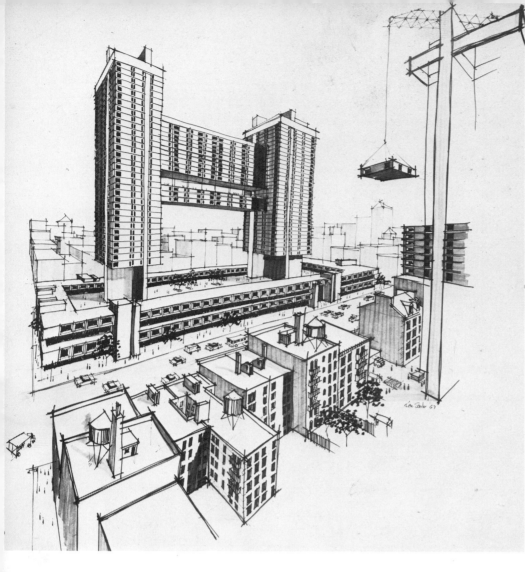

Fig. 18.19

Live-Work Project Proposed
for the City of New York
Frost Associates, Architects
rendered by Kenneth J. Sailor
Size: 30 x 40 in.
Media: Pentel and
Magic Marker

Fig. 18.20

Brighton Beach Competition
Brooklyn, N.Y.
Frost Associates, Architects
rendered by Kenneth J. Sailor
Size: 30 x 40 in.
Media: Pen, ink, Pentel,
and Magic Marker

Figure 18.19 illustrates the use of Pentel and Magic Marker and shows how one medium complements the other. Broad strokes of the Magic Marker are used for background and for an occasional plain surface, while Pentel is used for fine detail, scale figures, and tree foliage.

Drawn with pen and ink, Pentel, and Magic Marker, Fig. 18.20 again illustrates the fact that several carefully selected media can be used on a single project, each contributing to the total effect.

Fig. 18.21

Interior, World of Birds
Bronx Zoo, New York
Morris Ketchum, Jr.,
& Associates, Architects
rendered by
Wallace Toscano, A.I.A.
Media: Pencil and Pentel

In order to create Fig. 18.21, Mr. Toscano devised still another technique, in which he first covered his illustration board with gesso, a plasterlike mineral substance mixed with glue that dries very hard and smooth. The drawing was inked with a Pentel, and the shades and shadows were pencilled in with graphite pencil, the texture of the gesso giving a very crisp pencil stroke.

In Fig. 18.22, Mr. Toscano used a technique similar to that used for Fig. 18.21, except that tracing paper was used instead of gessoed board.

Fig. 18.22

Married students housing
State University Agricultural
& Technical College,
Morrisville, N.Y.
Morris Ketchum, Jr.,
& Associates, Architects
rendered by
Wallace Toscano, A.I.A.
Media: Pencil and Pentel

Fig. 18.23A
Fig. 18.23B
Fig. 18.23C

Essex County College
Newark, N.J.
(Aerial view and two
detail views)
The Grad Partnership,
Architects
rendered by Kenneth A. Licht
Size: 24 x 36 in.
Media: Photograph with
tempera
Photo: Louis Checkman

For Fig. 18.23A, the procedure was as follows:

1. An aerial photograph of a three-block area was obtained.

2. An undetailed cardboard model of proposed construction was prepared. The model was then photographed at approximately the same angle as the aerial photograph to approximate the same perspective. The photograph of the model was rubber-cemented to the aerial photograph and a new photograph was taken of the entire project. The photograph was enlarged to approximately 24 x 36 in., matte finish.

3. Tracing paper was applied over the composite photograph, and vanishing points were established. Mr. Licht then proceeded to lay out proposed buildings in detail, with sidewalks, fountains, trees, etc. The tracing was then transferred to the new photograph. The entire proposed construction was rendered in color, using tempera colors with Flex-Opaque to make the paint adhere to the photograph.

4. Black and white 8- x 10-in. photographs were made for distribution.

5. As the rendering is small in scale, several "closeup," or detail, renderings were made by Mr. Licht. (See Fig. 18.23B and C.) To obtain detail, the Graflex camera was moved in very close to the photograph. The renderings were made directly on the photographs, again using a few drops of Flex-Opaque in the tempera to keep it from crawling. The "looseness" in the detail renderings is due to magnification.

Fig. 18.24

House for builder client
Herman H. York, A.I.A.,
Architect
rendered by
Charles J. Spiess, Jr.
Size: 12 x 24 in.
Media: Chinese ink and
charcoal on illustration board
Photo: Gil Amiaga

Chapter 13, Rendering with Chinese Ink, is devoted to a description of this medium exclusively. In Fig. 18.24 some parts of the rendering, such as shadows, windows, lawn, and background, were painted by the usual wash method. However, trees were painted directly with a small pencil-type brush, using Chinese ink of various intensities. After the basic washes were applied to the ground areas, variations were introduced over the base washes. Window details, columns, battens, and the driveway at the right of the picture were drawn with straightedge, ruling pen, and Chinese white. The sky was made by wetting the sky area and, when it was damp but no longer wet, introducing a fairly dark Chinese ink wash into it. Finally, the foreground and parts of the sky area were slightly darkened by applying powdered charcoal with a piece of cotton. Because of the use of charcoal, the entire drawing was then "fixed."

Figures 18.25 and 18.26 illustrate the use of pen, waterproof ink, and Chinese ink wash. In both of these illustrations, Mr. Spiess III first drew a large portion of the buildings with pen, waterproof ink, and straightedge. Shades and shadows were applied with washes, while brickwork was indicated by the use of straightedge and pen and ink. It is interesting to note that Mr. Spiess III varies his treatment of trees and foliage. In Fig. 18.25, for the most part, trunks and branches are kept light against the dark background, while in Fig. 18.26 trunks and branches of most of the trees are rendered dark against the light building. Here we also find an interesting comparison of foreground delineation. In Fig. 18.25 the darkness of the foreground is limited and is quite textural, while in Fig. 18.26 the foreground is quite dark and understated.

Fig. 18.25
Hayden-on-Hudson
Apartment House
New York, N.Y.
Henry Kibel, Architect
rendered by
Charles Joseph Spiess III
Size: 30 x 40 in.
Media: Black and white
line drawing with
Chinese ink wash
Photo: Gil Amiaga

Fig. 18.26
67th Precinct Station House
& Engine Company 248,
Brooklyn, N.Y.
Knappe & Johnson,
Architects
rendered by
Charles Joseph Spiess III
Size: 30 x 40 in.
Media: Ink line drawing with
Chinese ink wash

Fig. 18.27

Apartment tower for DAP,
Inc., Sub. of Plough, Inc.
Dayton, Ohio
Harold R. Roe, A.I.A.,
Designer
rendered by
Howard Associates
Harold R. Roe, A.I.A.,
Project Manager
Size: 20 x 30 in.
Media: Casein and colored
pencil on colored board

Figures 18.27 and 18.28 illustrate a combination of casein and colored pencil presented on colored illustration board. In general the procedure is as follows:

A sky is floated on the board by first wetting the board thoroughly, then washing into the wet area a thin casein phthalocyanine blue modified by white and yellow ochre. Contrast is developed around the building areas by lightening the sky with a thin yellow ochre/white mixture or darkening with an ultramarine blue/yellow ochre mixture. By now the board will have begun to buckle, and extra moisture is soaked up with tissues. It should be kept in mind that sky colors should be thin enough to allow the color of the board to determine the intensity of the sky. Many illustration boards are not adequate for such a wet technique. The board most often used by Howard Associates is Crescent stone gray 975 or saddle tan 983.

The building, which is the center of interest, is then rendered in a usual casein technique, using casein in an opaque manner. As a comparison to the precision of the building and the softness of the sky, entourage, trees, bushes, water, etc. are crisply rendered in both Prismacolor and Verithin pencils in a broad stroke chisel-pointed style. Final highlights, trees, shrubbery, and foliage are then added by using casein paint. Cars and people, if any, are also rendered with paint and brush.

Fig. 18.28
"Entara Entrance" brochure
Kawneer Company, Inc.,
A Sub. of American Metal
Climax, Inc., Niles, Mich.
Richard P. Howard, Designer
Harold R. Roe, A.I.A.,
Architect
rendered by
Howard Associates
Harold R. Roe, A.I.A.,
Project Manager
Size: 18 x 26 in.
Media: Casein and colored
pencil on colored board

Chapter 19

Rendering plans

Ink and Water Color Plans

Excellent results may be obtained by rendering plot plans in pen and ink and water color. Such a drawing may be applied to a cold-pressed stretch or an illustration board with the same surface. The plan of the building is first placed upon the sheet in graphite pencil. Each contour line is drawn with a clean pencil line and textures such as those for the terrace, tile, etc., are laid out. Trees and other details such as rock outcroppings are first drawn in pencil. Shadows are applied upon the ground as if the plan were cut 4 ft above the first floor level. The entire grass area is first rendered, in the same number of light washes as there are contours. The first pale wash of this color is applied to the highest contour, and after this is dry, to the highest two contours, then the highest three, four, etc., until the lowest contour has been given one wash. In this way the rise and fall of the ground is shown. Bodies of water are rendered in the same way so that the lowest contour is given the most washes, the highest contour a single wash.

After the ground area has been rendered, the walls, partitions, and furniture are ruled in in waterproof black ink. The shadow of the building is then cast upon the ground in a darker tone of the color used for the ground washes. Shadows cast upon road areas will, of course, be a darker tone of the road color.

Fig. 19.1

Plan of a residence rendered by Milton R. Edelin Student project

Fig. 19.2

Plan of a residence
rendered by Leslie Feder
Student project

Flagstones and concrete textures are next applied with a ruling pen
and diluted ink. The trees are rendered with a small brush by working
directly from the palette, first giving each wooden member of the tree a
flat wash, then modelling each member with a darker wash on the shade
side. The foliage of the tree is usually shown with a transparent wash so
that the architecture may be seen through it. Low planting is painted
directly from the palette and the various plant forms are indicated in the
same way.

Often several kinds of tree indications are used on the same plan.
Deciduous trees are given a different indication from conifers; large conifers
a different indication from small ones. The structure of some trees is sometimes shown and at other times omitted. Variation adds charm and interest
to the rendered plan.

As in all rendering, it is all too easy to fall into the realistic color scheme
of bright green grass, blue water, etc., but sophisticated color schemes such
as those illustrated have a much greater appeal to the client. The grass
areas, for instance, in Fig. 19.1, Plate XVIII and Fig. 19.2 are, respectively,
blue-green, yellow-green, and gray-green. Water is shown in each, but it is
gray-blue rather than brilliant blue. Furniture in Fig. 19.1 and Plate XVIII
is blue and grayed orange, while that in Fig. 19.2 is brown and black. The
terraces in Fig. 19.2 are pale blue; those in Plate XVIII and Fig. 19.2 are
grayed orange. In other words, the colors used in all parts of each rendering
are all obtained from a previously determined color scheme, as in Chapter 14. These are all mixed together for each hue, the shade desired determining the exact amount of each color that is to be included in the mixture.

A *gallery of professional renderings*

Fig. 20.1

A plan house
Rudolph A. Matern, Architect
rendered by Charles Spiess, Jr.
Medium: Pencil

Fig. 20.2

Proposed Aerospace Building
University of Michigan,
Project No. 299
Ann Arbor, Mich.
James L. Coquillard
& Associates,
Architects-Engineers
Warren E. Poole, A. I. A.,
Acting University Architect
rendered by
Howard Associates,
Harold R. Roe, A.I.A.
Project Manager
Medium: Pencil

Fig. 20.3

Cazenovia College
Student Residence #6
and Dining Unit
Cazenovia, N.Y.
The Moore & Hutchins
Partnership, Architects
rendered by
Charles J. Spiess, Jr.
Size: 14 x 28 in.
Medium: Pencil on gray
illustration board

Fig. 20.4

Proposed chapel,
St. Francis College,
Biddeford, Maine
Brother Cajetan,
J. B. Baumann, O.F.M. (Dec.)
Architect
rendered by
Charles J. Spiess, Jr.
Medium: Pencil

Fig. 20.5

Vacation ski house
Stratton Mountain, Vt.
Alexander McIlvaine,
Architect
rendered by Minor L. Bishop
Medium: Pencil

Fig. 20.6

Proposed memorial to a
great American
Washington, D.C.
Alan Davoll, ALM, AWS,
Designer, and
Marcel Villaneuva, A.I.A.,
Architect
rendered by Alan Davoll
Medium: Water color

Fig. 20.7
Proposed hotel design
Walter Karl (Dec.) Architect
rendered by
Walter Karl (Dec.)
Medium: Transparent
water color

Fig. 20.8
Design for a house
Larry J. Dalton, Designer
rendered by Karl Visuals,
Jane Karl
Medium: Designer's gouache

PLAN MG 4-5 ELEVATION B

Fig. 20.9

Finland House, New York
Kahn & Jacobs, Architects
rendered by Marcel Mutin
Medium: Tempera

Fig. 20.10

Proposed design for
Woodward & Lothrop,
Prince Georges Plaza
Lathrop Douglass, Architect
rendered by Marcel Mutin
Medium: Tempera

Fig. 20.11

Vilas Communication Hall
University of Wisconsin,
Madison, Wis.
Campus Mall Shopping
Center, Lake Park Corp.,
John J. Flad & Assoc.,
Architects, Engineers
& Planners
rendered by Marcel Mutin
Medium: Tempera

Fig. 20.12

Shopping center project,
Montrose, Pa.
Robert Doerner, A.I.A.,
Architect
rendered by Robert C. Nelsen
Size: 30 x 40 in.
Medium: Tempera

Fig. 20.13A 1st Phase
Fig. 20.13B 2nd Phase

Newark College of
Engineering, Newark, N.J.
Epple & Seaman, Architects,
Brooks D. Kaufman,
Project Architect
rendered by Kenneth A. Licht
Medium: Tempera

Fig. 20.13C 3rd Phase

Fig. 20.14

Design for an industrial plant
Kempa and Schwartz,
Architects
rendered by Robert Schwartz
Medium: Tempera

kempa and schwartz · architects

Fig. 20.15

Medical Center
Babylon, N.Y.
Kempa and Schwartz,
Architects
rendered by Robert Schwartz
Medium: Tempera

Fig. 20.16

Clubhouse Entrance,
Monticello Raceway
Monticello, N.Y.
August Lux and Associates,
Architects
rendered by Vincent Furno
Medium: Tempera

Fig. 20.17

Monticello Raceway
Monticello, N.Y.
August Lux and Associates,
Architects
rendered by Vincent Furno
Medium: Tempera

Fig. 20.18

Research and engineering
building, Sterling Forest, N.Y.
Ives, Turano & Gardner,
Architects
rendered by
George Cooper Rudolph
Medium: Tempera

Fig. 20.19

Union Junior College
Union, N.J.
Frederick A. Elsasser,
Architect
rendered by
George Cooper Rudolph
Medium: Tempera

Fig. 20.20

Clarkstown Junior High School
New City, N.Y.
Perkins & Will, Architects
rendered by Pierre Lutz
Medium: Tempera

Fig. 20.21

Bath and Tennis Club
Westhampton Beach, N.Y.
Irving J. Berger, Architect
rendered by Marcel Mutin
Medium: Tempera

Fig. 20.22
Scheme for new passenger
terminal at
LaGuardia Airport
Port of New York Authority
Aviation Planning Division
rendered by Elliott Glushak
Medium: Tempera

Fig. 20.23
Office building for
H. H. Robertson Company
Ambridge, Pa.
Designed by Oscar F. Wiggins
rendered by Elliott Glushak
Medium: Tempera

Fig. 20.24

Chizuk Amuno Congregation
Baltimore, Md.
Daniel Schwartzman,
Architect
rendered by Elliott Glushak
Medium: Tempera

Fig. 20.25

Hudson Harbor Apartment
Complex—Aerial view
Edgewater, N.J.
Keith I. Hibner, Architect
rendered by Keith I. Hibner
Medium: Tempera

Fig. 20.26
Point Lookout Concession
Complex
Keith I. Hibner, Architect
rendered by Keith Hibner
& Arthur Taylor
Medium: Tempera

Fig. 20.27
Hudson Harbor Apartment
Complex (Street level view)
Edgewater, N.J.
Keith I. Hibner, Architect
rendered by
George Cooper Rudolph
Medium: Tempera

Fig. 20.28

Gem Shopping Plaza,
San Juan, Puerto Rico
McClintock & Thun
rendered by Pacifico Bacalzo
Size: 30 x 40 in.
Media: Casein and acrylic
on illustration board
Photo: Gil Amiaga

Fig. 20.29

Prototype of
tropical vacation cottage
Various Caribbean Islands
Geo. McClintock, Architect
McClintock & Thun,
Architects
rendered by Pacifico Bacalzo
Size: 20 x 30 in.
Media: Casein and acrylic
Photo: Gil Amiaga

Fig. 20.30A
Fig. 20.30B
Francisco & Sons
Garden Shop, Tenafly, N.J.
A. Existing conditions
B. Proposed alterations
on photograph
Harsen & Johns, Architects
rendered by Kenneth A. Licht
Medium: Tempera with
Flex-Opaque
Photo: Millard J. Meyers

A. Existing conditions

B. Proposed alterations
on photograph

Fig. 20.31

Proposed Hemisphere
Hotel
St. Croix, Virgin Islands
A. J. DiSanto &
Associates, Architects
rendered by Peter Rahill
Medium: Tempera

Fig. 20.32

Encyclopaedia
Britannica Pavilion,
Expo 70 World's Fair,
Osaka, Japan
A. J. DiSanto,
Associate Designer
A. J. DiSanto &
Associates, Architects
rendered by Peter Rahill
Medium: Tempera

Fig. 20.33

First National Bank
of Highland,
Poughkeepsie Branch
Flemming & Silverman,
Architects
rendered by Peter Rahill
Medium: Tempera

Fig. 20.34

Colony Square,
A development of
Cushman Corporation,
Atlanta, Ga.
Jova/Daniels/Busby,
Architects
rendered by
Robert E. Schwartz
Medium: Tempera

Fig. 20.35

Wisconsin Alumni Research
Foundation Office Building
John J. Flad & Associates,
Architects, Engineers
& Planners
rendered by Pierre Lutz
Medium: Tempera
Photo: Wollin Studios

Fig. 20.36

Christian Science Church
Center, Boston, Mass.
I. M. Pei & Partners,
Architects
Araldo A. Cossutta,
Partner-in-Charge
rendered by
Robert E. Schwartz
Medium: Tempera

Fig. 20.37
National Guardian Life
Insurance Company
Home Office, Madison, Wis.
John J. Flad and Associates,
Architects, Engineers
& Planners
rendered by Pierre Lutz
Medium: Tempera

Fig. 20.38
Chung Khiaw Bank,
Singapore
I. M. Pei & Partners,
Architects
rendered by
Robert E. Schwartz
Medium: Tempera

Fig. 20.39

Echo Park Pool Complex
Town of Hempstead,
Long Island, N.Y.
Planning Associates, Inc.,
Recreation Consultants
Keith I. Hibner, A.I.A.,
Consulting Architect
rendered by
George Cooper Rudolph
Rudolph, Russell & Fleury, Inc.
Media: Water color,
tempera and ink

Fig. 20.40

One Beacon St., Boston, Mass.
(Employers-Commercial Union
Companies, Owner)
Skidmore, Owings & Merrill,
Architects
rendered by John E. Russell
Rudolph, Russell & Fleury, Inc.
Size: 22½ x 32 in.
Medium: Opaque water color
(brownstone all brushwork)

Fig. 20.41

West Islip Office,
Central Federal Savings
& Loan Assn., West Islip, N.Y.
Ralph E. Leff, A.I.A.,
Architect
rendered by
Charles J. Spiess, Jr.
Size: 17 x 34 in.
Medium: Tempera
Photo: Gil Amiaga

Fig. 20.42

Apartment house
at Wilshire Heights,
Jefferson Parish, La.
S. J. Kessler & Sons,
Architects & Engineers
rendered by
Charles J. Spiess III
Size: 30 x 40 in.
Media: Ink line and tempera

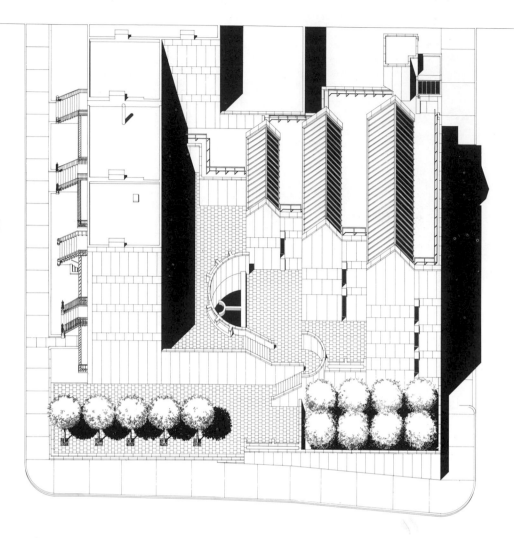

Fig. 20.43
New York State Bar Center
(Headquarters for the
New York State Bar
Association)
Albany, N.Y.
A perspective plan
James Stewart Polshek
and Associates,
rendered by
Ron Williams, Onyx
Medium: India ink on board
and/or Mylar

Fig. 20.44
Wilberforce University,
Wilberforce, Ohio
Dalton-Dalton-Little,
Architects
rendered by
Art Associates, Inc.
Ronald W. Rose & Rod Dullum
Medium: Casein
on colored board

Fig. 20.45

Park Central Apartments
Cleveland, Ohio
Dalton-Dalton-Little,
Architects
rendered by
Art Associates, Inc.
Ronald W. Rose & Rod Dullum
Medium: Casein
on colored board

Fig. 20.46

Hidden Lagoon Hotel
St. Croix, Virgin Islands
Welton Becket and
Associates, Architects
rendered by Longarevic
Size: 24 x 48 in.
Medium: Shiva casein (tube)
Photo: Gil Amiaga

Fig. 20.47

"Entara Entrance" brochure
for Kawneer Company, Inc.,
A Sub. of American Metal
Climax, Inc., Niles, Mich.
Richard P. Howard, Designer
Harold R. Roe, A.I.A.,
Architect
rendered by
Howard Associates
Harold R. Roe, A.I.A.,
Project Manager
Size: 20 x 30 in.
Media: Casein and colored
pencil on colored board

Fig. 20.48

W. Alton Jones Cell Science
Center, The Tissue Culture
Association,
Lake Placid, N.Y.
James L. Coquillard
& Associates,
Architects-Engineers
rendered by
Howard Associates
Harold R. Roe, A.I.A.,
Project Designer
Medium: Casein

Fig. 20.49

Plan for the
State University College
at Geneseo, N.Y.
Miller, Snibbe & Tafel,
Architects & Planners
Size: 20½ x 32 in.
rendered by Dave Morgan
Medium: Casein on
Crescent "dusk" illustration
board (a cool gray-green)

Fig. 20.50

Medical Tower,
New York, N.Y.
Hamby, Kennerly, Slomanson
& Smith, Architects
Size: 20 x 27½ in.
rendered by Dave Morgan
Medium: Casein on Crescent
white illustration board

Fig. 20.51

710 Fifth Avenue,
New York, N.Y.
Hamby, Kennerly, Slomanson
& Smith, Architects
Size: 20 x 29 in.
rendered by Dave Morgan,
Media: Pencil, rendering
with water color washes on
D'Arches watercolor board

Fig. 20.52

Design for
proposed restaurant
Mathew Pollack,
A.M.R. Management Co.,
New York, N.Y.
rendered by Al Lorenz,
Size: 30 x 40 in.
Media: Pen and ink, airbrush
with transparent water color
Photo: Gil Amiaga

Fig. 20.53

White Plains
Telephone Building
White Plains, N.Y.
Haines, Lundberg & Waehler,
Architects
rendered by Juri Kirsimagi
Size: 26 x 29 in.
Media: Pen and ink, airbrush

Fig. 20.54

Hoffman La Roche,
Research and Quality Control
Laboratory, Nutley, N.J.
Haines, Lundberg & Waehler,
Architects
rendered by Juri Kirsimagi
Size: 30 x 21 in.
Media: Pen and ink, airbrush

Fig. 20.55
New office building,
Allied Chemical Corporation,
Morristown, N.J.
Haines, Lundberg & Waehler,
Architects
rendered by Juri Kirsimagi
Size: 32 x 18 in.
Media: Pen and ink, airbrush

Fig. 20.56
Howe Avenue Nursing Home,
New Rochelle Hospital
New Rochelle, N.Y.
Frost Associates, Architects
rendered by Kenneth J. Sailor
Size: 15 x 22 in.
Media: Pen and ink,
airbrush (black and white)
Photo: Gil Amiaga

Fig. 20.57

Materials Research Center for
Allied Chemical Corporation,
Morristown, N.J.
James Stewart Polshek,
Architect
rendered by
Richard Thompson
Size: 36 x 14 in.
Media: Pen and ink,
airbrush (color)
Photo: Gil Amiaga

Fig. 20.58

Competition for the
Yale Mathematics Building
New Haven, Conn.
Frost Associates, Architects
rendered by Kenneth J. Sailor
Size: 20 x 30 in.
Media: Pentel and Magic
Marker (black and white)
Photo: Gil Amiaga

Fig. 20.59
Las Vegas City Hall,
Las Vegas, Nev.
Enlarged Detail
Daniel, Mann, Johnson &
Mendenhall,
Architects & Engineers
rendered by Uri Hung
Size: 33 x 24 in.
Medium: Designer's gouache

Fig. 20.60
Houston Center,
Texas Eastern Transmission
Corp., Houston, Tex.
Wm. L. Pereira & Assoc.,
Architects
rendered by Uri Hung
Size: 28 x 17 in.
Medium: Designer's gouache

Fig. 20.61
Ford Dearborn Project,
Ford Motor Co.,
Dearborn, Mich.
Wm. L. Pereira & Assoc.,
Architects
rendered by Uri Hung
Size: 24 x 18 in.
Medium: Designer's gouache

Bibliography

Adams, Maurice B., "Architectural Drawing," Royal Institute of British Architects *Transactions.* Vol. I, New Series, 1885.

Architekturzeichnungen, Berlin: Verlag Ernst Wasmuth, 1912.

Birren, Faber, *The Story of Color: from ancient mysticism to modern science.* Westport, Conn.: The Crimson Press, 1941.

Birren, Faber, *New Horizons in Color.* New York: Reinhold Publishing Corp., 1955.

Blomfield, Reginald, *Architectural Drawing and Draughtsmen.* London: Cassell & Co., 1912.

Brisebach, August, *Carl Friedrich Schinkel.* Leipzig: Insel-Verlag, 1924.

Burford, James, "The Historical Development of Architectural Drawing to the End of the Eighteenth Century," *The Architectural Review,* August 1923.

Capart, Jean, *Egyptian Art.* London: Geo. Allen & Unwin, London, 1923.

Carter, H. and Gardiner, A. H., "The Tomb of Rameses IV and the Turin Plan of a Royal Tomb," *Journal of Egyptian Archaeology,* IV, 1917.

Cole, Rex Vicat, *Perspective.* The practice and theory of perspective as applied to pictures, with a section dealing with its application to architecture. Philadelphia: Lippincott, 1927.

Color As Seen and Photographed: A Kodak Color Data Handbook. Rochester: Eastman Kodak Co., 1950.

Columbia Encyclopedia, 2nd Edition. Ed. William Bridgewater and Elizabeth J. Sherwood. New York: Columbia University Press, 1950.

Davies, N. de Garis, "The Rock Tombs of El Amarna," *Archeological Survey of Egypt,* XIII, Part I. London: Egypt Exploration Fund, 1903.

du Cerceau, Jacques Androuet, *Les plus excellents bastiments de France,* nouvelle ed. Paris: A. Levy, 1868. Original ed. 1607.

The Encyclopedia Britannica. Vol. V, pp. 992; Vol. XIV, pp. 1006; Vol. XVII, pp. 1006; Vol. XXIII, pp. 999. New York: Encyclopedia Britannica, 1933.

Falda, Giovanni Battista, *Le chiesa di Roma.* Rome: Giovanni Giacomo Rossi, 1680.

Ferriss, Hugh, *Power in Buildings.* New York: Columbia University Press, 1953.

Fouche, Maurice, *Percier et Fontaine, biographie critique.* Paris: H. Laurens, 1904.

Frey, Dagobert, *Bramantes St. Peter entwurf und seine apokryphen.* Wein: Schroll, 1915.

Gandy, Joseph, *Designs for Cottages, Cottage Farms and Other Rural Buildings, Including Entrance Gates and Lodges.* London: John Harding, 1805.

Gardner, Helen, *Art Through the Ages,* 3rd ed. New York: Harcourt, Brace, 1948.

Giedion, Siegfried, *Space, Time, and Architecture.* Cambridge: Harvard University Press, 1941.

Goodspeed, George S., *A History of the Babylonians and Assyrians.* New York: C. Scribner's Sons, 1927.

Guptill, Arthur L., *Color in Sketching and Rendering.* New York: Reinhold Pub. Corp., 1945.

Guptill, Arthur L., *Drawing with Pen and Ink*. New York: Pencil Points Press, 1930.

Guptill, Arthur L., *Sketching and Rendering in Pencil*. New York: Reinhold Pub. Corp., 1944.

Hunter, Dard, *Papermaking: The history and technique of an ancient craft*. New York: Alfred A. Knopf, 1943.

Jacobson, Egbert, *Basic Color: An interpretation of the Ostwald color system*. Chicago: Paul Theobald and Company, 1948.

Jacoby, H., *New Architectural Drawings*. New York: Frederick A. Praeger, Inc., 1969.

Jordan, Henricus, *Forma urbis Romae, regionum XIII*. Berlin: A.M.D. CCCLXXIIII.

Kautzky, Ted, *Painting Trees and Landscapes in Watercolor*. New York: Reinhold Pub. Corp., 1952.

Kautzky, Ted, *Pencil Broadsides: A manual of broad stroke technique*. New York: Reinhold Pub. Corp., 1940.

Kautzky, Ted, *Pencil Pictures*. New York: Reinhold Pub. Corp., 1947.

Kip, Johannes, *Britannia Illustrata: Views of all the king's palaces, several seats of the nobility and gentry; all the cathedrals of England and Wales*. London: Overton, 1727.

le Pautre, Anthoine, *Les oeuvres d'architecture d'Anthoine le Pautre*. Paris: Chez Iombert, 1751. Text by Augustin Chas. d'Aviler. (First edition published 1652, without text.)

Limbach, Russell T., *American Trees*. New York: Random House, 1942.

Luckiesh, Mathew, *Color and Colors*. New York: D. Van Nostrand Co., 1938.

Magonigle, Harold Van Buren, *Architectural Rendering in Wash*. New York: C. Scribner's Sons, 1929.

Malton, James, *An Essay on British Cottage Architecture*. London: Malton, 1804.

Mariani, Valerio, *La Facciata Di San Pietro Secondo Michelangelo*. Roma: Fratelli Palombi, 1943.

Moller, Georg, *Bemerkungen über die aufgefundene originalzeichnung des domes zu Koeln*. Darmstadt: Heyer und Leske, 1818.

Munsell, A. H., *A Color Notation: A measured color system, based on the three qualities, hue, value, and chroma, with illustrative models, charts, and a course of study arranged for teachers*, 2nd ed. Boston: Geo. H. Ellis Co., 1907.

Munsell, Albert, *A Grammar of Color*. Mittineague, Mass.: Strathmore Paper Co., 1921.

Munsell, Albert H., *On a Scale of Color-Values and a New Photometer*. 1904.

Munsell, Joel, *Chronology of the Origin and Progress of Paper and Paper Making*. 5th ed. Albany: J. Munsell, 1876.

Munsell Book of Color. Munsell Color Co., Baltimore, Md.

Piranesi, Giovanni Battista, *Roman Architecture, Sculpture and Ornament*. Selected examples from Piranesi's monumental work first published in Rome, 1756. London: E. & F. N. Spon, 1900.

Pitz, Henry C., *Drawing Trees*. New York: Watson Guptill Publications, 1956.

Sargent, Walter, *The Enjoyment and Use of Color*. New York: Chas. Scribner's Sons, 1923.

Schmitz, Hermann, *Baumeisterzeichnungen des 17 und 18 jahrhunderts*. Berlin: Ehemals Staatliche Museen Berlin, Kunstbibliothek, 1937.

"Techniques and Tradition in British Architecture," *Country Life*, 81, Jan. 16, 1937.

Uffizi, *Disegni di architettura (Civile e Militaire)* (Texte) 1885, pp. 231. Rome: Presso I, Principali Lebrai. Firenzi, 1904, pp. 14; 117 pl.

Vincent, Jean Anne, *History of Art: A survey of painting, sculpture and architecture in the Western World*. New York: Barnes & Noble, 1955.

Viollet le Duc, Eugene Emmanuel, *Compositions et dessins de Viollet-le-Duc*. Paris: Libraire centrale d'architecture, 1884.

Willis, Robert, *Facsimile of the Sketchbook of Wilars de Honecort*. London: John Henry and James Parker, 1859.

Zevi, Bruno, *Architecture as Space*. New York: Horizon Press, 1957.

Index